James Williams

Wills and Intestate Succession

A Manual of Practical Law

James Williams

Wills and Intestate Succession
A Manual of Practical Law

ISBN/EAN: 9783337232740

Printed in Europe, USA, Canada, Australia, Japan

Cover: Foto ©Suzi / pixelio.de

More available books at **www.hansebooks.com**

WILLS AND INTESTATE SUCCESSION

WILLS

AND

INTESTATE SUCCESSION

A MANUAL OF PRACTICAL LAW

BY

JAMES WILLIAMS, B.C.L., M.A.

OF LINCOLN'S INN, BARRISTER-AT-LAW, FELLOW OF LINCOLN COLLEGE, OXFORD

LONDON
ADAM AND CHARLES BLACK
1891

PREFACE

THE justification of the appearance of another volume on the well-worn theme of succession is the belief of the writer that there exists no work which attempts in a small compass to deal at once with the history and principles for which the student looks, and with the practical law essential to the layman, who is pretty sure at some time in his life to be a testator, an executor, or an administrator. Special features are, the notice of Scotch and Irish Law, and—where the subject admits of it—of the Conflict of Laws (the *Statuten-Kollision* of German jurists), or Private International Law, as some prefer to call it, and a list of the best authorities. The writer trusts that the statement of the law is as accurate as can be expected where limitations of space prevent that complete development of principles by cases which is the object of works of a more technical nature. Cases are seldom cited unless they are of unusual interest or importance. It has not been thought necessary in a book of this character to give a reference to more than one report in which a case occurs.

The expectation may here be expressed that, under the present editorship, this volume will form the first of a series of similar manuals, devoted to the most important branches of the law. It is believed these handbooks will be found of service to lawyers and laymen alike. They will be undertaken by members of the English bar who have become authorities on the subjects treated by them.

Among other branches of the law it is proposed to deal with Real Property, Bankruptcy, Education, Public Health and Social Legislation, Principal and Agent, Master and Servant, Marriage and Family Relations, Railways, Insurance, Partnership and Companies, Patent and Copyright, Banking and Negotiable Instruments.

J. W.

2 PUMP COURT, TEMPLE,
December 1890.

CONTENTS

AUTHORITIES	xi
LIST OF CASES CITED	xiii
INTRODUCTION	1

CHAP.
1. THE HISTORY OF THE WILL IN ENGLAND . . . 9
2. THE HISTORY OF INTESTATE SUCCESSION IN ENGLAND . 23
3. THE WILL IN GENERAL 28
4. THE WILL OF LANDS 39
5. THE WILL OF PERSONALTY . . . 58
6. THE CODICIL 63
7. REVOCATION 65
8. WILLS OF A SPECIAL NATURE 70
9. THE CONSTRUCTION OF WILLS 84
10. INTESTATE SUCCESSION TO—
    (1) REAL ESTATE 109
    (2) PERSONAL ESTATE 114
    (3) TITLES OF HONOUR 117
11. ADMINISTRATION IN A COURT OF PROBATE—
    (1) PROBATE 121
    (2) ADMINISTRATION 133

	PAGE
12. THE RIGHTS AND DUTIES OF EXECUTORS AND ADMINISTRATORS—	
(1) Rights	140
(2) Duties	148
13. ADMINISTRATION IN A COURT OF EQUITY . . .	157
14. CRIMINAL LAW	166
15. SUCCESSION IN ITS RELATION TO THE REVENUE—	
(1) Probate Duty	169
(2) Account Duty . . .	170
(3) Legacy Duty	171
(4) Succession Duty	175
(5) Estate Duty	179
(6) Other Duties . . .	180
16. CONFLICT OF LAWS . .	182
17. SCOTLAND	192
18. IRELAND . .	204
APPENDIX	209
INDEX . .	275

AUTHORITIES

ELEMENTARY.—Stephen, *Commentaries*, vols. i and ii (11th ed., 1890); Williams, *Real Property* (16th ed., 1887); Williams, *Personal Property* (13th ed., 1887); Digby, *History of the Law of Real Property*, c. viii (3d ed., 1884); Goodeve, *Modern Law of Real Property* (1883); Goodeve, *Modern Law of Personal Property* (1887); Challis, *Law of Real Property* (1885).

EARLY WILLS.—Nicholas, *Testamenta Vetusta* (1826); Furnivall, *The Fifty Earliest English Wills in the Court of Probate, 1387-1439* (1882).

EARLY PRACTICE.—Swinburne, *Brief Treatise on Testaments and Wills* (1590).

GENERAL.—Jarman (4th ed., 1881); Theobald (3d ed., 1885).

WILLS OF PERSONALTY.—Flood (1887).

CONSTRUCTION.—Wigram, *Admission of Extrinsic Evidence in Aid of the Interpretation of Wills* (4th ed., 1858); Hawkins, *Construction of Wills* (1863); Stroud, *Judicial Dictionary* (1890).

LEGACIES.—Roper (4th ed., 1847).

EVIDENCE OF SUCCESSION.—Hubback (1844).

MORTMAIN.—Tudor, *Law of Charities and Mortmain* (3d ed., 1889); Tyssen, *Law of Charitable Bequests* (1888).

PERPETUITIES. — Lewis (1843, Supplement, 1849); Marsden (1883).

PRIMOGENITURE.—*Two Essays on the Law of Primogeniture*, by Kenny and Laurence (1878).

PROBATE.—Browne (1873); Dixon (2d ed., 1886); Tristram and Coote (10th ed., 1888).

EXECUTORS AND ADMINISTRATORS. — Wentworth (4th ed., 1829); Toller (7th ed., 1839); Williams (8th ed., 1879).

ADMINISTRATION OF ASSETS.—Ram on Assets (1837); Eddis (1880).

ORIGINATING SUMMONS.—Marcy and Dodd (1889).

REVENUE.—Hudson, *Succession Duty Acts*, etc. (4th ed., 1872); Hanson, *Succession Duty Acts*, etc. (3d ed., 1876); Hanson. *Revenue Acts*, 1880 and 1881 (1881); Trevor, *Taxes on Succession* (4th ed., 1881); Layton, *Guide to the Payment of Legacy and Succession Duties* (8th ed., 1890).

CONFLICT OF LAWS.—Story, *Conflict of Laws* (7th ed., 1872); Foote, *Private International Jurisprudence* (1878); Dicey, *Law of Domicil* (1879); Phillimore, *International Law*, vol. iv (3d ed., 1889); Nelson, *Select Cases on Private International Law*, notes to *Doe v. Vardill, Enohin v. Wyllie, Thomson v. Advocate-General* (1889).

SCOTLAND.—Watson, *Law of Succession* (1826); Sandford, *Law of Heritable Succession* (1830); M'Laren, *Wills and Succession* (1868); Bell's *Principles* (8th ed., 1885); and other elementary works.

IRELAND.—Smith, *Guide to the Practice of the Probate Division* (5th ed., 1890).

FORMS.—Hayes and Jarman, *Concise Forms of Wills* (9th ed., 1883); Davidson, *Precedents in Conveyancing*, vol. iv. (3d ed., 1880); Davidson, *Concise Precedents* (15th ed., 1890); Prideaux, *Precedents*, vol. ii. (14th ed., 1889); Bythewood and Jarman, *Precedents*, vol. vii. (4th ed., 1889); Key and Elphinstone, *Precedents*, vol. ii. (3d ed., 1890). For Scotland, *Juridical Styles*, vols. i. and ii. (5th ed., 1881, 1883).

LIST OF CASES CITED

Ackroyd v. Smithson, 161
Alderson v. Maddison, 36
Ancaster, Duke of, v. Mayer, 161
Atkinson v. Anderson, 190
Attorney-General v. Baxter, 53
,, v. Ironmongers' Co., 104
,, v. Kent, 190
,, v. Stewart, 186
Aylesford, Earl of, v. Morris, 37
Aylesford's Estates, Re Earl of 117

Bernina, The, 143
Beverley's Case, 81
Boyes, Re, 64
Bradford v. Young, 120
Braybrooke, Lord, v. Attorney-General, 177
Bremer v. Freeman, 182
Brice v. Stokes, 144
Brodie v. Brodie, 182
Buckhurst Peerage, 119
Butter and Baker's Case, 38

Campden Charities, Re, 104
Cigala's Trusts, Re, 190
Clergy Society, Re, 93
Clook, Re, 128
Cooper v. Stuart, 52

Cowan v. Milbourn, 55
Curtis v. Hutton, 186

Dias v. De Lievera, 73
Dixon, Re, 73
Doe v. Laming, 91
,, v. Mills, 34
,, v. Vardill, 185, 191, 200
Duncan v. Lawson, 186

Egerton v. Earl Brownlow, 44, 99
Enohin v. Wylie, 187
Ewing v. Orr-Ewing, 187, 188

Ferguson-Davie v. Ferguson-Davie, 30
Fleetwood, Re, 53
Fordyce v. Bridges, 187
Fulton v. Andrew, 82

Gavelkind, Case of, 204
George III, In the goods of, 71
Goodman's Trusts, Re, 186, 191
Grant v. Grant, 93
Grove, Re, 186

Hall v. Hall, 31
Hamilton v. Dallas, 184
Hampton v. Holman, 104
Hillersdon v. Lowe, 102

LIST OF CASES CITED

Hog v. Lashley, 186

Incorporated Society v. Richards, 205

Jex v. McKinney, 186
Jupp, Re, 73

Landsdown v. Landsdown, 114
Leach v. Jay, 91, 106
Legat's Case, 48
Lyons, Mayor of, v. East India Co., 186

Mar Peerage, 119
Moore, Re, 100
Muggleton v. Barnett, 112, 113

Newburgh, Earl of, v. Newburgh, Countess of, 106

Occleston v. Fullalove, 95, 100
Oldenburg, In the goods of Prince, 71

Phillips v. Homfray, 152
Pinchon's Case, 21

Pinney v. Hunt, 120
Price, Re, 72
Printing, etc., Co. v. Sampson, 105

Robinson v. Ommaney, 60

Shelley's Case, 61, 97, 103, 106, 199
Skottowe v. Young, 190
Smee v. Smee, 81
Smith, Re, 72
Speight v. Gaunt, 147
Sugden v. Lord St. Leonards, 132

Tanistry, Case of, 204
Thomson v. Shakespeare, 52

Vera Cruz, The, 143

Whitby v. Mitchell, 49
Wild's Case, 95
Williams v. Arkle, 155
,, v. Williams, 148
Willock v. Noble, 72
Wingrove v. Wingrove, 32

Yeap Cheah v. Ong Cheng, 52, 187

INTRODUCTION

THE place of succession in a scientific system of law is not altogether easy to determine. In the arrangement of Savigny it is classed among the legal relations (*Rechtsverhältnisse*) which arise from a simple change in the subject of the relation.[1] By other authorities it is classed among modes of acquiring property, by others among normal as distinct from abnormal rights. It is at least safe to say that it is a mode of acquisition of property arising from no act of the successor himself, such as a right under a contract, but from the act of another person or by mere operation of law. In Roman law succession to the estate of a deceased person was always universal (*successio in universum jus quod defunctus habuit*), the *hereditas* or inheritance descending as an undivided whole. The legatee of a particular part only took through the *heres*. Some modern systems, like the Scotch, draw a distinction between universal and singular succession, but this was unknown to Roman, as it is to English, law. The conception of the *hereditas* as a mode of universal succession determined its place in Roman law, where it is classed among the modes of acquiring property *per universitatem*.

The origin of succession, like that of so many other

[1] *System des Heutigen Römischen Rechts*, vol. iii, 8 (Berlin, 1840).

legal ideas, is probably to be traced to a religious basis. According to the opinion of many authorities[1] it is derived from primitive animism, the source of the worship of the House-Spirit, always a male, generally an ancestor.[2] The vesting of the succession in the heir, himself originally, like the House-Spirit, always a male, was necessary for the purpose of continuing the family rites and observances on which, according to primitive belief, the very existence of the family depended. Property and *sacra* were indissolubly combined. It was a point of family honour that the spirit of the deceased, and through him the House-Spirit, was to be propitiated by ritual observances. Such observances were neglected at the peril of the survivors, for the family was one and indivisible, the dead members were still members in a sense, and the heir was simply a co-proprietor with the deceased.[3] The theory of the unity and perpetuity of the family is in fact the key to the early rules of succession. It also explains the joint liability of the kindred, known to have existed in England until superseded by the joint liability of the hundred,[4] and the law of what has been called, perhaps not very correctly, primogeniture. Many, if not most, legal systems recognised a right in the oldest son (sometimes the eldest agnate in case of

[1] See Fustel de Coulanges, *La Cité Antique*, bk. ii, c. 7 (English translation by S. Adams, Boston, 1874); Hearn, *The Aryan Household*, c. vi (1879); Maine, *Early Law and Custom*, c. iv (1883); Markby, *Elements of Law*, c. xviii (4th ed., 1889).
[2] A survival of ancestor worship in a civilised society in historical times was the festival of the *Parentalia* at Rome.
[3] This appears from some of the texts of Roman law. For instance, in *Inst.* iii, 1, 3, the words used are *statim morte parentis quasi continuatur dominium*, the death of the parent was as it were only the death of one of the partners, and the partnership continued as before.
[4] The liability of the hundred to compensate the owner of property in the hundred for damage done by rioters existed up to 1886, when it was abolished by 49 and 50 Vict., c. 38.

the infancy of the eldest son [1]) to the succession, but in ancient law the succession was to office, in modern to property. The eldest son was the most proper person to keep up the *sacra*. This view of the position of the eldest son is especially noticeable in the old Hindu law-books. Athenian law recognised the πρεσβεία, or right of the eldest son to the father's house, and the Mosaic law the double portion as the birthright of the eldest son (Deut. xxii, 17). The succession of the eldest son to the father's benefice under the feudal system is a kind of link between the ancient and modern systems. It was succession to an office which carried property with it. The supreme importance of succession as a means of continuing the family was recognised even at a late stage of Roman law by the rules that a vacant inheritance might be acquired by usucapion in one year, and that torture might be applied in cases affecting the inheritance to an extent beyond that allowed in other cases. Possibly the universality of the view that the House-Spirit was a male throws light on the importance of agnatic as distinguished from cognatic relationship. The distinction, though not always recognised by the Aryan nations, was at least of vast importance in Hindu and Roman law. Agnates were those who were related exclusively through males, whether the relationship were natural or artificial. An adopted son would be an agnate of the *paterfamilias*, a daughter's son would not be. Cognates were those related by ties of blood, whether their relationship was through males or females. The tendency of law has been to supersede agnatic by cognatic relationship. At Athens this was done by the legisla-

[1] As in the case of the Irish tanist, p. 204.

tion of Solon, at Rome by the prætor in his judicial capacity. He was an officer of the state, who perhaps wished to exalt the state at the expense of the *gens*. In modern English law relationship is estimated purely on the cognatic basis.

It might be expected from what has been said, and the expectation is confirmed by what is known of archaic law, that intestate succession is earlier in time than testate. The earliest examples of wills were probably those by which the inheritance was transferred to an artificial member of the family, made so by adoption, where there was in existence no natural member qualified to continue the *sacra*. But such a creation could at first take place only during the life of the testator. As Sir Henry Maine points out, the primitive Roman will, at any rate that made by *mancipatio*, where a plebeian was testator, differed from the modern will in three matters of the highest importance. It took effect at once as a present conveyance, because the form of *mancipatio* did not originally admit of modification by any condition or limitation in point of time. It was also a public act, and it was not revocable.[1] The patrician will was equally a public irrevocable conveyance, and probably equally incapable of conditional modification. If the *gens* were, as seems likely, only an extended family, it is evident why the primitive Roman will made by a patrician testator could only be made in the *comitia curiata*, or parliament of the *gentes*, and why the *gens* succeeded in default of agnates of a certain degree. The early Roman patrician will was, in fact, a local and personal act passed by the legislature; the plebeian a conveyance *inter vivos*. A great step in advance was

[1] *Ancient Law*, c. vi.

DEFINITION OF A WILL

taken when the will of either kind only came into operation after death. It then began to bear the meaning which it bears in modern law.

A will or testament may be defined as an instrument by which a person regulates the rights of others over his property or family after his death. In strictness, will, at any rate in England, is a general term, while testament applies only to dispositions of personal property. But this distinction is seldom observed, and it is a common form to head a will, "The last will and testament of A. B." "Will" is a translation of the Latin *voluntas*, which was a term used in the texts of Roman law to express the intention of a testator. It is curious that the abstract term has come to mean the document in which the intention is contained. The same has been the case with several other English law terms, the concrete has superseded the abstract—obligation, bond, contract, are examples. "Testament" is a translation of the Latin *testamentum*, derived by the Romans from *testatio mentis*, but more correctly derived directly from *testor*, i.e. that which witnesses or declares an intention. In the definition of a will by Modestinus in the Digest of Justinian, *testamentum* is defined by means of *voluntas*; it is *voluntatis nostræ justa sententia de eo quod quis post mortem suam fieri velit*.[1] The word "codicil" is derived from Roman law, but with a different meaning, the Roman *codicilli* were an informal will, the English codicil is an addition to a will. "Executor" and "administrator" are Latin words, but the Latin *executor* and *administrator* were used in signification very different from those which they suggest to an English lawyer. The former meant a prosecutor, the latter a provincial governor.

[1] *Digest*, xxviii, 1, 1.

Strangely enough, the two words occur in the titles of two of the constitutions of Justinian in immediate sequence.[1] The Roman *heres* included both the English terms and more besides, in fact the *heres* partook of the nature of heir, devisee, executor, administrator, and legatee, and was all or some of these according to circumstances.

The conception of complete freedom of disposition by will, familiar as it is in modern England, is by no means universal. In England freedom of disposition has only been attained by slow degrees,[2] in other countries it is the exception rather than the rule. Legal systems founded on Roman law, such as those of Scotland, France, and Louisiana, allow alienation of the whole property only where the deceased leaves no widow or near relations. In France this restriction has been the subject of much comment by legal and economical writers. It has been condemned by resolutions of Chambers of Commerce, and by jurists of the highest eminence. M. Troplong, for instance, holds that *un peuple n'est pas libre s'il n'a pas le droit de tester, et la liberté du testament est la plus grande preuve de la liberté civile*.[3]

The will, if not purely Roman, at least owes to Roman law its complete development—a development which, in

---

[1] *De Administratoribus*, Novel 95 ; *De Executoribus*, Novel 96. "Executor," as used in the well-known passage in Shakespeare, Henry V, act 1, sc. 2, differs both in meaning and accent from the legal use of the word.

[2] A trace of the period when the issue could not be entirely disinherited is found in the vulgar error that it is necessary "to cut off with a shilling" a child of the testator. This is a faint survival of the rule existing at one period of Roman law, that a child could not be entirely disinherited, though he might receive nothing more than a nominal gift.

[3] *Traité des Donations entre-vifs et des Testaments* (1855).

most countries, was greatly aided at a later period by ecclesiastics versed in Roman law, in England especially by the judges of the Court of Chancery. The effect has been that, as Sir Henry Maine expresses it, "the English law of testamentary succession to personalty has become a modified form of the dispensation under which the inheritances of Roman citizens were administered."[1]

In the Mosaic law the will, if it existed at all, was of a very rudimentary character, in spite of the assertion of Eusebius that Noah made a will disposing of the whole world.[2] In India, according to the better opinion, it was unknown before the English occupation. It was, according to Tacitus, not in use among the ancient German tribes. The will is, on the other hand, recognised by Rabbinical, Mohammedan, and Brehon[3] law. At Athens, under the legislation of Solon, a will could only be made where the testator left no children. Eleven out of the twelve extant orations of Isæus are on claims to an inheritance. In some cases he argues in favour of the validity of the will, in others against it.[4] The Romans were essentially a will-making people. An immense space in the *Corpus Juris* is occupied with testamentary law. The whole of part v of the Digest (books xxviii-xxxvi) deals with the subject, and there are many constitutions in addition in the Code and Novels. In Roman law the will was a transfer of the inheritance as a whole; the testator must dispose of all or

[1] *Ancient Law*, c. vi. The main differences between English and Roman law will be found summarised in Appendix E.
[2] The testaments of Adam and of the Twelve Patriarchs were at one time received as of at least apocryphal authority.
[3] See p. 207.
[4] If an Athenian died sonless and intestate, but leaving a daughter, she became an ἐπίκληρος, or orphan heiress, and the right and duty of the nearest kinsman to marry her often became the subject of litigation. See Maine, *Early Law and Custom*, c. iv.

none; he could not (unless a soldier) die partly testate and partly intestate.

The effect of the introduction of Christianity upon succession was very marked. Even before its introduction as the religion of the Roman State, the temples of the pagan gods had often enjoyed the right of custody of wills. This right passed to the Christian churches, and it became very common to deposit a will in a church. The influence of the priesthood was shown in both Roman and canon law by various provisions to the advantage of the Church, *e.g.* that the Church and not the Crown was *ultimus heres* to the estate of a clerk, that Church property could not be bequeathed, that gifts to the Church were not subject to the deductions necessary in other cases in favour of the wife and children, and that a will made *in pias causas* was valid without the usual number of witnesses.[1] The tendency of the ecclesiastical tribunals was to give a very liberal interpretation to bequests of a kind which modern English law would brand with the name of "superstitious uses."

[1] The canon law on the subject is contained chiefly in *Decretals*, bk. iii, cc. 26 and 27.

CHAPTER I

THE HISTORY OF THE WILL IN ENGLAND

LIBERTY of alienation by will is found at an early date in England. The pre-Conquest will was good whether verbal or written. No definite number of witnesses seems to have been prescribed. The will after death was published in the county court, and established by its authority. Intestacy appears to have been unusual at the time of Canute, one of whose laws implies that the only causes for it must have been neglect or sudden death.[1] How far the liberty of testation extended is uncertain; according to some authorities complete disposition of goods by will was allowed, according to others limited rights of the widow and children were recognised, subject in either case to the lord's heriot, a kind of tax in kind upon succession. As to land, it is generally supposed that free testamentary disposition of bocland (*i.e.* land of private proprietors) was allowed, of folcland (*i.e.* land belonging to the state) only by the king's licence. Whatever be the truth as to this, it is certain that after the Conquest a distinction, the result of the change in the tenure of land introduced by that event,

[1] *Secular Dooms*, 70.

arose between real and personal property, or immoveables and moveables.[1] A complete history of the English will still remains to be written; a short sketch of the more prominent events in that history is all that can be attempted in this place.

Real Estate.—After the Conquest direct alienation of real estate by will became impossible, as it was contrary to one of the express doctrines of feudalism, viz. that there could be no alienation without the consent of the lord.[2] Any attempt at alienation by will was an attempt to deprive the Crown or the lord of land from which feudal services were due, and so indirectly of the feudal services themselves. In fact, alienation *inter vivos* was considerably restricted until the passing of the Statute of *Quia Emptores* in 1290. There were also other reasons for restricting alienation by will—one, the discouragement of death-bed gifts to the church, another, the impossibility of the testator giving seisin to the devisee. The effect was that between the Norman Conquest and the reign of Henry VIII lands were not directly devisable by will, with certain exceptions. These exceptions were gavelkind land (chiefly in Kent), and land situated in certain ancient boroughs or manors.[3] Of the rights

[1] Immoveables and moveables, terms derived from Roman law, are seldom used as English technical terms, though they perhaps express better than any others what may be called the natural difference in the classification of property. They are not quite equivalent to real and personal property, or realty and personalty; for instance, a leasehold estate is in its nature an immoveable, but is regarded by English law as personalty. Another division, recognised by the legislature, is into real and personal estate. It is, however, to some extent misleading, as there can be no estate properly so called in personal property.

[2] This restriction seems to have applied at first only to land inherited by the deceased, not to land purchased. But gradually the restriction appears to have included purchased as well as descended land.

[3] In manors the distinction just noticed between land inherited

in boroughs, that of free devise possessed by citizens of London was the most important. Though, however, direct devise was not competent, more than one mode of giving effect to an indirect devise was discovered. One was to direct the executors of the will of the deceased (in whom of course the personalty of the deceased vested at his death) to purchase land and convey it to a particular person. Another and more usual mode was to make a conveyance during life to a feoffee to hold on uses to be declared by will, the will taking the form of a declaration to uses, similar to that of a conveyance to uses *inter vivos*, and not unlike the Scotch disposition and settlement. This no doubt explains why a will of lands was at one time sealed,[1] and also the law that, up to 1838, a will of lands passed only lands in the possession of the testator at the time of making it, while a will of personalty passed after-acquired property. To pass after-acquired real estate needed republication, which was practically equivalent to a new will. The same reason serves to explain why a will before 1838 could be revoked by presumption of an alteration in circumstances, and by a subsequent conveyance *inter vivos* of land devised by the testator, even though the conveyance were void, the attempt to make it being presumed to prove an *animus revocandi*. The doctrine of the use of land, as distinguished from its nominal ownership, would not be difficult to ecclesiastics familiar with the usufruct of

and land purchased seems to have existed at least into the 14th century. Two cases of devise of *terra acquisita* or *terra prequisita*, according to the custom of the manor of King's Ripton, are recorded in 1301 (*Select Pleas in Manorial Courts*, published by the Selden Society, vol. ii., 125, 127).

[1] See rule 6 of Lord Coke's rules, p. 37.

Roman law, and it was by such ecclesiastics that the doctrine of uses was probably introduced. After the passing in 1535 of the Statute of Uses (which contained an exception in favour of wills of uses made before May 1536), the alienation of land by devise of the use became impossible, as the use was in the same position with regard to devisability as the land itself, and the court had not yet construed the statute in a way not foreseen by its framers, a construction by which the trust succeeded to the legal position of the old use.[1] The restraint on alienation being found inconvenient, if not intolerable, especially when a large amount of land had come into the market after the dissolution of the monasteries, a modified power of devise was introduced by two statutes of 1540 and 1542 (32 Hen. VIII, c. 1, 34 and 35 Hen. VIII, c. 5), which are still law as to wills made before 1838. These acts were very partial in their operation, for they applied in the case of lands held by tenure of chivalry only to two-thirds of such lands, only those held in socage being wholly devisable. A reservation was made of primer seisins, reliefs, and other feudal dues, and of wardship of one-third of the lands held by knight-service. When the act of 12 Car. II, c. 24, turned all the old tenures in chivalry (with a few exceptions) into free and common socage, the whole lands of a deceased became devisable.[2] It was therefore necessary to enforce a certain amount of solemnity in the execution of wills, the acts of Henry

[1] See the work on *Real Property* in this series.
[2] The only exceptions at the present day appear to be (1) entailed estates where the entail has not been duly barred, an entail not being barrable by will, 3 and 4 Will. IV, c. 74, s. 40; (2) entailed estates granted for public services under the provisions of private Acts of Parliament, such as Blenheim and Strathfieldsaye, and rendered inalienable by such acts.

VIII only exacting that the will should be in writing. Simple notes in another person's handwriting, if published by the testator as his will, were sufficient to satisfy the acts. Accordingly, by the Statute of Frauds (29 Car. II, c. 3), it was required that devises of land should be signed by the testator, or by some other person for him in his presence and by his express direction, and that they should be subscribed in his presence by three or four credible witnesses. Owing to a series of decisions of the courts on the credibility of witnesses under the act, it was enacted by 25 Geo. II, c. 6, that gifts to attesting witnesses were void, but that the witnesses still remained credible, and that creditors were credible witnesses. The Statute of Frauds still governs wills made before January 1838, now a rapidly diminishing quantity. A will of lands did not need probate, the original will being itself a document of title. Such probate, in exceptional cases, was introduced for the first time by the Court of Probate Act, 1857. It might, however, be admitted to probate, where an executor was appointed. Many technical constructions of terms used in wills were altered by the Wills Act.[1] Up to 1838 a man could make a will at fourteen, a woman at twelve.

The liability of the devisee for the debts of the testator has only been established by slow degrees. In the time of Glanvill (who wrote in the reign of Henry II), the heir of a deceased person was, according to the better opinion, bound to the extent of his inheritance to warrant the reasonable gifts of his ancestor to the grantees and their heirs, and to pay such of the debts of his ancestor as the ancestor's estate was in-

[1] See chap. ix.

sufficient to satisfy. But this state of the law was gradually trenched upon, partly by the courts and partly by the legislature. A rude kind of remedy was given by the Statute of Merchants in 1285 (13 Edw. I, st. 3), which empowered a merchant to seize the lands of a deceased debtor under a statute-merchant, and exclude the heir until he had satisfied his debt. It became a rule of the courts, dating from about the same period, and applying to others besides merchants, that the heir was not bound (except to the Crown) unless charged by the deed of his ancestor. Where the heir was so charged by deed under seal, wherein he was expressly named (by specialty, as it was called), he was bound to the extent of the lands descended, but no further.[1] Such lands became *assets* in his hands, and were all in the nature of real estate that the creditors had to resort to unless the testator had charged his lands by will with payment of his debts. In such a case the lands were called *equitable assets*, and simple contract creditors were allowed by the Court of Chancery to rank equally with specialty creditors. Various acts were passed at different times to remedy the unjust exclusion of all but specialty creditors, but the devisee was not liable to debts until 1691, and it was not until 1833 that lands of all persons alike became subject to all debts, but with a preference (in the absence of a charge of debts upon the land) to specialty creditors. Simple contract and specialty creditors did not rank equally until 1870. Estates *pur autre vie* and trust estates were first made assets by descent by the Statute of Frauds.

---

[1] The heir of lands conveyed to uses was not so bound until the Statute of Uses. That statute for the first time made the use assets of the deceased.

Two subjects are of sufficient interest to demand a special notice, viz. copyholds and mortmain. Before the present Wills Act, testamentary alienation of copyholds, which were first made devisable in 1815 by 55 Geo. III, c. 192, was generally made by surrender to the use of the will of the copyhold tenant. The surrender was made into the hands of the lord, and the steward entered a presentment of the surrender (if made out of court, as it generally was) on the court rolls of the manor. After the decease of the tenant the devisee generally brought the will into court, and a presentment was made of the tenant's decease and of the terms of his will. This presentment was made unnecessary by 4 and 5 Vict., c. 35. By the Wills Act, copyholds may be devised directly like lands of any other tenure. Copyholds devised were not subject to debts until 1833, even where charged with the payment of debts, and even in favour of the Crown. A fine is generally payable on admittance of any copyholder succeeding by descent. But in many cases enfranchisement has abolished the right to the fine. The right to a heriot, either the tenant's best beast, or a pecuniary composition in lieu thereof, still exists in some manors. It is said to be of Danish origin.

The Mortmain Acts constitute a series of measures dictated by public policy, their object being to prevent the accumulation of real estate in the hands of corporations. Lands belonging to corporations were said to be in *mortuâ manu* or in mortmain, because, owing to the perpetual existence of the corporation, they produced no benefit to the feudal lord by escheat or otherwise. Mortmain proper only applies to gifts to corporations, though the term is often used with regard to gifts of land for any purpose where the alienation of the land would be restricted. Restraints on gifts to corporations were well known to Roman law. For instance, in the time of the Pagan emperors only certain deities could be instituted heirs, and in the time of the Christian emperors gifts to ecclesiastical corporations, such as monasteries, were bound to be duly registered. The earliest mortmain provision in England is the Constitutions of Clarendon (1164), the latest the Mortmain and Charitable Uses Act, 1888 (chiefly a consolidating act). The Constitutions of Clarendon by § 2 enact that no gift is to be taken by the Church without the licence and assent of the Crown, the earliest mention of a licence in mortmain. Between 1164 and 1888 the law passed from a stage of absolute to one of limited disqualification, and the modern tendency is to allow testamentary gifts of personalty to charities in all cases and gifts of realty up to a limited amount to charities of a certain kind.[1] The most important act before 1888 was 9 Geo. II, c. 36, much of which is re-enacted by the act of 1888. The terms used in the two acts as to personalty savouring of realty are, however, sufficiently different to make it a question whether the law as to personalty savouring of realty has been in any way altered by the later act. There appears to be a divergence of opinion among text-writers on the subject.

Personalty.—The history of wills of personalty to a certain extent moved in parallel lines. In both real and personal property partial preceded complete power of disposition. The opinion of the best authorities is that by the common law of England a testator could only dispose of his whole personal property if he left no wife

[1] See p. 45.

or children; if he left either wife or children he could only dispose of one-half, and one-third if he left both wife and children. The shares of wife and children were called their *pars rationabilis*, which is recognised by *Magna Carta*.[1] At what period the right of disposition of the whole personalty superseded the old state of the law is uncertain; that it did so is certain, and the places where the old rule still existed, the province of York, the principality of Wales, and the City of London, were regarded as exceptions. The right of bequest in these places was not assimilated to the general law until comparatively recent times by acts passed between 1693 and 1726. At different times limited powers of disposition over goods not alienable by will at common law were given by various Acts of Parliament, some of which are still law, though practically superseded by the larger powers of the Wills Act of 1837. Among these earlier acts are the Statute of Merton, 1235 (20 Hen. III, c. 2), enabling widows to bequeath the corn on their lands, and 28 Hen. VIII, c. 11. s. 4 (1535), enabling incumbents to bequeath the profits of corn sown on their glebes. At one time a will of personalty was not valid unless an executor was appointed, but this rule has long been obsolete. In early wills an overseer as well as an executor was often appointed.

At common law a will might be either written or verbal (otherwise called nuncupative). A written will must have been published, that is, declared in the presence of witnesses, as the ·testator's last will; a nuncupative will was simply recited and might be proved by the evidence of those who had heard it. The

[1] *Omnia catalla cedant defuncto, salvis uxori ipsius et pueris suis rationalibus partibus suis*, § 26 of the *Magna Carta* of John.

Statute of Frauds provided that no nuncupative will should be good where the estate bequeathed should exceed the value of £30, unless proved by the oaths of three witnesses at least, who were present at the making thereof. There were also other restrictions, the most important perhaps being that the words of a nuncupative will must be committed to writing within six days. A will in writing could not be altered by word of mouth. If holograph, that is, entirely in the writing of the testator, it was valid without signature. The effect of legislation and custom combined was that before the Wills Act there were ten different ways in which a will could be made, and the Real Property Commissioners in 1833 strongly recommended uniformity.[1] Up to 11 Geo. IV and 1 Will. IV, c. 40, the executor took for his own benefit any residue undisposed of as the general representative of the testator; since that act he holds it as trustee for the next of kin.

The jurisdiction over probate of wills of personalty was until 1858 in the ecclesiastical courts. This was a relic of the old theory by which the personalty of the deceased was regarded as being *primâ facie* a fund for providing masses for his soul.[2] The ecclesiastical jurisdiction was of very ancient origin; it is noticed by Glanvill, and is generally supposed to have been assumed after the Conquest by the prelates and their officers, in accordance with the general law of Christian Europe. The courts which had jurisdiction were those of the

---

[1] Fourth Report, 12.
[2] In pre-Reformation wills a bequest for masses is almost invariable, and by the statute of 1357 (see below), the surplus was to be applied to such purposes. The statutory sanction of masses for the soul was finally withdrawn in the reign of Edward VI by the act making gifts for masses superstitious (see below).

ordinary,[1] who might be archbishop, bishop, or archdeacon. The jurisdiction of the archdeacon, though mentioned by Chaucer in his "Friar's Tale," had become obsolete long before 1858, and the only courts (with the exception of certain peculiars and local courts)[2] which had jurisdiction up to that date were the court of the archbishop of the province (called the Prerogative Court), and the court of the archbishop or bishop of the diocese (called the Consistory Court). If the deceased had *bona notabilia, i.e.* goods to the value of more than one hundred shillings,[3] in two distinct dioceses, the will had to be proved in the Prerogative Court, in other cases the Consistory Court had jurisdiction. The archbishops and bishops did not sit as judges in person, but by their representatives, the chancellors or commissaries of dioceses, the official principals of the Prerogative Courts. The judge of the Provincial Court of Canterbury was the Dean of Arches, not necessarily, but by virtue of long custom.[4] The Prerogative Court was an appellate court from the diocesan courts, but as a matter of fact

[1] In ecclesiastical law the ordinary is a judge who exercises immediate and not delegated jurisdiction; the word is derived from Roman law, and no doubt depends for its meaning in the last resort on the distinction familiar in the Roman system between *judicia ordinaria* and *judicia extraordinaria*.

[2] From 1258 to 1688 wills made in the City of London were proved and enrolled in the Hustings or Husting Court, with or without having been proved in the Court of the Ordinary. The proof in the Hustings Court was in open court on the oath of a witness. See the *Calendar of Wills proved and enrolled in the Court of Husting*, by R. R. Sharpe, 1889. Wills of members of the Universities were at one time proved in the Chancellors' Courts.

[3] In the diocese of London, *bona notabilia* were by custom double this amount.

[4] The original jurisdiction of the Dean of Arches was confined to peculiars of the province of Canterbury. Of some of these peculiars he was judge of first instance, of others commissaries were judges, an appeal lying from them to the Court of Arches.

contentious cases generally came before it in the first instance, either because the goods were in most cases *bona notabilia*, or because letters of request were issued by the diocesan court to remove the case for trial to the Prerogative Court. Such duties as are now performed by registrars then devolved upon surrogates. An appeal lay from the Prerogative Court to the Delegates, commissioners appointed by the King in Chancery, to whom by 25 Hen. VIII, c. 19, appeals from the archbishop were to be made. From 1832 to 1858 the appeal was to the Judicial Committee of the Privy Council. The practice was wholly in the hands of advocates and proctors, barristers and solicitors had no right of appearance or audience in the ecclesiastical courts. The jurisdiction of the ecclesiastical courts was entirely confined to wills of personalty; if they attempted to assume jurisdiction over wills of land, they were subject to writs of prohibition from the temporal courts. The same was the case even in wills of personalty, if the ecclesiastical court construed a statute in a manner not approved by the temporal courts. The judge of the Prerogative Court was appointed by the archbishop, the chancellor or commissary of the diocesan court by the archbishop or bishop. Many of the early judges, if one may rely upon the language of statutes,[1] laid themselves open to prosecution for corruption and extortion, and in the reign of James I Sir John Bennet was impeached for corruption in his office as judge of the Prerogative Court. These proceedings appear to have dropped, but in 1622 he was

---

[1] For instance, 31 Edw. III, st. 1, c. 4 (1357), and 21 Hen. VIII, c. 5 (1529), the latter act attempting a reform by fixing the fees demandable in probate and administration.

fined £20,000 by the Star Chamber. He afterwards obtained a pardon from Charles I.[1] The proceedings of the ecclesiastical courts, even where the judges were above suspicion, were dilatory and expensive, and the abolition of their jurisdiction in testamentary matters was regretted by few. In 1857, by the Court of Probate Act of that year, the ecclesiastical jurisdiction was transferred to the court created by the act; and in 1875, by the Supreme Court of Judicature Act, 1873, the jurisdiction of the Court of Probate was merged in that of the High Court of Justice, and specially assigned to the Probate, Divorce, and Admiralty Division of that court. Contentious jurisdiction in probate was first conferred upon the County Courts by the act of 1857.

The liability of executors and legatees for the debts of the deceased seems to have been established at least as early as that of heirs and devisees. It existed in the time of Bracton, who wrote in the reign of Henry III and is treated as clear law by Lord Coke in 1612.[2] In the period of formal pleading no action could have been brought against an executor in any case in which the testator, if living, could have waged his law.[3] For that reason an action of debt on a simple contract lay against the executor only in the Court of Exchequer, where wager of law was not allowed. Power to sue for torts to the property of the deceased was first given to executors by 4 Edw. III, c. 7. They were allowed an action of account by 13 Edw. I, c. 23, but no

[1] An account of the proceedings will be found in 2 State Trials, 1146, and in the Dictionary of National Biography, *s.v.* Bennet, Sir John.
[2] *Pinchon's Case*, 9 Coke's Rep., 86.
[3] That is, have sworn that he did not owe the debt, confirming his oath with that of eleven of his neighbours, who swore that they believed his denial to be true.

such action lay against them until 4 and 5 Anne, c. 16. All these statutes have been superseded by later acts, as will appear in a subsequent chapter.

Before recent legislation a married woman was under certain testamentary disabilities. She could not at common law make a will of any property, for it was not hers to leave. Equity, however, allowed her to dispose by will (under certain restrictions) of property settled to her separate use. In some cases the husband could dispose of her property by will, in others not. A provision was often inserted in the marriage settlement —where there was one—enabling the wife to make an appointment disposing of personalty below a certain value. She could always make a will under a power of appointment, or, when executrix, continue the representation by appointing another executor. She could not act as executrix or take a grant of probate without her husband's concurrence. Her position was gradually ameliorated by the Married Women's Property Acts of 1870 and 1874, and still more by the act of 1882.[1] It seems to have been completely assimilated to that of the unmarried woman by the rule of the Probate Division of 29th March 1887, under which it is not necessary to recite in a grant of probate of the will of a married woman that she was entitled to separate estate.

[1] See p. 71.

CHAPTER II

THE HISTORY OF INTESTATE SUCCESSION IN ENGLAND

THE law of sucession to real estate depends on what, for want of a better word, may be called feudal principles, the law of succession to personal estate is based on that existing in the later period of Roman law, when cognatic had taken the place of agnatic relationship. As in the case of wills, it will be necessary to consider separately the history of succession to the two kinds of property. A short sketch of the history is necessary for explaining much of the significance of the existing law.

Real Estate.—In the pre-Conquest period land descended as a rule, that is, where no custom modified the general law, to all the sons equally, the rule of primogeniture being of Norman introduction.[1] By the reign of Henry II (when Glanvill wrote) the law had become

[1] Both the Mosaic and the Mohammedan law occupy a position midway between pre- and post-Conquest law in England. By the former the eldest son had a double portion for his birthright, by the latter a son had double the portion of a daughter, but the eldest son had no special privilege. In the United States the right of the eldest son has been abolished in all the States, and real and personal property generally descend in the same manner, the main differences appearing in variations of the law as to the respective rights of succession of the husband and the wife. Bills for the assimilation of the succession in real estate to that of the succession in personal estate have often been introduced into the House of Commons of the United Kingdom, but hitherto without success.

established in the form which still prevails. Under this law the rule as to succession of the eldest son is strict and uniform, and now applies to freeholds of all kinds (with a few exceptions to be noticed later), though in Glanvill's time affecting only military tenures.[1] By the time of Bracton the rule of succession of the eldest son had become established with regard to lands of socage tenure. In default of a son the rules of succession laid down by Glanvill remained unaltered until they were amended by Parliament in 1833, unless any general or local custom, such as gavelkind or borough-English, sanctioned a different mode of descent. The three main points in which the law, before the act of 1833, differed from that now prevailing were these. The descent was from the person last seised, instead of from the purchaser, in accordance with the old legal maxim *Seisina facit stipitem;* after failure of issue the collaterals succeeded to the exclusion of the ancestor; the half-blood was entirely excluded.

The right of the successor to the whole estate of the ancestor was limited in freeholds by relief, curtesy, and dower, and in copyholds by fine and heriot, as already mentioned. Relief was a sum of money paid to the lord on succession, consisting generally of a year's rent. A relief might be payable by special custom in succession to copyholds. Curtesy, in full curtesy of England, was the life tenancy of a husband of the whole of the estates in possession of his deceased wife, whether legal or equitable (in gavelkind lands of one-half), provided there had been issue of the marriage born alive who might by possibility have

---

[1] Glanvill's words are, *Si miles fuerit vel per militam tenens tunc secundum jus regni Angliæ primogenitus filius patri succedat in totum.*

been heir to the wife. Dower was a life estate of a widow in one-third part of the lands of her deceased husband, in gavelkind lands of one-half. Rights analogous to curtesy and dower may exist by custom in copyholds. In the latter case the right is generally called freebench. None of these limitations of the full enjoyment of succession are now of much practical importance. Relief is represented by a payment in exceptional cases of one year's quit-rent, generally a nominal sum. It is doubtful whether tenancy by the curtesy can exist after the changes in the law made by the Married Women's Property Act, 1882. The power of barring the widow's right to dower (either by provision in lieu of it, or by simple declaration in a deed or will) given by the Dower Act of 1833, has made the existence of estates in dower very rare.[1] In most cases clauses in the marriage settlement prevent any question as to curtesy or dower arising.

Personalty.—There is a difference of opinion as to the origin of the rights of the Church over the personal estate of an intestate. Blackstone derives it from delegated prerogative, the Crown being originally entitled to such goods as *parens patriæ*. But whether the rights of the Church were inherent or delegated, there is no doubt that they existed in full vigour at an early date, and were recognised in the *Magna Carta* of John, § 27 of which provides that if a free man die intestate, his chattels shall be distributed among his relations, parents, and friends *per visum ecclesiæ*, with a saving for payment of his debts. The goods of the deceased were vested in the ordinary, who was not accountable to any authority

---

[1] Tenancy in dower is, however, still common in some of the States of the United States.

for the mode in which he distributed them. This led to continual complaints that the Church took the whole residue (after payment of two-thirds to the widow and children) for its own benefit, leaving the debts unpaid. In fact, this became the established canon law in England.[1] To remedy this state of things numerous statutes were passed, the earliest of which was that of Westminster the Second in 1285 (13 Edw. I, c. 19), by which provision was made for payment by the ordinary of the debts of the intestate, as far as his goods extended, in the same manner as executors would have been bound to have done, had he left a will. The residue after payment of debts still remained at the disposition of the ordinary until 31 Edw. III, c. 11 (1357), enacted that in case of intestacy the ordinary should depute the nearest and most lawful friends of the deceased to administer his goods.[2] This was the origin of administrators in intestacy. They were merely the deputies or nominees of the ordinary, as they are now of the Probate Division. The Statute of 21 Hen. VIII, c. 5, allowed the judge to choose the widow or the next of kin as administrator at his discretion. Before the reign of Charles II, there was a difficulty in compelling the administrator to make a distribution. Any bond to duly distribute among the next of kin, if entered into by the administrator before the ecclesiastical court, was held void by the temporal courts. Nor was there any statutory definition of the next of kin. In order to remedy these inconveniences the Statutes of Distribution

[1] *In Britanniâ tertia pars bonorum descendentium ab intestato in opus ecclesiæ et pauperum dispensanda est.*—*Decretals*, v. 3, 42.
[2] Any debts due to the intestate and recovered by such friends were by the act still to be administered and dispended for the soul of the dead.

were passed, under which the distribution of the surplus personal estate is to be made by the administrator to the next of kin in a certain order.[1] Administration is now wholly under the jurisdiction of the High Court or a County Court. All customary modes of administration were finally abolished by 19 and 20 Vict., c. 94.

[1] See p. 134.

CHAPTER III

THE WILL IN GENERAL

THE main authority for the law and the formalities of execution of a will is the Wills Act passed July 3, 1837, principally owing to the exertions of Lord Langdale. The whole act is still law, except s. 12, repealed by 28 and 29 Vict., c. 112, and ss. 2 and 36 by the Statute Law Revision Act, 1874. The act extends to England and Ireland, but not to Scotland. What the act did was to make certain amendments in the law, chiefly relating to real property, and to enforce a uniform system of formalities of execution in the case of wills of all kinds. Any differences of procedure arise subsequently; as far as execution is concerned, the law demands the observance of the same formalities, whatever be the nature of the property disposed of. In the great majority of cases a will deals with personalty only or personal and real property together, a will of lands only is comparatively rare. By the Stamp Act, 1870, wills are exempt from stamp duty, but probates and letters of administration must be stamped, as will appear in a later chapter. The will of a living testator may by the Court of Probate Act, 1857, be deposited for safe custody in the principal registry at Somerset House.[1]

[1] 20 and 21 Vict., c. 77, s. 91. The fee for such deposit is ten

TESTAMENTARY CAPACITY

The requisites for the validity of a will are :—
(1) Testamentary capacity of the testator;
(2) Testamentary character of the instrument;
(3) Knowledge and approval of the instrument by the testator;
(4) Absence of undue influence;
(5) Due execution and attestation.

These requisites depend partly on common law, partly on the Wills Act and a later act of 1852.

(1) Every person of the age of twenty-one or upwards is *primâ facie* capable of disposing of his or her property by will. Since the Naturalisation Act, 1870, and the Married Women's Property Act, 1882, this appears to be true of the alien and of the woman married since January 1, 1883. The main, if not the only, exception to the rule as thus laid down is the case of insanity. Insanity is a question of fact, and there appears to be no presumption of sanity until the contrary be shown. The disability of an infant is subject to certain exceptions; a soldier in actual military service or a mariner at sea may make a valid will at fourteen,[1] and a depositor in a savings bank or member of a friendly, etc., society, may make a nomination (which has the effect of a will) at sixteen.[2]

(2) Certain kinds of instruments cannot operate as wills, because they are not of a completely testamentary character. The tests for determining such character

---

shillings. In the office of the inspector of seamen's wills there is, under the Order in Council of December 28, 1865, a depository for the wills of seamen and marines. A will deposited in a public office is the nearest approach in England to the *testament mystique* of the French Code Civil, § 976, a will sealed and deposited with a notary.

[1] See Ch. VIII, where these exceptional wills are more fully treated.
[2] See p. 139.

appears to be whether the document in question is revocable, and whether it is intended to take effect only on the testator's death. If these tests be applied, even a document in form a deed may be in legal effect a will. Mere instructions for a will, or even orders on a banker or letters, if duly executed as a will, may take effect as such. So may a document expressly said to be temporary, *e.g.* one containing the words "until a formal will be made by a lawyer." On the other hand, in a recent case a document duly executed as a will but headed, "This is not meant as a legal will, but as a guide," was held not to be a valid testamentary document, and probate was refused.[1] Evidence is admissible to show either that a document *primâ facie* testamentary is not so, or that a document *primâ facie* not testamentary is so. There is no definition of a will in the Wills Act other than that in the interpretation clause, by which the word "will" is to extend to a testament, and to a codicil, and to an appointment by will or by writing in the nature of a will in exercise of a power, and also to a disposition by will and testament, or devise of the custody and tuition of any child, by virtue of 12 Car. II, c. 24, and the corresponding Irish act, and to any other testamentary disposition.[2] It is not necessary that a will should be a single document. "Sometimes a testator for greater security executes his will in duplicate, retaining one part and committing the other to the custody of another person (usually an executor or trustee); and questions have not unfrequently arisen as to the effect of his subsequently destroying one of such papers, leaving the duplicate entire. In these cases the

[1] *Ferguson-Davie* v. *Ferguson-Davie*, Law Rep. 15 Probate Div., 109 (1890). [2] S. 1.

presumption generally is that the testator means by the destruction of one part to revoke the will, but the strength of the presumption depends much upon circumstances."[1]

Documents may be incorporated as part of the will, but they must be documents actually existing at the time of making the will, and identified by express reference in the will. A will may be contingent, that is, may depend for its validity on the happening of a future event or even on the option of another person than the testator. A will may also be joint, subject to revocation by either of the joint makers or by the survivor. Mutual wills may also be made, that is, wills remaining revocable during the joint lives of the makers, but irrevocable after the death of one of them, provided that the survivor takes advantage of the will of the deceased.

(3) At the time of making the will the testator must be able to understand the nature of the business in which he is engaged, such as the effect of the document, the property intended to be left, and the persons to be benefited. In the absence of proof of fraud or coercion, a will read over to a testator is presumed to have been approved by him, and this although the attesting witnesses, when called to give evidence in court, have no recollection of the circumstances.

(4) The use of undue influence may avoid a will. What is undue influence is a question difficult to answer in the abstract. Roman law expressed it by the words, *Quamvis si liber esset noluisset, tamen coactus voluit.* In a case of *Hall* v. *Hall*, tried before Lord Penzance in the Court of Probate in 1868,[2] that learned judge laid down the law as follows. "To make a good will a man must

[1] 1 Jarman, c. vii.   [2] Law Rep., 1 Probate, 481.

be a free agent. But all influences are not unlawful. Persuasion, appeals to the affections or ties of kindred, to a sentiment of gratitude for past services, or pity for future destitution, or the like,—these are all legitimate and may be fairly pressed on a testator. On the other hand, pressure of whatever character, whether acting on the fears or the hopes, if so exerted as to overpower the volition without convincing the judgment, is a species of restraint under which no valid will can be made. Importunity or threats, such as the testator has not the courage to resist, moral command asserted and yielded to for the sake of peace and quiet, or of escaping from distress of mind or social discomfort, these, if carried to a degree in which the free play of the testator's judgment, discretion, or wishes is overborne, will constitute undue influence, though no force is either used or threatened. In a word, a testator may be led but not driven; and his will must be the offspring of his own volition and not the record of some one else's." In a later case Sir James Hannen directed a jury that in order to establish undue influence it must be shown that the will of the testator was coerced into doing what he did not desire to do.[1] The burden of proof rests on those who assert the exercise of undue influence, and proof must be given that fraud or coercion has been exercised with regard to the will itself. It is always a suspicious circumstance that a person who prepared a will, especially if a solicitor, is greatly benefited by its provisions. Such a person has thrown upon him the *onus* of showing the righteousness of the transaction. An agreement for a reward to use influence over a testator on behalf of a particular person is void.

[1] *Wingrove* v. *Wingrove*, Law Rep., 11 Probate Div., 81 (1886).

(5) By the terms of the Wills Act no will is valid unless in writing and executed in accordance with the provisions of the act. The requisites of execution are as follows :—

(*a*) Signature at the foot or end thereof by the testator or by some other person in his presence or by his direction. The signature may be in pencil, or may be by mark or by a stamp, or even in an assumed name. The will may be written on any substance capable of being written on. No sealing is necessary, and sealing alone is not a sufficient signature, unless the seal be one bearing the testator's name or initials and acknowledged by him as his hand and seal. It is usual, though not compulsory, for the testator and the witnesses to sign each sheet of a will where there are more than one, and to sign or initial all interlineations, which should also be expressly referred to in the attestation clause. Interlineations are presumed to have been made after execution. Where only the last sheet is attested, the presumption is that the others were in the room and formed part of the will at the time of execution. Owing to some difficulties having arisen as to the interpretation of the words "at the foot or end thereof," an Act of Parliament was passed in 1852 (15 and 16 Vict., c. 24), which enacts in short that the will is to be considered valid if it be apparent that the testator intended to give effect by his signature to the writing signed as his will.

(*b*) Signature or acknowledgment in the presence of two witnesses, both present together, before either of them attests.

The requisites of attestation are as follows :—

(*a*) Capacity of the witnesses. Any one is a capable witness, even idiots and lunatics are not excluded by law, though for obvious reasons testators do not make choice of such perons. An infant, if able to write, is a good witness. So is the husband or wife of the testator, an executor, or a creditor. Under the Wills Act, s. 14, a will does not become void owing to the incompetency of a witness, and by s. 15, if a will be attested by any person to whom, or to whose wife or husband, any beneficial interest be given (except a mere charge for payment of debts), the person attesting will be a good witness, but the gift of such beneficial interest to such person, or the wife or husband of such person, will be void. Under this section even a power to a solicitor, who was an attesting witness, to make professional charges was held to be void. Subsequent marriage of two attesting witnesses does not avoid a gift to either or both. A legatee benefited by a will may attest a codicil under which he takes nothing, and conversely a gift may be made by a subsequent codicil to the witness of a will. A gift to an attesting witness is void although there are more witnesses than are necessary; for instance, a gift to one of three attesting witnesses would be void, notwithstanding that the attestation of the others is sufficient for the validity of the will.[1]

(β) The sight, or opportunity of sight, by the witnesses of the signature of acknowledgment of the testator. It is sufficient if the witnesses might have seen had they looked.

(γ) Signature by the witnesses in the presence of the testator, though not necessarily in one another's presence. No form of attestation is prescribed. The usual form,

[1] *Doe* v. *Mills*, 1 Moody and Robinson's Rep., 288 (1833). But the court will admit evidence to prove that the third name was not signed in the capacity of witness.

however, implies that all the three parties were present together and signed in one another's presence.

(δ) Intention to attest as witnesses is necessary. The witness must therefore be aware that it is a will that he attests, though he need not be informed of the contents. Initials, description, or a mark constitute a sufficient signature. By s. 21 of the act no obliteration, interlineation, or other alteration made in any will after its execution is to have any effect (except so far as the words of the will before such alteration shall not be apparent), unless such alteration be executed in the same manner as a will. The alteration may be executed and attested in the margin or on some other part of the will opposite to or near such alteration, or at the foot or end of or opposite to a memorandum referring to such alteration, and written at the end or some other part of the will. Unattested alterations or interlineations are presumed to have been made after execution.

Other sections of the Wills Act dealing with the general law (not treated under special heads) are the following:—

By s. 3 all real and personal estate to which the testator is entitled either at law or in equity may be disposed of by will. This includes property acquired between the execution of the will and the death of the testator.[1]

By s. 13 every will executed in accordance with the act is valid without republication.

By s. 23 a conveyance or other act subsequent to the execution of a will (except an act of revocation) does not prevent the operation of the will over such

---

[1] As a general rule a testator can leave by will only what he could give in life. The one exception appears to be a freehold to commence *in futuro*, which can legally be the subject of a devise, but not of a conveyance *inter vivos* at common law.

real or personal estate as the testator has power to dispose of at his death.

By s. 34 the act does not extend to wills made before January 1, 1838, and a will re-executed or republished or revived by codicil is, for the purposes of the act, to be deemed to have been made at the time of re-execution, republication, or revival; nor does the act extend to the estate *pur autre vie* of any person dying before January 1, 1838.

It should be noticed that there may be a good contract to make a will or a devise or bequest in favour of a particular person. Such a contract has been enforced by action for specific performance, or by action for damages against the representatives of the deceased. The contract must be valid by the Statute of Frauds where that statute requires writing. On this principle a mere verbal promise to make a will in favour of a housekeeper in reward for her services was held to give no right of action against the heir of the promiser on his dying intestate. Neither the continuance of the plaintiff in the service of the deceased after the promise, nor the execution by the latter of a document intended to operate as a will in the plaintiff's favour, but invalid for want of proper attestation, was regarded by the House of Lords as sufficient part performance to exclude the operation of the Statute of Frauds.[1] In the case of a will obtained by a promise to dispose of property in a particular way, the court gives effect to the verbal arrangement by affecting with a trust the property devised or bequeathed.

A contract to dispose of a succession in favour of a particular person is good,[2] subject always to the pro-

[1] *Alderson* v. *Maddison*, Law Rep., 7 Appeal Cases, 174 (1883).
[2] By the law of France and other countries which follow the Roman law such a contract is invalid.

tection afforded by the courts to expectant heirs, who have been relieved from unconscionable bargains even where such bargains have been made after they have attained their majority. In one well-known case the heir-apparent to an earldom, when twenty-two years of age, had borrowed money at sixty per cent on the security of his interest in the property which would be his at his father's death. After the death of the father, the lender commenced actions on his bills, but it was held by the Court of Appeal in Chancery that the actions must be restrained and the bills delivered up on payment of the sums actually advanced with interest at five per cent.[1]

A will defective in form is defective for every purpose. In some cases a court of equity will interfere to grant relief where an instrument is not duly executed, but this is never the case where the instrument is a will. The date of a will may, however, be supplied or corrected by a court having jurisdiction in probate after hearing the evidence of an attesting witness. The powers given by a will are sometimes extended by a private Act of Parliament, chiefly in the direction of increased powers of leasing and of sale of heirlooms. But there appears to be no instance where an act has given validity to a will invalid in form. In a few cases private acts have been passed for better effecting the purposes of wills, Parliament assuming to a limited extent the jurisdiction of a court of construction.

The rules for the guidance of testators given by Lord Coke are still of value, and it will not be amiss to set them out at length.

"1st. Make it by good advice, in your perfect memory,

[1] *Earl of Aylesford* v. *Morris*, Law Rep., 8 Chancery, 484 (1873).

and inform your counsel truly of the estates and tenures of your lands, and by God's grace the resolution of the judges in this case [1] will be a good direction to learned counsel to make your will according to law, and thereby prevent questions and controversies.

"2d. It is good, if your will concern inheritance, to make it indented,[2] and to leave one part with a friend, lest after your death it be suppressed.

"3d. At the time of the publication of the will,[3] call credible[4] witnesses to subscribe their names to it.

"4th. If it may be, let all the will be written with one and the same hand, and in one or the same parchment or paper, for fear of alteration, addition, or diminution.

"5th. Let the hand and seal[5] of the devisor be set to it.

"6th. If it be in several parts, let his hand and seal be put, and the names of the witnesses subscribed, to each part.

"7th. If there be any interlining or rasure in the will, let a memorandum be made of it and signed by the testator.

"8th. If you make any revocation of your will, or of any part of it, make it by writing, by good advice; for on a revocation by word[6] follow controversies, some of the witnesses affirming it to be in one manner, and some in another manner."

---

[1] *Butler and Baker's Case*, 3 Coke's Rep., 25a (1591), to the report of which these rules are added as a note. The case dealt with the requisites of a will, and what real estate might at that time be devised.

[2] The advice to indent the copy is a relic of the old theory of a will as a conveyance. See p. 11. A deed of grant is generally by indenture.

[3] Publication is not now necessary.

[4] Credibility is not a condition of valid attestation since the Wills Act. See p. 13.

[5] There is no need to seal a will, though it may be sealed if the testator please. Sealing without signing is not a sufficient execution.

[6] Such revocation would not be valid in any case since the Wills Act.

CHAPTER IV

THE WILL OF LANDS

THE law of what may be called the external and internal validity of the will of lands (under which any kind of real estate is included) depends partly on decisions of the courts, mostly on statute. The principal part of the law depending on decisions is that dealing with the internal validity of the will where questions of public policy arise.

The will of lands differs fundamentally from the will of personalty in being itself evidence, while the probate copy is the only legal evidence of the will of personalty, or of the will of both lands and personalty combined. A will of lands thirty years old, coming from the proper custody, will be presumed to have been duly executed. In two cases only is probate of a will of lands granted: (1) where executors are appointed to carry out its provisions, (2) where the probate is in solemn form pursuant to the Court of Probate Act, 1857.[1] The same act provides that in any case where it would be necessary, according to the then existing law, to produce and prove an original will, in order to establish a devise or other testamentary disposition of or affecting real

[1] P. 125.

estate, the party intending to give such proof may give to the opposite party ten days at least before the trial notice of his intention to give in evidence the probate in solemn form, and such probate shall be sufficient evidence of the will, and of its validity and contents, unless the opposite party, within four days after receiving the notice, give notice that he intends to dispute the validity.[1] An action will lie in the Chancery Division to perpetuate the testimony of the attesting witnesses, where a devisee apprehends an attempt on the part of the heir to impeach the validity of the will. Where land devised by a will is in one of the register counties (Middlesex and Yorkshire), in order to give it validity as a document of title a memorial should be registered in the registry of the county or riding, containing, *inter alia*, the dates of the will and of the testator's death, the names and addresses of the witnesses, a description of the lands affected by the will, and the names of the parishes where they are situated. The Registry Acts do not apply to devises of copyholds, and the Middlesex Act does not apply to the City of London. It is provided by the Vendor and Purchaser Act, 1874 (37 and 38 Vict., c. 78, s. 8), that where the will of a testator devising land in Middlesex or Yorkshire has not been registered within the period allowed by law in that behalf (in ordinary cases six months from the testator's death), an assurance of such land to a purchaser or mortgagee by the devisee, or by some one deriving title under him, shall, if registered before, take precedence of and prevail over any assurance from the testator's heir-at-law.

A devise by will may be either immediate or executory. An executory devise is one the operation of which

[1] S. 64.

is postponed until a certain time after the testator's death. "To take a common instance; a man may by his will devise lands to his son A, an infant, and his heirs; but in case A should die under the age of twenty-one years, then to B and his heirs. In this case A has an estate in fee simple in possession, subject to an executory interest in favour of B. If A should not die under age, his estate in fee simple will continue with him unimpaired. But if he should die under that age, nothing can prevent the estate of B from immediately arising and coming into possession, and displacing for ever the estate of A and his heirs."[1] The difference between an executory devise and a contingent remainder is of smaller importance than it was, as by an act passed in 1877, (40 and 41 Vict., c. 33), a contingent remainder is capable of taking effect as an executory devise in the event of the particular estate determining before the contingent remainder vests.[2] It can of course take effect only where the executory devise could take effect, and if the executory devise would be void for remoteness, the remainder will be equally void.

The sections of the Wills Act affecting real estate are the following:—

"The words 'real estate' shall extend to manors, advowsons, messuages, lands, tithes, rents, and hereditaments, whether freehold, customary freehold, tenant right, customary, or copyhold, or of any other tenure, and whether corporeal, incorporeal, or personal, and to any undivided share thereof, and to any estate, right, or interest (other than a chattel interest) therein."—S. 1.

[1] Williams on *Real Property*, pt. ii, ch. iii, s. 1. Another example is afforded by a devise in case of death without issue as construed by s. 29 of the Wills Act. See p. 88.
[2] See the work on *Real Property* in this series.

The power of devising real estate extends to all real estate to which the testator shall be entitled either at law or in equity at the time of his death, and which, if not so devised, would devolve upon the heir-at-law or customary heir of him, or, if he became entitled by descent, of his ancestor. It also extends to customary freeholds and copyholds without surrender and before admittance, and also to such as could not at the time of the passing of the Act have been disposed of owing to the want of a custom to devise or surrender, or to the custom that a will or surrender should continue in force for a limited time. The power also extends to estates *pur autre vie*[1] of whatever tenure, to contingent, executory, or other future interests, and to rights of entry. (S. 3.) This section gives the right to dispose of all kinds of real estate, whether in possession, reversion, or remainder, even those to which he has only a possessory title. The only exception seems to be estate of which there is a joint tenancy, for on death of one joint tenant the estate passes to the survivor or survivors, and the power of devise is confined to the last survivor. Heirlooms[2] and fixtures are, though in their nature personal, regarded by the law as real property, except as far as, in the case of fixtures, exceptions have been introduced by Act of Parliament.

Where any real estate of the nature of customary free-

---

[1] That is, an estate dependent on the life or lives of another, or others, called *cestui que vie* or *cestuis que vie*. Such estates were at one time commonly granted by certain corporations, such as colleges and deans and chapters, but are now comparatively rare. An estate *pur autre vie* is a freehold.

[2] Heirlooms are properly such chattels as by local custom pass with the inheritance. But the term is often applied, and less correctly, to gifts of such chattels as jewels and pictures intended by the testator to devolve with land. Heirlooms of the latter kind may by leave of the court now be sold by a tenant for life under the powers given by s. 37 of the Settled Land Act, 1882.

hold or tenant right or customary or copyhold might have been surrendered to the use of a will, and the testator has not surrendered it to the use of his will, no person entitled thereto is to be admitted except on payment of such stamp duties and fees as are chargeable in respect of a surrender or the presenting, registering, or enrolling of such surrender. Where the testator was entitled to have been but was not admitted, the person entitled under the will is liable to the stamp duties and fees which would have been payable on admission of the testator in addition to those payable on his own admission. (S. 4.)

Wills or extracts of wills disposing of a customary freehold or tenant right or customary or copyhold are to be entered by the lord or steward of the manor on the court rolls; and the lord is entitled to the same fine, heriot, dues, duties, and services from the devisee as would have been due from the customary heir had the estate descended. (S. 5.)

If no disposition by will be made of an estate *pur autre vie* of a freehold nature, the same is chargeable, if it come to the heir by special occupancy,[1] as assets by descent; in the absence of a special occupant of any estate *pur autre vie*, whether freehold or otherwise, and whether a corporeal or incorporeal hereditament,[2] it goes to the executor or administrator of the party that had the

[1] The heir entering and holding possession of an estate *pur autre vie* granted to the grantee and his heirs is known as the special occupant, as distinguished from the personal occupant, that is, the first person entering after the death of the tenant for life of an estate *pur autre vie*, who until the coming into operation of the Statute of Frauds was entitled to hold it as his own. The Statute of Frauds abolished general occupancy.

[2] Incorporeal hereditaments, which cover much the same ground as the *res incorporales* of Roman law, are such property as is (to use the language of the text-books) of an intangible nature, *e.g.* rents, annuities, advowsons.

estate thereof by virtue of the grant, and is assets in his hands, distributable in the same manner as the personal estate of the testator or intestate. (S. 6.)

The remaining sections of the Wills Act which refer to real estate are instances of statutory construction, and will be found in the chapter on construction.

Recent legislation has dealt to a considerable extent with the power of devising real estate. The interpretation clause of the Settled Estates Act, 1877, includes "will" under "settlement," so that the powers of the act may be exercised over property devised by will. The same is the case with the larger powers of disposition of settled land given by the Settled Land Act, 1882. The latter act also includes under "settlement" an estate or interest not disposed of by a settlement, and reverting to the settlor or descending to the testator's heir. By the Conveyancing Act, 1882, s. 10, a restriction is placed on executory limitations.[1]

It may be useful to group together certain cases in which the law from motives of public policy refuses to give validity to certain devises and bequests. Whether or not a particular devise or bequest is of this nature is a question of construction, and some part of the law will more properly fall under that head.[2]

(1) *Public policy in general.*—This would practically include all cases not included under classes of a more special nature,—for instance, such as *Egerton* v. *Earl Brownlow*.[3] It generally comes to be considered under the head of devises upon condition. There are, however, one or two statutes restricting express devises on the ground of their being against public policy. The most interesting is perhaps 53 Geo: III, c. 49, forbidding devises for the

[1] See below.   [2] P. 98.   [3] P. 99.

purpose of multiplying votes for Parliament. This has become of comparatively small importance since recent alterations in the law have made it impossible henceforth to create forty-shilling rent-charges for the purpose of giving votes.

(2) *Mortmain.*—The law of mortmain now depends chiefly on the Mortmain and Charitable Uses Act, 1888 (51 and 52 Vict., c. 42), which partly, but not altogether, consolidates the previous law on the subject. The effect of the act is that in general real estate or personal estate "savouring of realty"[1] cannot be left by will for charitable purposes and that no corporation can hold land in mortmain unless by licence from the Crown or by statute, under penalty of forfeiture to the Crown or a mesne lord. No gift to a corporation or charity, involving the acquisition of land even indirectly, can be made unless in accordance with the terms of the act. Thus gifts of money to erect a schoolhouse, a chapel, a dispensary, etc., have all been held void under previous mortmain acts. By the present act every assurance of land or of money to be laid out in the purchase of land to or for the benefit of any charitable uses must be by deed *inter vivos* executed in the presence of at least two witnesses, and must, unless it be made in good faith and for valuable consideration (which may take the form of a rent or rent-charge), be made at least twelve months before the death of the assuror. If the assurance be of stock in the public funds, it must be made six months

---

[1] Sometimes called "impure personalty." It includes leaseholds, mortgage debts, and emblements. Whether debentures and bonds in a company are pure or impure personalty depends on the remedies against the real estate of the company given to the debenture-holders and bond-holders. So strict is the rule as to impure personalty that even legacy duty on a charitable bequest given free of duty cannot be paid out of impure personalty.

before the death of the assuror. If the assurance be of land or personal estate other than stock in the public funds, it must within six months after execution be enrolled in the central office of the Supreme Court of Judicature. The exemptions from the provisions of the act (as far as regards the law of wills) are as follows :—

(*a*) Assurances of land by will to an extent not exceeding twenty acres for a public park, and two acres for a public museum, and one acre for a schoolhouse for an elementary school, provided that a will containing such an assurance must be executed not less than twelve months before the death of the assuror, or be a reproduction in substance of a devise made in a previous will in force at the time of such reproduction, which was executed not less than twelve months before the death of the assuror, and must be enrolled in the books of the Charity Commissioners within six months after the death of the testator.

(*b*) Assurances of land or personal estate to be laid out in the purchase of land to or in trust for any of the Universities of Oxford, Cambridge, London, Durham, and the Victoria University, or any of the colleges or houses of learning within any of those universities, or in trust for any of the colleges of Eton, Winchester, and Westminster, for the better support and maintenance of the scholars only upon the foundations of those last-mentioned colleges, or to or in trust for the warden, council, and scholars of Keble College.

Further exceptions from the policy of the Mortmain Act are made by numerous Acts of Parliament, many of which relate to gifts of land for Church purposes. Thus by 3 and 4 Vict., c. 60, a licence in mortmain is not required in cases of endowment unless the endowment exceeds the clear annual value of £300. In some cases a limit of amount is fixed, in others not. 43 Geo. III, c. 108, empowers a testator, by will duly executed at least three months before his death, to devise land not exceeding five acres, or goods and chattels not exceeding in value £500, towards the erecting or providing any church or chapel.[1] Occasionally relief from the provisions of the Mortmain Act is given in an indirect manner, as by s. 37 of 7 and 8 Vict., c. 37, which enacts that where a grant has been made for a school site the death of the grantor within twelve months does not avoid the grant.

Many of the exceptions from the Mortmain Act affect chiefly or wholly gifts by deed *inter vivos*. This is the case with the Church Building Acts, the New Parishes Acts, the act of 17 and 18 Vict., c. 112 (enabling grants of land to the extent of one acre to be made to literary and scientific societies), and the Companies Act, 1862 (enabling companies formed for art, etc., not for profit, to hold land not exceeding two acres, and more with the licence of the Board of Trade). Numerous public and charitable institutions are exempted by special Acts of Parliament. Among these are the British Museum, the Governors of Queen Anne's Bounty, the Ecclesiastical Commissioners, the Conservators of the Thames, the Prison Commissioners, University College, London, the Guardians of the Poor of Plymouth, and certain hospitals, as Westminster, St. George's, Greenwich, the Foundling, and Bath. In most of these cases there is a limit fixed to the amount which may be left by will. By the custom of London

---

[1] All the law relating to such gifts, as far as they are for church building purposes, will be found in 1 Stephens's *Laws Relating to the Church and Clergy*, 137, *s. v.* "Benefactions."

a citizen of London may still devise land in the city of London to a corporation other than a charity. A will relating to a charity may, by the Charitable Trusts Act, 1855, be enrolled by the Charity Commissioners. It should be noticed that the power of the Crown to grant licences in mortmain applies only to mortmain proper, *i.e.* the holding of land by a corporation, not to charitable uses. Bequests for charitable purposes have been upheld under circumstances where they would have been void for uncertainty had the legatees been private persons. For instance, bequests for charitable and deserving objects—to the poor, to the poor inhabitants of a particular parish, etc.

(3) *Perpetuity.*—The Mortmain Act deals specially with devises and bequests to corporations and charities.[1] The law which forbids property to be tied up for more than a limited period in a particular line of succession depends to a great extent on the same principles, but is the creation of the courts rather than of statute, as there appear to be only two Acts of Parliament forbidding perpetuity. The law, it has been said, abhors perpetuities: in the words of Lord Coke, "Perpetuities . . . were born under an unfortunate constellation, for as soon as they have been been brought in question, judgment has always been given against them, and none at any time given for them."[2] It was to conditions

---

[1] Charities in all cases, and corporations with a licence to hold in mortmain, either from the Crown or under an Act of Parliament, are of course exceptions to the ordinary rules of law as to perpetuities. Charitable uses are any of those mentioned in the preamble to 43 Eliz., c. 4. This act was repealed by the Mortmain Act of 1888, but it was enacted by the latter act that references to charities in Acts of Parliament within the meaning, purview, and interpretation of the act of Elizabeth, are still to be construed by reference to the preamble of that act.

[2] *Legat's Case*, 10 Coke's Rep. 113*b* (1639).

restraining tenants in tail from alienation that the term "perpetuity" was first applied.[1] Such attempts at creating perpetuity were looked upon with disfavour by the courts of common law; and finally, in the reign of Edward IV, they allowed a tenant in tail, by suffering a common recovery—a fictitious judicial proceeding,—to bar the entail, in spite of the terms of the statute *De Donis Conditionalibus*. The tenant in tail in remainder was on coming of age enabled, with the concurrence of the tenant in tail in possession, to bar the entail by a recovery. On a similar principle it has become the rule that the latest period at which an estate limited by way of executory use can be allowed to vest is twenty-one years after the expiration of some life or lives in being at the time when the devise was made, with a further period allowed for the time of gestation, in case of a person entitled being *en ventre sa mère* when his right accrues. This rule forbids the tying up of an estate for a longer period than until the unborn child of some living person shall come of age. A gift to the first son of A, a living person, who shall attain the age of twenty-four, will be altogether void—void for remoteness, as it is termed, not simply void for the three years beyond the legal limit. The rule as to creation of contingent remainders is that no estate can be given to an unborn person for life, followed by an estate to the child of such person. No remainder, in fact, can be given to the child of a person not in existence. This is called, in old legal language, limiting a possibility upon a possibility, or a double possibility; and the rule exists, it has been recently held,[2] independently of the rule

[1] Third Report of the Real Property Commissioners, 30 (1830).
[2] *Whitby* v. *Mitchell*, Law Rep., 44 Chancery Div., 85 (1890).

against perpetuities, though the principle of both the rules is, from the view of public policy, the same. The act of 1877, already referred to, appears not to preserve the contingent remainder if the particular estate on which it depends be defeated by its determination owing to remoteness before the remainder vests.[1] The Conveyancing Act, 1882,[2] enacts that where a person is entitled to land for an estate in fee, or for life, or a term of years absolute or determinable with life, with an executory limitation over on default or failure of issue, the executory limitation is to become void as soon as there is living any issue who has attained the age of twenty-one. This enables him to alienate without the concurrence (previously necessary) of those taking under the limitation. Where a question of perpetuity arises from the exercise of a power of appointment, the calculation of the time from which perpetuity is reckoned varies as the power is general or special. The donee of a general power has the same capacity of disposition as an absolute owner, therefore the date from which the perpetuity is to be reckoned is that of the exercise of the power. But where the power is special, *e.g.* among members of a class, such as the children of A, the appointment is not valid unless it would have been unobjectionable in point of remoteness if it had been contained in the instrument creating the power. A general power exercisable only by will is on the same footing in this respect as a special power. As a will speaks from the death of the testator, a power created by will may be duly exercised when it would have been too late had it been exercised by deed on

---

[1] Lewin on *Trusts*, c. xvi, s. 12.
[2] 45 and 46 Vict., c. 39, s. 10.

the day of the execution of the will. With regard to accumulations of income, an act passed in 1800 (39 and 40 Geo. III, c. 98), known as the Thellusson Act,[1] forbids the accumulation of income for any longer term than the life of the grantor or settlor, or twenty-one years from the death of the grantor, settlor, devisor, or testator, or during the minority of any person living or *en ventre sa mère* at the death of the grantor, etc., or during the minority only of any person who under the settlement or will would for the time being, if of full age, be entitled to the income directed to be accumulated. The act extends to income of both real and personal property, but not to any provision for the payment of debts, or for raising portions for children, or to any direction touching the produce of timber or wood. A direction to accumulate is, if it transgress the limits named, not void altogether, like an executory devise beyond the limits allowed by law, but is valid to the extent of the time allowed by the act.

Many of the cases as to perpetuity have arisen on testamentary trusts for keeping tombs in repair. A distinction has been drawn between tombs outside and tombs inside the walls of a church. A trust for the former purpose is void, but for the latter purpose good, as it is for the benefit of the congregation that it should be kept in good repair. It is a charitable gift, which the former is not, as no living person is benefited by it. One of the most interesting cases on the question

[1] The act was passed in consequence of the will of a Mr. Thellusson, the terms of which directed an accumulation of the testator's income during the lives of all his children, grandchildren, and great-grandchildren who should be living at the time of his death, for the benefit of descendants who should be living at the time of the death of the last survivor of those named. The probable amount of the accumulated fund was estimated at £19,000,000.

of perpetuity was that of which Shakespeare's house was the subject. A testator bequeathed £2500 to be invested to keep the house in repair, a further sum of £2500 to form a museum there, and an annuity of £60 out of the rents of real estate for paying the wages of a keeper or guardian, among whose duties should be that of attending to visitors and offering them "a bound-up volume with pen and ink to inscribe, on certain conditions, such lines in verse or prose as the fancy of each visitant may induce him to write." It was held by the Court of Appeal in Chancery, that inasmuch as the house was private property and the museum was intended to be perpetual, the trust for it was void, and that the gift of £60 per annum was also void as a perpetuity.[1] The principle of perpetuity has been extended to gifts of houses in the Straits Settlements. In the case in question there was a devise of the upper story of four houses or shops as a family house for the use of two separate families, without any limitation of the period of occupation. There was also a devise of two plantations to be reserved as the family burying-place and of a house for performing religious ceremonies to the testatrix and her late husband. All these devises were held void for perpetuity.[2] Whether a grant by the Crown in England or a colony is affected by the rule against perpetuities appears to be an unsettled point.[3]

[1] *Thomson* v. *Shakespeare*, 1 De Gex, Fisher and Jones' Rep., 399 (1860). Had the house been public property, the result would probably have been different.

[2] *Yeap Cheah* v. *Ong Cheng*, Law Rep., 6 Privy Council, 381 (1875). This case is very interesting, as showing the primitive religious conceptions which may have to be dealt with by a court of justice even in modern times. The gift, it should be noticed, was held void on the ground of perpetuity, not on the ground of its being to superstitious uses.

[3] *Cooper* v. *Stuart*, Law Rep., 14 Appeal Cases, 286 (1889).

(4) *Superstitious Uses.*—A distinction is to be drawn between superstitious uses or trusts proper and uses or trusts for the promotion of religious views forbidden by law. Under the first head come devises or bequests for the benefit of the soul of the testator. Such devises or bequests were almost a matter of course in wills before the Reformation, and often took the form of founding chantries for a priest to sing in. They were forbidden by numerous statutes in the sixteenth century (especially by 1 Edw. VI, c. 14, which abolished chantries), and there is a considerable number of reported cases decided upon the construction of the acts. All the cases, with one or two exceptions, relate to gifts by Roman Catholic testators. The exceptions are gifts by Jewish testators, but the effect is the same. The promotion of the views of Joanna Southcote has been held to be not a superstitious use. There has never been any decision in England as to the Mormon faith. In one case in the reign of Charles II, Lord Keeper North held that a gift of £600 to Richard Baxter to be distributed among sixty of the ministers ejected in 1662, and also a legacy for the purpose of publishing his *Call to the Unconverted*, were void as superstitious, but this decision was reversed by the Lords Commissioners.[1] As lately as 1880 a gift of £10 for masses for the soul of the testator was held void.[2] Uses or trusts for the promotion of religious views forbidden by law rest on somewhat different principles. Gifts for superstitious uses are simply void, those for unlawful religious views are applied by the Crown for the purposes of some religious purpose permitted by the law. Most of the cases have arisen with

---

[1] *Attorney-General* v. *Baxter*, 1 Vernon's Rep., 248 (1684).
[2] *Re Fleetwood*, 15 Chancery Div., 596.

regard to gifts to religious orders of men, which by the Roman Catholic Relief Act of 1829 (10 Geo. IV, c. 7), are illegal associations.[1] The Roman Catholic Charities Act, 1860 (23 and 24 Vict., c. 134), enacts that no gift of real or personal estate upon any lawful charitable trust for the exclusive benefit of persons professing the Roman Catholic religion shall be invalidated by reason only that the same estate has been or shall be subjected to any trust or provision deemed to be superstitious or otherwise prohibited by the laws affecting persons professing the same religion; but in every case it shall be lawful for the Chancery Division or a judge thereof at chambers, upon the application of the Attorney-General, or of any person authorised by the Charity Commissioners, or for the Commissioners themselves, to apportion the estate or the annual income so that a proportion thereof may be exclusively subject to the lawful charitable trusts declared by the donor, and the residue become subject to such lawful charitable trusts for the benefit of persons professing the Roman Catholic religion, to take effect in lieu of such superstitious or prohibited trusts, as the said court or a judge or the said board may consider to be most just. In cases other than Roman Catholic cases the courts have held trusts or legacies for the benefit of dissenters valid, as long as they are not subversive of all religion and morality. A legacy for the best essay on the sufficiency of natural theology treated as a science was held void as subversive of Christianity. Although in recent prosecutions for blasphemy a more liberal view of the liability to the criminal law of persons actively attacking Christian doctrine has

[1] Nothing in the act is to extend to any order, community, or establishment of females bound by religious vows.

been taken, it is probably still correct to affirm with the late Chief Baron Kelly that "there is abundant authority for saying that Christianity is part and parcel of the law of the land."[1]

(5) *Restriction on Alienation.*—It is a cardinal principle that conditions or limitations repugnant to the estate to which they are attached are void. If an estate be devised in fee simple, with a condition prohibiting the grantee and his heirs, or the grantee himself, from alienation, either by his own act or the act of the law, such a condition is merely void. It would also be void from its tending to create a possible perpetuity. The repugnancy of the estate is, however, the ground on which Lord Coke considers such a condition invalid.[2] A condition against alienation by act of the law, *e.g.* a condition that the estate of a devisee shall not be subject to the bankrupt laws, is equally void, as contrary to the policy of the law. An estate may, however, be limited until bankruptcy. The policy of the common law in respect of restriction on alienation has in some cases been adopted by statute. Thus the Settled Land Act, 1882 (45 and 46 Vict., c. 38, s. 51), enacts that any provision in a will purporting or attempting by way of direction, declaration, or otherwise, to forbid a tenant for life to exercise any power under the act, or tending by any limitation, etc., to prohibit or prevent him from exercising, or to induce him to abstain from exercising such power, is to be deemed to be void. To the general rule against attaching conditions repugnant certain exceptions are admitted. A condition that the devisee shall not alien to a named person appears to be valid.

[1] *Cowan* v. *Milbourn*, Law Rep., 2 Exchequer, 234 (1867).
[2] Coke upon Littleton, 222, 223.

Whether a condition that he shall not alien during a particular time is valid or not appears to be uncertain, there being a conflict of authority on the question. In the case of married women an exception introduced by the Court of Chancery has long been admitted. Property devised to the separate use of a married woman may be made subject to a restraint on anticipation. In such a case any attempted disposition by her during the continuance of the marriage is absolutely void. The law is not altered by the Married Women's Property Act, 1882, s. 19 of which provides that "nothing in this Act contained shall . . . interfere with or render inoperative any restriction against anticipation at present attached to, or to be hereafter attached to the enjoyment of any property or income by a woman under any . . . will." A restriction against anticipation contained in a settlement of a woman's own property is, by the same section, not to be valid against ante-nuptial debts, but this part of the section does not apply to a restriction on anticipation contained in a will. In some cases the court has been empowered by recent legislation to exercise certain powers irrespective of a restraint on anticipation. The Settled Estates Act, 1877, s. 50, enacts that no clause or provision in any settlement[1] restraining anticipation shall prevent the court from exercising, if it think fit, any of the powers given by the act. The Settled Land Act, 1882, s. 61, provides that a restraint on anticipation in the settlement shall not prevent the exercise by a married woman of any power under the act. By the Conveyancing Act, 1881, s. 39, notwithstanding that a married woman is restrained from anticipation,

[1] By the interpretation clauses of these acts "settlement" includes "will."

the court may, if it thinks fit, where it appears to be for her benefit, by judgment or order, with her consent, bind her interest in any property. The restraint on anticipation applies only to married women; it was at one time attempted to extend it to men, and without respect to their being married or not, but the law has long been established as it has been already stated.

(6) *Restraint of Marriage.*—This subject will be treated in a subsequent chapter.[1]

(7) *Indefiniteness of subject or object.*—This generally makes the devise void, subject to an exception in favour of charities and to explanation by extrinsic evidence of the indefiniteness in certain cases.[2]

[1] P. 98. [2] P. 93.

CHAPTER V

THE WILL OF PERSONALTY

THE only sections of the Wills Act dealing specially with personalty are the interpretation clause (s. 1) and the sections preserving the privilege of soldiers and sailors as to the disposal of their personal estate.[1] By s. 1 "the words 'personal estate' shall extend to leasehold estates and other chattels real, and also to moneys, shares of government and other funds, securities for money (not being real estates), debts, choses in action, rights, credits, goods, and all other property whatsoever which by law devolves upon the executor or administrator." This allows the testator to make a bequest of all his personal property of whatever kind, whether in possession or in action.[2] At one time, as has already been said,[3] the appointment of an executor was necessary to the validity of a will of personalty, but this rule has long been obsolete, and now, where no executor is appointed, administration *cum testamento annexo* is granted.[4] Any personal estate left by a will is called a legacy or bequest as opposed to the devise, which is properly used only of real estate.[5] But legacy may be used of real

[1] P. 77. [2] P. 141. [3] P. 17. [4] See p. 137.
[5] Originally devise and bequest were used indiscriminately. Thus in the Assize of Northampton (1176), § 4, *divisa* is used for a bequest.

estate, if there be nothing else named in the will to which it can apply. Legacies are of several kinds. A general legacy is one payable out of the general assets of the testator, such as a bequest of £100, or a bequest of the residue not already disposed of. A demonstrative legacy is a gift of a certain sum to be satisfied from a particular fund, such as a gift of £100 to be paid out of a certain sum in consols. A specific legacy is a bequest of a named sum or chattel, such as £100 now standing to the testator's credit at a particular bank, or a particular piece of jewellery, furniture, etc. General legacies are liable to abatement in case of a deficiency of assets, and the legatees may be bound, subject to the provisions of 22 and 23 Vict., c. 35,[1] to refund the whole or a part of the legacy, even after payment, should debts owing by the estate afterwards come to light. A demonstrative legacy is not liable to abatement as long as any part of the fund out of which it is payable exists. A specific legacy does not abate until after exhaustion of the general and demonstrative legacies, but it is liable to be adeemed by the testator disposing of it during his lifetime. By 3 and 4 Will. IV, c. 105, s. 12, legacies to widows in satisfaction of dower are entitled to priority over other legacies. Legacies may also be optional, substitutional, or contingent. An optional legacy is one in which the legatee has a choice between two or more chattels, or between a larger and a smaller sum. In the latter case he is entitled to the larger sum. A substitutional legacy is one given to

---

of chattels, and in the pleas of the Manorial Court of King's Ripton (see p. 3), and in many of the wills of the fourteenth century contained in Sir H. Nicholas' *Testamenta Vetusta*, *legatum* is used for a devise of land. The *legatum* of Roman law applied to both kinds of property.   [1] P. 146.

B in case of A, the original legatee, predeceasing the testator, in order to prevent the legacy falling by lapse into the residue, which otherwise it would do, except in the cases provided for by s. 33 of the Wills Act. Lapse will not be prevented merely by the addition of the words, "and his executors, administrators, and assigns," for these words are but surplusage. A contingent legacy is one left on a condition, such as one left to the legatee if or when he shall attain the age of twenty-one, or "to A if he shall be in my service at my death." A legacy may also, like a devise, be executory, that is, may create an interest to arise at a future time, not immediately on the death of the testator. An instance would be a life interest in a term of years, or a sum of money, by annuity or otherwise, with a limitation over after the death of the original legatee. There can be no limitation of articles *quæ ipso usu consumuntur*, such as wine. Nor can there be any entail of a chattel interest, *e.g.* a gift of a term of years to A and the heirs of his body confers on A the term absolutely, and on his death it goes to his personal representatives. By the Apportionment Act, 1870, all periodical payments in the nature of income are to be considered as accruing from day to day. A bequest of an annuity would fall within this rule, and on the death of the first annuitant his representatives would be entitled to so much of the income as had accrued up to his death.[1] A bequest, like a devise, must be good in law, *i.e.* definite in subject and object, and not made for superstitious uses, or in restraint of alienation or marriage. Executory bequests must not transgess the rule as to perpetuities, or as to

[1] A legatee of chattels for life may be compelled to give an inventory to the legatee in remainder.

accumulation under the Thellusson Act.[1] In the exercise of powers of appointment the limits from which perpetuity is reckoned vary according as the power is general or special, i.e. confined to a particular class, as children of a particular person. In the former case the rule against perpetuities has no application until a settlement is executed in pursuance of the power; in the latter case the limits of perpetuity are reckoned from the date of the creation of the power.[2] The rule in *Shelley's Case*, though primarily laid down as to real property, has been adopted, *mutatis mutandis*, in the law of personal property.[3] Thus a gift of money in trust for A for life, and after his decease in trust for his executors, administrators, and assigns, confers on A the absolute interest. It seems necessary, however, that the word "assigns" should be used in order that the rule should apply, differing in this respect from a gift of real estate.

Closely connected with the subject of legacies is that of *donationes mortis causâ*, though the gift in such cases takes effect in addition to or in spite of a will, and not, like a legacy, by virtue of a will. The law as well as the name of *donationes mortis causâ* is founded on Roman law. A *donatio mortis causâ* is a gift of personalty made in contemplation of death, to be absolute only in case of the death of the giver. It could originally only have been of chattels the property in which passes by delivery. But certain exceptions have been engrafted on this state of the law, and it has been held that a debt secured by bond can be passed by delivery of the bond, and that a policy of life assurance, a banker's deposit-

[1] P. 51.   [2] P. 50.
[3] The doctrine of a possibility upon a possibility applies, however, only to estates in land.

note, a mortgage deed, and a bill or note payable to order and unindorsed can be given *mortis causâ*. A cheque on a banker is not a good *donatio* unless it be payable during the donor's lifetime. A *donatio* is revocable during life by the donor, and only takes effect in the event of his death. It is subject to his debts and to legacy duty. The assent of the executor is not necessary for the vesting of the property in the donee. An imperfect testamentary instrument cannot be made effectual by treating it as a *donatio mortis causâ*. If not made *bonâ fide* three months before the death of the donor, a *donatio* is now chargeable with account duty.[1]

A legacy or *donatio mortis causâ* cannot be sued for in the Probate Division, but must be claimed in a court of equity (or, after assent by the executor) in the Queen's Bench Division.[2] A county court has jurisdiction where the amount does not exceed £50.[3]

[1] P. 170.   [2] 51 and 52 Vict., c. 43, s. 58.
[3] This is apart from its equitable jurisdiction, in which the limit is £500. See p. 164.

CHAPTER VI

THE CODICIL

THE English codicil has little but the name in common with the Roman *codicilli*. It may be defined as an addition to a will or a supplementary will. Its usual object is to modify the effect of an antecedent will. For most purposes the law of codicils is identical with that of wills, and much of what follows in this chapter applies to wills proper as well as to codicils. The interpretation clause of the Wills Act (as does also that of the Conveyancing Act, the Settled Land Act, and other acts) includes codicil under will. Codicils require the same formalities of execution as wills, and are subject to the same law as to undue influence, probate, and other matters. A will may be confirmed, revived, or revoked by codicil, subject to the provisions of ss. 20 and 22 of the Wills Act. Unattested or insufficiently attested instruments may be incorporated in a codicil, and so become operative testamentary instruments. But where a codicil refers to a will duly executed and to unattested instruments, only the will is incorporated, though no doubt by express words effect could be given to any instrument. An instrument to be incorporated must be in existence at the date of the execution of the codicil. A testator cannot reserve to himself by will the power of making a subsequent disposition of his property by unattested paper, if such paper be intended to have a testamentary effect. A frequently occurring case of this kind is the attempt of a testator to impose a secret trust on persons *primâ facie* taking beneficially. If a devisee or legatee be expressly on the face of the will constituted a trustee, but the trusts are not thereby declared, no trusts afterwards declared by a paper not duly attested can be binding. If the trust were not declared when the will was made, it is essential, in order to make it binding, that the devisee or legatee should have had notice of the trust in the testator's lifetime, and should have accepted the particular trust. "It may possibly be that he would be bound if the trust had been put into writing and placed in his hands in a sealed envelope, and he had engaged that he would hold the property given to him by the will upon the trust so declared, although he did not know the actual terms of the trust."[1] In case of the failure of the trust, if the trustee be obviously not intended to hold the property for his own benefit, he becomes a trustee of a resulting trust for the heir or the next of kin, according as the property is real or personal. A devisee or legatee may be compelled to disclose in a court of equity whether he takes on a secret trust for superstitious uses, or for the benefit of a Roman Catholic patron of a living who is disabled from presenting.[2] The destruction of a codicil which has revived a revoked will does not necessarily avoid that will, in the face of declarations by the testator of his desire to adhere to the will.

[1] *Re Boyes*, Law Rep., 26 Chancery Div., 536 (1884).
[2] 3 Jac. I, c. 5; 13 Anne, c. 13.

CHAPTER VII

REVOCATION

A WILL is always revocable or ambulatory (as it is sometimes expressed), even though the testator expressly declare it not to be so, unless, indeed, there be a contract not to revoke. A will is revoked in many ways, which may be divided into two great classes—revocation by testamentary act, and revocation by non-testamentary act. Revocation by testamentary act is the subject of part of s. 20 of the Wills Act, which enacts that no will or codicil, or any part thereof, shall be revoked otherwise than as aforesaid (*i.e.* by marriage under s. 18), or by another will or codicil executed in manner thereinbefore required, or by some writing declaring an intention to revoke the same, and executed in the manner in which a will was thereinbefore required to be executed, or by the burning, tearing, or otherwise destroying the same by the testator, or by some person in his presence and by his direction, with the intention of revoking the same. In all cases revocation is a question of intention, and the will is not revoked unless the act, *primâ facie* one of revocation, have been done *animo revocandi*. Thus the presumption of intention will be rebutted by evidence that the act was done under a mistake, such as that the will revoked was invalid or useless, or that another instrument not valid is valid. It may also be rebutted by showing that the testator was not of sound mind when the act was done, and that therefore there could have been no *animus revocandi*. What has been called by the somewhat cumbrous name of the doctrine of "dependent relative revocation" is this. A revocation made with the view of making or reviving another disposition can only take effect if such other disposition be effectually made or revived. The testator must consider the substitution of a valid disposition as part of the act of revocation. The original will is not revoked unless the other disposition of the property is an effective one. Evidence is always admissible in this, as in other cases of presumed revocation, to prove the intention of the testator; for instance, to prove that he destroyed a particular will in order to make a fresh will. There is no revocation unless and until a new will duly executed exists. The principle is the same where alterations have been made in the amount of a legacy; there the original legacy remains if the alterations have not been properly executed and attested. In such a case the court will endeavour to discover—if necessary, by physical means, such as magnifying glasses—what the original words were. If the original bequest have been covered with a piece of paper pasted over it, on which a new bequest was written, but as to which the witnesses can give no information, the court will order probate to issue in blank as to the substituted bequest. A case of dependent relative revocation may also be raised by proper evidence in case of substitution of the name of a legatee differing from that originally written. The rules as to dependent relative revocation apply to similar questions arising in the Chancery Division as the court of construction, except that in the latter no external evidence is admissible to prove dependent relative revocation. The intention must appear on the face of the instrument. A subsequent will must revoke the former will completely where both wills are in existence; if there be several wills not inconsistent with one another, they must be read together as the last will. The naming of the latest instrument the last will is not of itself sufficient revocation of previous ones. Considerable difficulty has arisen as to the effect of revival of a revoked will by a codicil. If both wills be in existence, a codicil revokes an intermediate will. If the first will have been destroyed, the question arises whether the intermediate will is revived, the one purporting to be revived having been destroyed, and there being therefore nothing on which the codicil can operate. The cases on the subject are not very easy to reconcile, but the decision seems to depend on whether the codicil does or does not contain provisions inconsistent with the intermediate will. The instrument of revocation need not be a formal will or codicil. A duly signed and attested letter requesting a friend to destroy a will is a good testamentary revocation.

Revocation by non-testamentary act may be effected by marriage, s. 18 of the act, and by almost any means indicating an intention to revoke, as long as it is one of the means named in s. 20. Presumption of an alteration in circumstances is no longer sufficient to revoke. The act of revocation by destruction of some kind must be done, if by the testator's direction, in his presence. Thus a direction in a letter to a friend would not be a good revocation unless executed as a will. Tearing off or obliterating the signature of the testator or the witnesses is sufficient, but it is not sufficient merely to run a pen through the names. Of course destruction by any one other than the testator, unless under his direction, is not a good revocation. In such a case evidence may be given as to the terms of the destroyed will, and the court will grant probate of it as far as they can be ascertained. When only a portion of a will is destroyed, the question to be decided is whether the destroyed part is so important as to affect the validity of the whole document, or whether it is separable and unimportant. Where a will is made in duplicate, revocation of one copy is revocation of both.

There may be a good contract not to revoke a will just as there may be one to make a will. Such a contract will be valid if made on good consideration, *e.g.* as a mode of repayment of a loan. An action can be brought on such a contract or covenant, but it cannot be specifically enforced by a court of equity. A covenant not to revoke a will is not invalid as being in restraint of marriage.[1] On the marriage of the covenantor the will would of course be revoked, but an action on the covenant for any damages sustained by the revocation could be brought against the covenantor.

Marriage does not revoke a will in one case, that is, by s. 18 of the act, a will made in exercise of a power of appointment[2] when the real or personal estate thereby appointed would not in default of such appointment pass to the heir, customary heir, executor, or administrator, or the person entitled as next of kin

---

[1] *Robinson v. Ommanney*, Law Rep., 21 Chancery Div. 780 (1882).
[2] For such wills see the following chapter.

under the Statutes of Distribution. In all other cases marriage operates as a revocation, even though the will may have been distinctly made in view of a contemplated marriage which subsequently took place. Before the Wills Act, marriage and the birth of a child was necessary to revoke the will of a man. Marriage alone, as now, revoked that of a woman.

Revival of a revoked will is the subject of s. 22 of the act, which enacts that no will or codicil or any part thereof which shall be in any manner revoked shall be revived otherwise than by the re-execution thereof, or by a codicil executed in manner thereinbefore required and showing an intention to revive the same; and when any will or codicil which shall be partly revoked and afterwards wholly revoked shall be revived, such revival shall not extend to so much thereof as shall have been revoked before the revocation of the whole thereof, unless an intention to the contrary shall be shown.

CHAPTER VIII

WILLS OF A SPECIAL NATURE

The King.—It was resolved in Parliament in the 16th year of Richard II that the king, his heirs and successors, might lawfully make their testaments. This must no doubt be understood to include only such property as could at that date be alienated by will. In some cases parliamentary authority has been given to royal wills, in others not. The executors of Henry IV were confirmed in their office by letters-patent of Henry V, those of Henry V by Parliament. The widest testamentary powers ever conferred on an English king were given to Henry VIII by 28 Hen. VIII, c. 7, empowering him to limit and appoint the succession to the crown by letters-patent or by will, in default of children by Jane Seymour or any future wife. By a subsequent Act (35 Hen. VIII, c. 1) the princesses Mary and Elizabeth were put into the entail, but subject to such conditions as the king should appoint by will. In the exercise of this parliamentary authority, the king devised the crown in remainder, on the failure of issue of his three children, to the heirs of the body of his younger sister, the wife of Charles Brandon, Duke of Suffolk, to the exclusion of the descendants of his elder sister, Margaret Queen of Scots. The reasons. why the provisions of the will were not carried out are matter for the historian rather than the lawyer. By 39 and 40 Geo. III, c. 88, the king and his successor may devise or bequeath their private and personal property.[1] No court has, however, jurisdiction to grant probate of the will of a king. This was held by the Prerogative Court in 1822 in the case of the will of George III.[2] A queen consort had always the right of making a will denied to wives of lower position. Probate of an *acte définitif* of the royal family of Russia, disposing of the goods of a member of the family, was granted by Mr. Justice Butt in 1884, the *acte définitif*, or family compact, superseding the will of the prince.[3]

Married Women.—The law as it affected married women previously to the passing of the Married Women's Act, 1882, has already been briefly stated. The intention of the act was no doubt to place the married woman with regard to her testamentary powers on the same level as the unmarried woman. The words of the act are very extensive. "A married woman shall, in accordance with the provisions of this act, be capable of acquiring, holding, and disposing by will or otherwise of any real or personal property as her separate property in the same manner as if she were a feme sole without the intervention of any trustee."[4] In a case, however, before Mr. Justice Pearson in 1885 he held that these words give a married woman power to dispose by will only of property of which she is seised or possessed

---

[1] A collection of royal wills was printed for the Society of Antiquaries by J. Nichols (1780).
[2] *In the goods of His Late Majesty George III*, 1 Addams's Rep., 255.
[3] *In the goods of Prince Oldenburgh*, Law Rep., 9 Probate Div., 234. [4] 45 and 46 Vict., c. 75, s. 1 (1).

while she is under coverture, and that, notwithstanding s. 24 of the Wills Act, her will made under coverture is not, without re-execution after she has become discovert, effectual to dispose of property acquired during widowhood.[1] This is practically what had been held by the House of Lords before the act.[2] In a case in 1887 Mr. Justice Stirling held that the act of 43 Geo. III, c. 108 (enabling persons under certain circumstances to make gifts by will of land or goods for the erection of churches, with a proviso that such a gift should not be made by a married woman without her husband), was not, as far as regarded the proviso, affected by the Married Women's Property Act.[3] These cases are sufficient to show that the act has not, owing to judicial decision, given absolute and unqualified power of disposition by will to the married women in every case, whatever the intention of the framers of the act may have been. Other sections of the act which affect wills are these: "Every woman who marries after the commencement of this act (January 1, 1883) shall be entitled to have and to hold as her separate property, and to dispose of in manner aforesaid, all real and personal property which shall belong to her at the time of marriage, or shall be acquired by or devolve upon her after marriage, including any wages, earnings, money, and property gained or acquired by her in any employment, trade, or occupation, in which she is engaged, or which she carries on separately from her husband, or by the exercise of any literary, artistic, or scientific skill."[4]

"'The execution of a general power by will by a

---

[1] *Re Price*, Law Rep., 28 Chancery Div., 709.
[2] *Willock* v. *Noble*, Law Rep., 7 House of Lords, 580 (1875).
[3] *Re Smith*, Law Rep., 35 Chancery Div., 589.
[4] S. 2.

married woman shall have the effect of making the property appointed liable for her debts and other liabilities in the same manner as her separate estate is made liable under this act."[1] "Every woman married before the commencement of this act shall be entitled to have and to hold and to dispose of in manner aforesaid as her separate property all real and personal property, her title to which, whether vested or contingent, and whether in possession, reversion, or remainder, shall accrue after the commencement of this act, including any wages, earnings, money, and property so gained and acquired by her as aforesaid."[2] Whether this section alters the old legal rule of construction, whereby, under a gift to a husband and wife and a third person jointly, the husband and wife take only one moiety, is a question which has been differently decided by Chancery judges of first instance.[3] The rule is at least as old as Bracton, who gives as its explanation that *vir et uxor sunt quasi unica persona quia caro una et sanguis unus.* A married woman who is an executrix or administratrix alone or jointly may sue or be sued as if she were a *feme sole.* "For the purposes of this act the legal personal representative of any married woman shall, in respect of her separate estate, have the same rights and liabilities, and be subject to the

[1] S. 4.
[2] S. 5. It will be noticed that this section only applies to property accruing since January 1, 1883. With regard to property which accrued before that date, either the common law or the law as altered by the acts of 1870 and 1874 applies, according as the marriage was before or after 1870 or 1874.
[3] *Re Jupp,* Law Rep. 39 Chancery Div., 148 (1888); *Re Dixon,* Law Rep., 42 Chancery Div., 306 (1889). The later decision is in favour of the wife taking as a separate person. In some of the colonies whose law is based on Roman law there is no difficulty, the husband and wife take as separate persons. This is the case in Ceylon, *Dias* v. *De Lievera,* Law Rep., 5 Appeal Cases, 123 (1879).

same jurisdiction, as she would be if she were living."[1] "The word 'contract' in this act shall include the acceptance of any trust, or of the office of executrix or administratrix, and the provisions of this act as to the liabilities of married women shall extend to all liabilities by reason of any breach of trust or devastavit committed by any married woman being a trustee or executrix or administratrix either before or after her marriage, and her husband shall not be subject to such liabilities unless he has acted or intermeddled in the trust or administration."[2]

The effect of the act in relation to probate and administration has been to make some changes in the practice. For instance, before the act it was usual to limit the grant of probate to such property as the married woman had a right to dispose of and had disposed of by will, a *ceterorum* grant being subsequently made to the husband, but now a general grant is issued in the ordinary form. Nor need a husband now join in the administration bond where the administratrix is a married woman. But probate of the will of a married woman is still not obtainable through an Inland Revenue officer, but must be referred to the Principal or a District Registry. By the Divorce Act, 1857 (20 and 21 Vict., c. 85), a married woman who has obtained a protection order or a judicial separation may dispose of her property in all respects as a *feme sole*, and if she die intestate, it is to devolve as it would have done had her husband been then dead.

[1] S. 23.
[2] S. 24. The main clauses of the act dealing with "contract" are sub-sections (2), (3), and (4) of s. 1, and the effect of them is, shortly put, that a married woman may contract as if she were a *feme sole*, and that the contract is to be deemed to be a contract binding her separate property, including that afterwards acquired. For further information see the treatise on *Marriage* in this series.

Power of Appointment.—A will made under a power of appointment is not revoked by marriage when the real or personal estate thereby appointed would not, in default of appointment, pass to the testator's executor or administrator, or to the next of kin.[1] Before the Wills Act a will exercising a power of appointment was bound to conform to any special formalities named in the instrument conferring the power, but since the act the power is duly exercised if executed and attested like an ordinary will. An appointment by will insufficiently executed will not be aided by the court. In the exercise of powers given by instruments operating *inter vivos*, certain persons may be relieved from the effects of defective execution of a power in their favour. A will executed according to the Wills Act is a good execution of a power, though the will would be invalid by the law of the domicil of the testator. Whether the converse is true is uncertain, *i.e.* whether a testamentary appointment, good by the law of the domicil, but not fulfilling the conditions of the Wills Act, would be held valid by an English court. There are authorities on both sides. Where a will, disposing of property over part of which the testator had a power of appointment within the terms of s. 18 of the Wills Act, was revoked by subsequent marriage, the part of the will dealing with the property appointed still remains valid, and probate limited to that property may be granted.

Guardianship.—As a general rule wills dispose of property, but even at common law a will simply appointing a guardian was good. The common law was superseded by 12 Car. II, c. 24, under which a father, if of age, may dispose of the custody of his unmarried infant

---

[1] Wills Act, s. 18.

children by will. The Guardianship of Infants Act, 1886, extended such powers to the mother, but she can only appoint a guardian or guardians to act either (1) after the death of herself and the father of the infant or (2) jointly with the father of the infant; and in this case the court (that is, the Chancery Division in England and Ireland, the Court of Session in Scotland) may after her death, if satisfied that the father is for any reason unfitted to be the sole guardian, confirm the appointment of the guardian or guardians, or make such other order as the court shall think fit.

Aliens.—Before the Naturalisation Act, 1870, an alien enemy resident in England could only dispose of personal property by will with the king's licence. Real property he could not dispose of at all, as he could not hold it. By s. 2 of that act (33 Vict., c. 14) real and personal property of every description may be taken, acquired, held, and disposed of by an alien in the same manner in all respects as by a natural-born British subject, and a title to real and personal property of every description may be derived through, from, or in succession to an alien in the same manner in all respects as through, from, or in succession to a natural-born British subject. The section does not affect any estate or interest in real or personal property to which any person is or may be entitled in pursuance of any disposition made before the passing of the act (May 12, 1870), or in pursuance of any devolution by law on the death of any person dying before the passing of the act. The act appears to apply to aliens, whether subjects of a power at peace or at war with the United Kingdom, but it does not affect the will of an alien domiciled abroad; and in determining the validity of such a will, the principles of law existing prior to the act are still applicable, that is, put as briefly as possible, that its validity depends on the law of the domicil of the testator.

Soldiers and Sailors.—The Statute of Frauds and the Wills Act expressly reserved to soldiers in actual military service, and to mariners or seamen being at sea, the right of disposing of their personal estate as they might have done before the Acts. The statutes dealing with the subject, especially with exemption from probate, are numerous, and only the main provisions can be given here. The will of a soldier is, by the force of long custom, valid even if it be made by unattested or by unsigned writing, or by word of mouth, in the presence of one or more witnesses. 11 Geo. IV and 1 Will. IV, c. 41 (as amended by the Regimental Debts Act, 1863, and the Superannuation Act, 1887), enables the Secretary of State for War to pay any pension or prize-money, not exceeding £100, to the next-of-kin or representatives of an officer or soldier without probate or administration. The Regimental Debts Act, 1863, as amended by the Regulation of the Forces Act, 1881, defines certain preferential charges which, on the death of an officer or soldier, are to be paid in preference to other debts. It also provides for the collection and disposal of his effects. The personal estate of an officer or soldier dying on service in India, not exceeding £100 after the payment of preferential charges, is not liable to duty, nor need representation be taken out in the case of such a sum, but the amount due will be paid out for the benefit of the widow, children, or other persons entitled. The Pensions and Yeomanry Pay Act, 1884, extends the exemption from probate in the case of the same small amount of assets to any one who has been a soldier or officer, or the widow of such a person. By the Army Act, 1881, s. 44 (11), a soldier convicted by court-martial is not, save as provided by royal warrant, to be liable to any forfeiture under the Regimental Debts Act. The Military Savings Banks Act, 1859, enables regulations to be made concerning the retention or deposit in military savings banks of the effects of deceased soldiers, and for the payment or application thereof for the benefit of their orphans or other persons entitled.

As to sailors, the Wills Act provided that the act of 11 Geo. IV and 1 Will. IV, c. 20, as to the wills of petty officers and seamen in the royal navy, and of marines, so far as related to their wages, pay, prize-money, bounty-money, and allowances, should not be affected. The Act of George IV has, however, been repealed, and the law now depends upon the Navy and Marines (Wills) Act, 1865, 28 and 29 Vict., c. 72. "Seaman or marine" is defined by the act as "a petty officer or seaman, non-commissioned officer of marines or marine, or other person forming part in any capacity of any of Her Majesty's vessels, or otherwise belonging to Her Majesty's naval or marine force, exclusive of commissioned, warrant, and subordinate officers, and assistant engineers, and of Kroomen." A will made before entry into the service is insufficient to pass wages, prize-money, bounty-money, grant, or other allowance in the nature thereof, or other money payable by the Admiralty, or any effects or money in charge of the Admiralty. A will combined with a power of attorney is invalid. The requisites for the validity of a will under the act are that (1) it should be in writing and duly executed with the formalities of the Wills Act; (2) where it is made on board one of Her Majesty's ships, one of the two witnesses must be a commissioned officer, chaplain, or warrant or subordinate officer; (3) where it is made elsewhere, one of the two witnesses must be either one of those above-mentioned or the governor, agent, physician, surgeon, assistant-surgeon, or chaplain of a naval hospital, at home or abroad, or the incumbent, curate, or minister of a church or place of worship in the parish where the will is executed, or a British consular officer, or an officer of customs, or a notary public. If a seaman or marine is a prisoner of war, and the will is in writing, one witness is sufficient, provided the witness be a commissioned officer or chaplain belonging to Her Majesty's naval or marine or military force, or a warrant or subordinate officer in the navy, or the agent of a naval hospital, or a notary public. Such a will is good if it be made according to the forms required by the law of the place where it was made, or by the Wills Act. The Admiralty has a discretionary power to pay over wages, etc., to any person claiming to be entitled thereto, although the act has not been complied with. Similar authority is, by the Merchant Shipping Act, 1854, s. 200, conferred upon the Board of Trade in the case of a will made by a merchant, seaman, or apprentice, and not executed under the provisions of the act. The formalities required by the act are that the will must be in writing and witnessed, if made on board ship, by the master or first or only mate. If not made on board ship, two witnesses are necessary, one of whom must be a shipping master, or some minister or officiating minister or curate of the place where the will is made, or, in a place where there are no such persons, a justice of the peace, British consular officer, or officer of customs. By the Navy and Marines (Property of Deceased) Act, 1865, (28 and 29 Vict., c. 111), provision is made for the disposal of residue standing in the books of the Admiralty to the credit of a deceased officer, seaman, or marine. Where the residue does not exceed £100, representation to the deceased need not be taken out, and the Admiralty may dispose of it to the persons entitled to it, subject (in the case of a seaman or marine) to payment of his debts. Where the residue does not exceed £100 . no duty is payable. An order in council to carry out the provisions of the Act was made on 28th December 1865. By the Revenue Act, 1889 (52 and 53 Vict., c. 42), s. 30, the residue or any part thereof of the estate and effects of a deceased officer, seaman, or marine, remaining undisposed of or unappropriated for six years and a half from the date of the receipt by the Admiralty of notice of the death, is to be paid over to the Greenwich Hospital capital account. Subject to these acts, a seaman may make his will in the same way as a soldier at common law.

The principal difference between the soldier and sailor and non-privileged persons, is that the old law governs the testamentary age of the privileged class, so that a soldier or sailor may dispose of his personal property on actual military service or at sea at the age of fourteen, and that a will is only revoked, as under the old law, by marriage and the birth of a child, not by marriage alone. In the construction of the law the following are some of the more important points which have been decided. The term "soldier" in s. 11 of the Wills Act includes officers and surgeons. "Actual military service" means an expedition; accordingly, a will made by an officer quartered at home or in barracks abroad is not within the section. "Mariner or seamen" applies to any grade in the navy or merchant service. "At sea" includes the time of the vessel's being in port, as long as the sailor is not discharged. If the will include real estate, and be ineffectual to dispose of it, it may be good as to personalty, provided that the disposition of the latter be not made dependent on that of the former.

Depositors in Savings Banks, etc.—Nomination is equivalent to a will, and may be made at the age of sixteen.[1]

Lunatics.—The lunatic is not capable of making a will, unless during a lucid interval.[2] The court must be satisfied that the testator had a sound disposing mind, and was capable of deciding the persons to be benefited and the manner in which his property was to be distributed. The rational character of the will, if made by the testator himself, is evidence that it was made during a lucid interval. If subject to insane delusions, his will is not necessarily invalid, unless the delusions have influenced him to make a particular disposition which he would not otherwise have made. The burden of proving capacity to make a will rests upon those who propound the will, *a fortiori* when it appears that the testator was subject to delusions. The law is well illustrated by a remarkable case which came before the Probate Division in 1879.[3] The testator, though capable of transacting complicated and important busi-

---
[1] See p. 139.
[2] This was laid down as law as long ago as 1603, in *Beverley's Case*, 4 Coke's Rep., 123.
[3] *Smee* v. *Smee*, Law Rep., 5 Probate Div., 84.

ness, was under the delusion that he was a son of George IV. Sir James Hannen, having laid down the law to the jury in a summing up from which the statement of law as given above is mainly taken, the jury found that neither of the two contested wills was made when the testator was of sound mind. The Lunacy Regulation Act, 1853 (16 and 17 Vict., c. 70, s. 84), enacts that the Masters in Lunacy may, on being satisfied of a lunatic's death, open and read any paper deposited with them, and purporting to be his will, for the purpose of ascertaining the executor, and whether or not it contains any directions concerning his funeral, and then deliver the same to the registrar or other proper officer of the Probate Division.

Other Exceptional Cases.—A will made by a testator while in a state of drunkenness is in the same legal position as one made by a lunatic. "Intoxication is, in truth, temporary insanity," according to Sir John Nicholl in one of the cases. Of course, the disability only lasts while the state of intoxication continues. Wills made by blind, deaf and dumb, and illiterate persons are as good as any others; the only difficulty arising in such cases is one of evidence, viz., the proof that the testator thoroughly understood the nature of his intentions, and communicated those intentions in an intelligible manner to the person who wrote the will. There is no unyielding rule of law that, where it has been proved that a testator competent in mind has had a will read over to him, and has thereupon executed it, all further inquiry is shut out.[1] If this apply to a testator of competent mind, it appears to apply *a fortiori* to cases where there is any suspicion of incompetence.

[1] *Fulton* v. *Andrew*, Law Rep., 7 House of Lords, 448 (1875).

In the case where the rule just cited was laid down, "habitual drunkenness and disease of the brain" was set forth as one of the particulars delivered in support of pleas as to the competency of the testator, pursuant to rule 40 of the Probate Rules of 1865.

CHAPTER IX

THE CONSTRUCTION OF WILLS

THE construction or interpretation of wills is a subject of great difficulty, and the law depends upon a mass of cases, few of which are direct authorities except where the same or nearly the same words are used. The difficulty is increased by the distinction drawn in English law between the court of probate and the court of construction. The Probate Division has but limited powers of construction; its duties are almost confined to seeing that nothing but a duly executed document, made by a capable testator, is admitted to probate: the meaning of words used, the class of persons entitled to take, and similar matters fall within the jurisdiction of the court of construction, usually the Chancery Division. That court accepts the decision of the court of probate as to validity of execution, even where there is a devise of realty by the will which, as far as the realty is concerned, does not need probate. Nor can an unrevoked probate granted by the court of probate be impeached in the court of construction, even for fraud. The court of construction has, however, in some cases, by the exercise of its interpretative ingenuity, practically made null and void the provisions

THE EFFECT OF CASE LAW 85

of a will which has been duly admitted to probate.[1] The effect of case law on construction is well put by Mr. Theobald in the introduction to his well-known treatise on wills, in a criticism upon the view sometimes held, that construction of a will is to be left entirely to the discretion of an individual judge, unfettered by precedent and authority, or, as it has sometimes been put, that one man's nonsense affords no clue to the meaning of another man's nonsense.

"The principles of law applicable to the construction of wills must be the same as those applicable to other matters. Law is no more than the expression of the meaning of the acts of men in their relations with one another, when viewed by the most enlightened common sense of the day. There is no abstract law to be applied like a foot-rule to facts; but law is the facts viewed in their natural bearings with reference to each other. It follows that, if the facts are the same, the same consequences ought to be deduced from them. The difficulty consists in discovering whether the facts are the same or not. In one sense, no doubt, the facts never are absolutely identical. There must at least be a difference of time, and this in itself, considering the continual change in social life, is an important factor. But the question is not whether the facts are absolutely identical, but whether a fresh set of facts can be fairly distinguished from an earlier set. If not, judges have always considered themselves bound by the interpretation put upon such facts by their predecessors; and when there have been repeated adjudications upon similar sets of facts, by

[1] In the exercise of its discretion the court of construction may look at the original will in order to be assisted in arriving at its meaning, and may correct obvious mistakes, such as "with issue" used for "without issue."

a process of analysis and classification, rejecting immaterial distinctions, and selecting essential points of similarity, what may be called a rule of law is established. . . . Cases of construction are so numerous, originality even in 'nonsense' is so rare, that there will nearly always be similar cases, or at any rate cases instructive even by their distinguishability."

All that can be attempted in a work of this scope is to notice some of the principal and subsidiary rules of construction which have been adopted, and then to proceed to a brief mention of some words and phrases which offer any points of interest. To a limited extent construction has already been treated in dealing with the wills of soldiers and sailors. Those who wish to pursue the subject further will find most of the words and phrases which have received judicial interpretation contained in alphabetical order in a recent work of much research, Stroud's *Judicial Dictionary* (1890).

Rules of construction are mainly judicial; only to a limited extent statutory. The statutory rules are contained in the Wills Act, and are as follows, omitting only the interpretation clause, which defines the senses in which the words "will," "real estate," and "personal estate" are to be taken.[1]

"Every will shall be construed, with reference to the real estate and personal estate comprised in it, to speak and take effect as if it had been executed immediately before the death of the testator, unless a contrary intention shall appear by the will." (S. 24.)

"Unless a contrary intention shall appear by the will, such real estate or interest therein as shall be com-

[1] In the United States statutory interpretation has been carried much further than in England.

prised or intended to be comprised in any devise in such will contained, which shall fail or be void by reason of the death of the devisee in the lifetime of the testator, or by reason of such devise being contrary in law, or otherwise incapable of taking effect, shall be included in the residuary devise (if any) contained in such will." (S. 25.)

"A devise of the land of the testator, or of the land of the testator in any place or in the occupation of any person mentioned in his will or otherwise described in a general manner, and any other general devise which would include a customary copyhold or leasehold estate, if the testator has no freehold estate which could be described by it, shall be construed to include the customary copyhold and leasehold estates of the testator, or his customary copyhold and leasehold estates or any of them to which such description shall extend, as the case may be, as well as freehold estates, unless a contrary intention shall appear by the will." (S. 26.)

"A general devise of the real estate of the testator, or of the real estate of the testator in any place or in the occupation of any person mentioned in his will or otherwise described in a general manner, shall be construed to include any real estate, or any real estate to which such description shall extend (as the case may be), which he may have power to appoint in any manner he may think proper, and shall operate as an execution of such power, unless a contrary intention shall appear by the will; and in like manner a bequest of the personal estate of the testator, or any bequest of personal property described in a general manner, shall be construed to include any personal estate, or any personal estate to which such description shall extend (as the case may be), which he may have power to appoint in any manner he may think proper, and shall operate as an execution of such power, unless a contrary intention shall appear by the will." (S. 27.)

"Where any real estate shall be devised to any person without any words of limitation, such devise shall be construed to pass the fee-simple or other the whole estate or interest which the testator had power to dispose of by will in such real estate, unless a contrary intention shall appear by the will." (S. 28.)

"In any devise or bequest of real or personal estate the words 'die without issue,' or 'die without leaving issue,' or 'have no issue,' or any other words which may import either a want or failure of issue of any person in his lifetime or at the time of his death, or an indefinite failure of his issue, shall be construed to mean a want or failure of issue in the lifetime or at the time of the death of such person, and not an indefinite failure of his issue, unless a contrary intention shall appear by the will by reason of such person having a prior estate tail, or of a preceding gift being (without any implication arising from such words) a limitation of an estate tail to such person or issue or otherwise, provided that this act shall not extend to cases where such words as aforesaid import if no issue described in a preceding gift shall be born, or if there shall be no issue who shall live to attain the age or otherwise answer the description required for obtaining a vested estate by a preceding gift to such issue." (S. 29.) [1]

"Where any real estate (other than or not being a presentation to a church) shall be devised to any trustee

---

[1] The effect of this section is to create, not an estate tail, as was the case before the act, but an estate in fee-simple with an executory devise over on death without issue.

or executor such devise shall be construed to pass the fee-simple or other the whole estate or interest which the testator has power to dispose of by will in such real estate, unless a definite term of years absolute or determinable or an estate of freehold shall thereby be given to him expressly or by implication." (S. 30.)

"Where any real estate shall be devised to a trustee without any express limitation of the estate to be taken by such trustee, and the beneficial interest in such real estate or in the surplus rents and profits thereof shall not be given to any person for life, or such beneficial interest shall be given to any person for life but the purposes of the trusts may continue beyond the life of such person, such devise shall be construed to vest in such trustee the fee-simple or other the whole legal estate which the testator had power to dispose of by will in such real estate, and not an estate determinable when the purposes of the trust shall be satisfied." (S. 31.)

"Where any person to whom real estate shall be devised for an estate tail or an estate in *quasi* entail [1] shall die in the lifetime of the testator, leaving issue who would be inheritable under such entail, and any such issue shall be living at the time of the death of the testator, such devise shall not lapse, but shall take effect as if the death of such person had happened immediately after the death of the testator, unless a contrary intention shall appear by the will." (S. 32.)

"Where any person, being a child or other issue of the testator, to whom any real or personal estate shall be devised or bequeathed for any estate or interest not determinable at or before the death of such person,

---

[1] That is, an estate *pur autre vie* granted to a man and the heirs of his body.

shall die in the lifetime of the testator leaving issue, and any such issue of such person shall be living at the time of the death of the testator, such devise or bequest shall not lapse, but shall take effect as if the death of such person had happened immediately after the death of the testator, unless a contrary intention shall appear by the will." (S. 33.)

Most, if not all, of these sections of the Wills Act have themselves become the subject of judicial interpretation, an interpretation of an interpretation. For instance, it has been held under s. 24 that where a testator bequeathed a leasehold house, and after the date of the will purchased the reversion and took a conveyance of the same to himself in fee, the freehold interest in the house passed by the will. Also, where a testator made a gift of "all my ready money . . . and any other property that I may now possess," it was held that in spite of the use of the word "now" personal property acquired subsequently to the date of the will passed by the bequest. It will be noticed that in all the sections just cited, except ss. 30 and 31, the statutory construction is only to prevail in the absence of a contrary intention appearing by the will. In the excepted sections the statutory construction may be cut down by the gift of a definite term of years or an express limitation of the estate taken by the trustee.

The general principles which, apart from statute, govern the construction of wills are thus laid down by Mr. F. V. Hawkins.[1]

(1) In construing a will, the object of the courts is to ascertain, not the *intention* simply, but the *expressed intentions* of the testator, i.e. the intention which the

[1] *A Concise Treatise on the Construction of Wills* (1863).

will itself, either expressly or by implication, declares; or (which is the same thing) the meaning of the words, —the meaning, that is, which the words of the will, properly interpreted, convey.[1]

(2) In construing a will, the words and expressions used are to be taken in their *ordinary, proper*, and *grammatical* sense; unless, upon so reading them in connection with the entire will, or upon applying them to the facts of the case, an ambiguity or difficulty of construction in the opinion of the court arises; in which case the primary meaning of the words may be modified, extended, or abridged, and words and expressions supplied or rejected, in accordance with the presumed intention, *so far* as to remove or avoid the difficulty or ambiguity in question, but no further. It follows from (1) that in every case the words used must be *capable of bearing* the meaning sought to be put upon them.

(3) As a corollary to, or part of, the last proposition, *technical* words and expressions must be taken in their *technical* sense, unless a *clear* intention can be collected to use them in another sense, and that other sense can be ascertained.[2]

(4) Notwithstanding the last two propositions, the intention of the testator, which can be collected with reasonable certainty from the entire will, with the aid of extrinsic evidence of a kind properly admissible, must have effect given to it, beyond, and even against, the literal sense of particular words and expressions.

[1] The rule that the intention of the testator is to be observed is, in Lord Coke's words, the pole star to guide the judges, or, in the words of Lord Chief Justice Wilmot, the pole star for the direction of devises, *Doe* v. *Laming*, 2 Burrows' Rep., 1112 (1760).
[2] See *Leach* v. *Jay*, cited below.

The intention, when legitimately proved, is competent not only to *fix* the sense of *ambiguous* words, but to *control* the sense even of *clear* words, and to *supply* the place of *express* words, in cases of difficulty or ambiguity.

With regard to the explanation of the intention, this may be done in two ways, first by presumption, second by extrinsic evidence. There are certain presumptions which the law makes rebuttable by evidence, but in the absence of evidence conclusive. Among such presumptions are those that a debt is satisfied by a legacy of equal or larger amount, that legacies of an equal amount given in the same instrument are merely repetitions, and that legacies of unequal amount in the same instrument, or of equal amount in different instruments are *primâ facie* cumulative. Another example is the presumption against double portions; when a parent or person in *loco parentis* has covenanted to pay a portion to a child and afterwards gives a legacy of the same or a larger amount to that child, the legacy is *primâ facie* a satisfaction of the portion, and if of a smaller amount than the portion it is a satisfaction *pro tanto*. The donee is bound by the rules of equity to elect which of the two gifts he will take; he cannot take both. Where there is a gift by will, and after the making of the will and before death a gift to the child is made, the legacy is adeemed *pro tanto*. It is a revocable gift, and has been revoked by the conduct of the testator. The presumption against satisfaction or ademption does not arise in the case of strangers. As to evidence to explain intention, a distinction is drawn between direct evidence of intention and evidence of circumstances (such as foreign words, nicknames, local custom), from which the court may conclude what the intention must have been. The latter is commonly admissible, the former appears to be admissible only when the evidence given as to circumstances has raised an ambiguity by disclosing the existence of more than one subject or object to which the words are applicable. Further, a distinction is drawn between latent and patent ambiguity, first drawn, it is supposed, by Lord Bacon, who gives as an example of patent ambiguity a grant of land to *J. D. et J. S. et heredibus.*[1] Such a gift is void for uncertainty, whether the uncertainty be in the subject or the object of the gift. An instance of the former was "a handsome gratuity to my executors," of the latter "a gift for missionary purposes" or a bequest of "all." Latent ambiguity is, patent is not, explainable by evidence. A common case of latent ambiguity is where a description in the will applies to more than one person, or partly to one and partly to another. Thus in a gift to "my nephew Joseph Grant," on its being shown that the testator had a nephew of that name and that his wife's brother had a son of the same name, evidence was admitted to show which of the two Joseph Grants the testator had intended to benefit.[2] Where a legacy was left to "The Clergy Society," there being no society of that exact name, but several popularly called so, evidence was admitted to show which society was intended.[3] A further limitation of the admission of extrinsic evidence of intention is that it is admissible as a rule only to rebut a presumption or determine a latent ambiguity, not to establish

---

[1] 1 Spence, *Equitable Jurisdiction*, 562.
[2] *Grant* v. *Grant*, Law Rep., 5 Common Pleas, 380, 727.
[3] *Re The Clergy Society*, 2 Kay and Johnson's Rep., 740 (1856).

the contrary of a rule of construction, such as that in *Shelley's Case*, which will be mentioned later. And even where a latent ambiguity exists, evidence is admissible only to enable the court to decide which of several persons or things was intended under an equivocal description, not to show that both or all were intended to be included, to be used where there is a mere misdescription and no equivocation.

There are numerous minor rules of construction, many of them being little more that transcriptions of the Roman law. This is what might have been expected when it is remembered that for centuries probate was in the jurisdiction of the clergy, who were, as a rule, at least, superficially acquainted with the texts of Roman law. The object of these rules is of course to assist in arriving at the "expressed intention" of the testator. Whether they do so in all cases is a question that is open to considerable doubt. Among the more interesting and important of these rules are the following. In general they only apply where no contrary intention is shown.

A general devise of "lands" or of "rents and profits" includes emblements[1] and lands contracted to be purchased, also reversions and copyholds, and (under the Wills Act) leaseholds. It also includes incorporeal hereditaments as a rule (such as advowsons), when they are appendant or appurtenant to land, but not when they are in gross, *i.e.* exist independently of the tenancy of land.

"Money" or "moneys" includes money at the bank on current account or on deposit, but not stock in the funds or debts due. Where there is no personal estate,

---

[1] That is, the crops of agricultural land sown by the testator. It has been laid down as a rule of construction that although as between heir and executor the emblements go to the latter, in a general devise they pass to the devisee.

it may include the general residue. "Ready money" or "cash" is more restrictive, and does not include money on account current.

"Estate" includes all property, real and personal; "effects" or "goods" only personal.

"Children" means legitimate children,[1] and does not include grandchildren.

"Issue" is a wider term and includes descendants of every degree. In a gift of real estate both "children" and "issue" may be words of limitation. Thus a devise to A and his children or issue, where there is no issue at the time of the devise, confers on A an estate tail. The weight of authority is against the application of this rule (known as the rule in *Wild's Case*)[2] to personalty.

"Family" *primâ facie* signifies legitimate children.

"Heirs" in gifts of personalty may mean persons entitled under the Statutes of Distribution. A gift of personalty to "A or his heirs" means to the heirs by substitution if A dies before distribution.

"Next of kin" means the nearest blood relations and not the next of kin according to the Statutes of Distribution, so that those who would under the Statutes be entitled by representation are excluded.

Immediate gifts to children as a class include *primâ facie* those living at the testator's death. The same principle applies to grandchildren, brothers, nephews, and cousins. A gift not immediate admits others of the class coming into existence before the period of distribution. Those living at the death of the testator take vested interests subject to be partially divested in favour of after-born members of the class. Where the share is

---

[1] This must be read subject to the decision in *Occleston* v. *Fullalove*, p. 100.   [2] 6 Coke's Rep., 16 (1599).

made payable on attainment of a given age or marriage, attainment of the age or marriage of the first child doing so is the period of distribution. Where there are no children in existence at the period of distribution, or where the words "to be born" are used, an immediate gift becomes executory, and children born at any future date will take.

"Or" is often read as "and"; "and" as "or." Thus a gift to "A or his heirs" is a gift to A in fee.

There are many rules as to incidence of charges, such as that legacies are *primâ facie* payable out of the personal estate and that a charge of legacies on real estate *primâ facie* does not charge lands specifically devised. There are also many rules used to determine the time at which a legacy vests, and whether it is vested or contingent. Thus a legacy "to be paid" at twenty-one is vested, and if the infant die before that age it goes to his personal representatives, while if it be given "at" twenty-one or "when he attains" twenty-one, it is contingent, and on his death before that age it lapses, unless indeed interest be given in the meantime.

Clauses which cannot be made to bear an intelligible meaning must be treated as though they were not inserted; where there are two repugnant clauses which cannot by any interpretation be reconciled, the one which is the later in position is to be followed. In a deed the rule is the reverse.

The above is one example of differences in the rules of construction as they relate to wills and other instruments. Another is the rule as to *malum prohibitum* and *malum in se*, which differs according as the instrument is a will or a contract.[1] Another, which has been the

[1] P. 98.

ground of numerous decisions, is the mode of construction of executory trusts in marriage articles and in wills. In the former case the court has a clue to the intention from the nature of the contract, in the latter the court knows nothing of the object in view *a priori*, but must be guided to the intentions solely by the language of the instrument. Accordingly a limitation in marriage articles to the husband or wife, with remainder to the heirs of the body of either or both of them will be construed to mean first and other sons, and a settlement will be made upon the issue successively in tail as purchasers.[1] This is in order to prevent one or other of the parents from defeating the provision for the children by barring the estate tail. In a will, on the other hand, the same words will give an estate tail which can be barred in the ordinary way. Another difference is that in a deed an estate of inheritance can only be conferred by the words necessary for a grant, such as "A and his heirs," or "A and the heirs of his body," or (since the Conveyancing Act, 1881) "A in fee simple," "A in tail male," etc., while in a will it can be conferred by many other expressions in addition to these, *e.g.* "A and his assigns for ever," "A and his issue."

Conditional devises and bequests are subject to peculiar rules of construction. The construction varies according as the condition is precedent or subsequent and as the property left is real or personal. A condition is the addition of a declaration of intention by which the existence of a legal relation is made to depend on an uncertain event. It differs from a conditional limitation

---

[1] Such a settlement, called a strict settlement, appears to have been decreed in every case under marriage articles, to which *Shelley's Case*, to be presently mentioned, does not apply.

or an executory devise or bequest in that the estate reverts to the grantor or his representatives on breach of the condition, in the other cases it is limited over to other persons. A condition precedent is one in which the performance of the condition precedes the vesting of the property. A condition subsequent is one in which the failure to perform the condition determines the continued enjoyment of property already vested. A condition precedent, whether impossible, illegal, or impolitic, if attached to a devise, must be fulfilled in order that the estate may vest in the donee. In a gift of personalty a condition precedent involving physical impossibility or *malum prohibitum* is invalid and leaves the gift absolute. "But where the performance of the condition is the sole motive of the bequest, or its impossibility was unknown to the testator, or the condition which was possible in its creation has since become impossible by the act of God, or where it is illegal as involving *malum in se*,[1] in these cases the civil agrees with the common law in holding both gift and condition void."[2] In both real and personal property a condition precedent becoming impossible by the act of the testator is discharged. Impossible, impolitic, or illegal conditions subsequent are ineffectual, whether there be a gift over or not. Most of the cases have arisen with respect to conditions in restraint of marriage. In both real and

[1] The difference between *malum prohibitum* and *malum in se*, adopted from the civil law, is this. The latter is an act forbidden as being in its nature immoral, the former as an act which, if not forbidden by positive law, would not be immoral. As far as contract is concerned, the distinction between *malum prohibitum* and *malum in se* has long been exploded, but the citation above seems to show that it may still be of some importance in wills.

[2] 1 Jarman, 12. The rules of Roman law will be found, among other passages, in *Digest*, xxviii, 7; xxxv, 1; xxxvi, 1; *Code*, vi, 46.

personal estate, a condition attached to the gift that the donee shall not marry at all is void. A gift with a condition that it is to cease if the donee marry without consent, will cease if the gift be of real estate, but not if the gift be of personal estate, the condition being *in terrorem* unless there be a gift over. A condition not to dispute the will follows the same rule as one not to marry. A condition in restraint of a second marriage, *e.g.* that the testator's widow shall, after his death, retire into a convent, is valid. So is a condition in limited restraint of a first marriage, *e.g.* that the donee shall not marry a woman who is or has been a domestic servant. There seems to be no difference in the law as it affects men and women.

One of the most interesting of the numerous cases which have arisen is that of *Egerton* v. *Earl Brownlow*, decided by the House of Lords in 1853. The Earl of Bridgwater devised estates to trustees to make a settlement according to the limitations in the will. One of the limitations was to Lord Alford for a term of ninety-nine years, with certain remainders, and with a proviso that if Lord Alford should die without having acquired the title of Duke or Marquis of Bridgwater, then the use and estate to the heirs male of his body was to cease and be absolutely void. Lord Alford entered into possession of the estates—which were worth £70,000 a year—but died without acquiring any of the higher titles. It was held that his heir male was entitled to the estates discharged of the condition subsequent, for it was void as being contrary to public policy. The ground of the decision was that the condition tended to induce the donee of the estates to use improper means to influence the Crown, and the Crown itself to confer a particular title on a particular person, thus fettering its discretion as the fountain of honour.[1]

Another illustration of the doctrine of public policy, useful as showing what has been called the "progressive character" of English equity, is that of gifts to unborn illegitimate children. Such gifts were formerly regarded as void, but since the decision in *Occleston* v. *Fullalove*,[2] it appears now to be a question of intention rather than of policy, whether such gifts are to stand, the only point being whether the words of the will are clear enough to include such children as objects of the benefit. Only those children can take who come into existence before the death of the testator.

Two curious cases have been recently decided bearing on the question of restraint of marriage. It was held in 1884 that a covenant not to revoke a will was not void as being in restraint of marriage.[3] The Court of Appeal held in 1888 that a gift to a sister of the testator "during such time as she may live apart from her husband" of a weekly sum, was a limited gift of weekly payments to be made during a period, the commencement and duration of which were fixed in a way which the law does not allow, and that the gift was void.[4] The decision turned on the question whether the gift was on condition subsequent, or by way of limitation; had it been the former, the condition would have been void, but the gift good; the court, however, held it to be the latter, and accordingly the gift was void. It is always laid down in the text-books that a condition subsequent is to be distinguished from a conditional

---

[1] 4 House of Lords Cases, 1.
[2] Law Rep., 9 Chancery App., 147 (1874).
[3] *Robinson* v. *Ommanney*, *supra*, p. 68.
[4] *Re Moore*, Law Rep., 39 Chancery Div., 116.

limitation. The latter partakes of the nature of both a condition and a remainder. It is a condition in that it abridges the enjoyment of an estate, a limitation in that it passes the estate to a stranger on the occurrence of a contingency. An example of a conditional limitation is a gift until marriage or bankruptcy, or a gift of a personal annuity to a man and the heirs of his body. Such a gift as the last named, as it does not fall within the statute *De Donis Conditionalibus* (13 Edw. I, c. 1), cannot create an estate tail in the annuity, and so remains a gift on condition that the donee has heirs of the body. In the case of a conditional limitation of real estate, any estate in remainder becomes at once vested on the happening or non-happening of the contingency named; in the case of a condition subsequent, the person entitled to the estate in remainder must take some means to assert his rights, as by entry. At common law a stranger could not take advantage of a condition, though a different rule obtained in courts of equity. Both at common law and in equity a conditional limitation could be made in favour of a stranger, that is, some one other than the grantor or his heirs, or the heirs of his body.

Other rules of construction which may be shortly noticed are these. (*a*) *Falsa demonstratio non nocet quum de corpore constat.*[1] Thus "all my real estate" passes leaseholds if the testator has no real estate. But where

---

[1] This is an example of one of those Latin maxims, so frequently occurring in English text-books, which are not classical, but have only a specious resemblance to those actually used in the texts of Roman law. The nearest approaches to this maxim in Roman law are *falsâ demonstratione legatum non perimi* (*Institutes*, ii, 30, 20), and *nihil facit error nominis quum de corpore constat* (*Digest*, xviii, 1, 9, 1). The perils of an exclusively literal interpretation also appear in the frequently cited maxim, *Qui hæret in literâ hæret in cortice.*

there is nothing to answer to the description the gift fails, *e.g.* a devise of lands in the parish of A, all the testator's property being in the parish of B. The misdescription may be of many kinds; for instance, the amount of a debt due, the property left, or (what is most common) the name of the devisee or legatee. The misdescription, as has been already stated, may generally be corrected by evidence. (*b*) *Non accipi debent verba in demonstrationem falsam quum competunt in limitationem reram.* (*c*) General words following specific words will be limited by the latter to things *ejusdem generis.* (*d*) Where there are inconsistent devises or bequests, the latest governs. (*e*) That mode of construction is to be preferred which will prevent an intestacy, *ut res magis valeat quam pereat.* (*f*) The intention, if it cannot take effect altogether, is to take effect as far as possible. (*g*) The heir-at-law cannot be disinherited unless by express words or necessary implication. Mere negative words are not sufficient for the purpose.

The argument from absurdity is the weakest which can be urged in a question of construction. It is only to be used when all others have failed. The right of a testator to be capricious, said Vice-Chancellor Wigram, cannot be denied.[1] Weight can only be given to the absurdity of a clause if its literal interpretation would overthrow the whole scheme of the will as discoverable in other parts of it.[2]

One of the rules of construction, which has been the most keenly debated among jurists, is that known as the

---

[1] *Hillersdon* v. *Lowe,* 2 Hare's Rep., 566 (1843).
[2] At the end of the second volume of Jarman on Wills, the learned author lays down twenty-four rules of construction, which practically cover the same ground as that taken in this chapter.

rule in *Shelley's Case*.[1] The decision was to the effect that if the ancestor take an estate of freehold and in the same gift or conveyance an estate is limited, either mediately or immediately, to his heirs or the heirs of his body, these words are words of limitation and not of purchase, the ancestor thus taking in the first case an estate in fee-simple, in the second an estate tail. The rule applies even where there is an express declaration that the estate of the ancestor is not to extend beyond his own life. In order that the rule may apply, the limitations must be in the same instrument, and must be both legal or both equitable.

The construction of what are called "precatory trusts" in wills has been the subject of numerous decisions. A trust is implied from words of confidence, of request and entreaty, and even of advice and recommendation, as long as there is sufficient certainty on the property left and the persons to be benefited. The tendency of decisions is to refuse to construe doubtful expressions as importing trusts, *e.g.* a desire that the legatee will be kind to or do justice to a particular person. If the gift be subject to trusts, the donee takes what is not required for the purpose of the trusts. If the gift be upon trust, he is trustee of the whole and takes no part for his own benefit.

The doctrine of *cy-près* is an important one, and is applied in two ways. (1) Where there is, in favour of a charity, a gift which would in an ordinary case be void for uncertainty or failure of objects of the charity, the court will carry it out as nearly as may be to what it supposes would have been the testator's intention had he known that the gift could not have literal effect given

[1] 1 Coke's Rep., 93b (1581).

to it, provided it be not contrary to law. Altered social circumstances often makes it necessary to apply old benefactions *cy-près*, as in the case of universities and public schools. A good example of the application of the doctrine to a charity is afforded by a case decided by the Rolls Court in 1840. A testator in 1723 bequeathed a sum of money, part of the interest of which was to be applied "unto the redemption of British slaves in Turkey or Barbary." The court allowed the fund to be applied to the other charitable purposes mentioned in the will, the testator being, as it were, permitted to decide for himself as to the *cy-près* application of the fund when the original purpose for which it was left had ceased to exist.[1] A long continued unauthorised application of charity funds *cy-près* by trustees is no ground of objection to a scheme directing a different application.[2] (2) Where there are limitations of real estate void for perpetuity, the court will make them good as far as possible, e.g. by giving an estate tail in the direction marked by the testator. The principle applicable to the doctrine, in whichever way it is applied, is, in the words of Sir George Jessel, that "when you find two intents in a will which are inconsistent with each other, and you therefore cannot carry out both, you give effect to the general or paramount intent."[3]

From one point of view the doctrine of *cy-près* is one of construction, from another it is only a branch of the

[1] *Attorney-General* v. *Ironmonger's Company*, 2 Beavan's Rep., 313.
[2] *Re Campden Charities*, Law Rep., 18 Chancery Div., 310 (1881).
[3] *Hampton* v. *Holman*, Law Rep., 5 Chancery Div., 183 (1877). In the states of Pennsylvania and Georgia *cy-près* is the subject of statutory enactment. The only example of such an enactment in England appears to be the Roman Catholic Charities Act, 1860, cited p. 54.

larger doctrine of public policy. The two points of view, however, have this in common, that to a great extent what is or is not contrary to public policy depends itself on the construction put on certain words by the courts. There is no settled rule, and it by no means follows that what was held to be void as contrary to public policy a century ago would be held to be so at the present time. There is, in fact, an element of progress in the doctrine of public policy, as there is in many other legal principles. On the question of the judicial meaning of the phrase "public policy," Sir Frederick Pollock writes : " That question is, in effect, whether it is at the present day open to courts of justice to hold transactions or dispositions of property void, simply because in the judgment of the court it is against the public good that they should be enforced, although the grounds of that judgment may be novel. The general tendency of modern ideas is no doubt against the continuance of such a jurisdiction. On the other hand there is a good deal of modern and even recent authority which makes it difficult to deny its continued existence."[1] As far as regards contract, Sir George Jessel thus expressed the modern view : " You have this paramount public duty to consider, that you are not lightly to interfere with the freedom of contract."[2] A similar paramount public duty no doubt restrains the courts from indiscreet interference with testamentary freedom.

In spite of the liberal interpretation given by the courts to the language of testators, care in the use of

[1] Pollock on Contracts (4th ed., 1881), c. vi. (C).
[2] *Printing and Numerical Registering Company* v. *Sampson*, Law Rep., 19 Equity, 462 (1875).

technical terms is still to be recommended. There are dangers connected with the doctrine in *Shelley's Case*[1] and certain other doctrines where a strict meaning has been given to certain words and phrases. Technical terms are *primâ facie* used in their technical meaning. Thus the word "seised" was construed strictly, and it was held that a devise of real estate of which the testator was seised did not pass certain estate which another person had wrongfully entered, and held at the time of the testator's death, although the testator was entitled to it.[2]

It should be noticed that the court of construction has no authority to rectify a mistake in a will other than an obvious slip, though the court of probate has, as has been already stated, power to omit words introduced *per incuriam*, or by fraud or mistake, or conveying reflections on the character of survivors. The words of the will are not corrected, but the intention is as far as possible carried out, in spite of difficulties arising from the use of particular words. An instructive case on the point is *Earl of Newburgh* v. *Countess of Newburgh*.[3] An Earl of Newburgh devised to the countess an estate for life in his real estates in the counties of Sussex and Gloucester. The word "Gloucester" was accidentally struck out by the person who drew the draft of the will, and the person who made the fair copy for the testator to execute substituted "county" for "counties."

[1] The inconvenience of the rule in *Shelley's Case* has led to its express abolition by the legislature in most of the states of the United States.
[2] *Leach* v. *Jay*, Law Rep., 9 Chancery Div., 42 (1878).
[3] 5 Maddock's Rep., 364 (1820). This is in accordance with the general principle of law that where any legal transaction has been put into the shape of a formal document, informal documents preliminary to it cannot be looked at to discover intention.

The testator executed the will under the impression that it contained the words both "Sussex" and "Gloucester." In a suit to rectify the will, evidence for the purpose of correcting the mistake by producing the original draft was rejected.

The question of conversion, in one sense a question of construction, will be treated in a subsequent chapter.[1]

In addition to the presumptions governing the decision of the court of construction, there are certain presumptions made by the court of probate which to a certain extent are rules of construction. They are fully considered in His Honour Judge Pitt Taylor's treatise on the *Law of Evidence*,[2] and may be shortly added here, even at the risk of some repetition. The presumptions are, with the exception of (*b*), rebuttable by evidence to the contrary. They are primarily applicable only to wills of pure personalty, or of mixed personalty and realty, such as come within the jurisdiction of the Probate Division, but many of them would doubtless govern, *mutatis mutandis*, the construction of wills of realty only.

(*a*) On proof of the signature of the deceased, he will be presumed to have known and approved of the contents of the will.

(*b*) Where proof can be furnished that, prior to the execution of a will by a competent testator, it was read over to him or brought specially to his notice, the court will, in the absence of fraud, recognise a conclusive presumption that he approved of the contents.

(*c*) When several sheets of paper constituting a connected disposal of property are found together, the last only being duly signed and attested, the court will

[1] P. 161. [2] 8th ed., 1885, §§ 160-166.

presume that all formed part of the will at the time of its execution.[1]

(d) It is presumed that if the testator might have seen, he did see the witnesses subscribe their names.

(e) Alterations, interlineations, or erasures are presumed to have been made after execution, even of codicils to the will. But this does not apply to the filling up of blanks.

(f) A will last seen in the custody of the testator, and not forthcoming at his death, is presumed to have been destroyed by him, *animo cancellandi*.

(g) A testator is presumed to have known the value of his estate: accordingly on deficiency of assets the legacies must abate.

[1] In such a case an affidavit by an attesting witness that the separate sheets constituted the will of the testator is generally required.

CHAPTER X

INTESTATE SUCCESSION

INTESTACY is either total or partial. Total intestacy is caused by the absence of a will, or by the invalidity of a will for any reason, such as incapacity of the testator, informality of execution, or undue influence. Partial intestacy affects only a part of the property of the deceased, and arises from his disposing of only a part of his property, from lapse not within the provisions of the Wills Act, s. 33, or from informal execution of part of the testamentary document or documents. It will be convenient to divide intestate succession as a whole into three branches—succession to real estate, to personal estate, and to titles of honour. To the latter, intestate succession is the only kind of succession possible; in the case of intestate succession to real or personal property, the rules of succession are the same whether the intestacy be total or partial; the only difference is that in the latter case they can only affect that part of the property as to which there has been an intestacy.

(1) *Real Estate.*

The rules of descent of real estate[1] now depend on

---
[1] It should be remembered that not all real estate can be inherited by descent. For instance, an estate for life is real estate, but it can

the common law as amended by the Inheritance Act of 1833 (3 and 4 Will. IV, c. 106), 22 and 23 Vict., c. 35 (known as Lord St. Leonards' Act), and the Conveyancing Act, 1881 (44 and 45 Vict., c. 41). The Act of 1833 does not extend to descents taking place on the death of any person dying before 1st January 1834. To such descents the old law as set out by Blackstone, and shortly noticed in Ch. II above, is still applicable. The modern rules of descent are as follows—

(1) In every case the descent shall be traced from the purchaser.[1] The last owner is to be considered the purchaser unless the contrary be proved.

(2) Inheritance in the first place descends to the issue of the purchaser *in infinitum*.

(3) The male issue is preferred to the female.

(4) The eldest of the male issue of equal degree of consanguinity inherits, but the female inherit jointly as coparceners.

(5) All lineal descendants *in infinitum* represent the ancestor.

Thus far the rules apply to the descent of estates tail as well as of estates in fee-simple. The remaining rules affect only the latter.

(6) On failure of lineal descendants, the inheritance goes to the nearest lineal ancestor.

(7) The father and all male paternal ancestors and

---

obviously not be inherited. An estate tail is descendible only to a limited extent within the bounds of the entail. The rules as given here are adopted, with slight alterations, from Williams' *Real Property*, Part I, c. iv, where a useful diagram will be found.

[1] " Purchaser" signifies any one taking otherwise than by descent. Purchase is sometimes known as conquest. The title "conqueror," applied to William I, probably only signified that he was a conqueror in the sense of not succeeding by descent.

REAL ESTATE 111

their descendants are admitted before any of the female paternal ancestors.

(8) Brothers and sisters do not inherit directly, but by representation of the parent.

(9) The half blood takes next after the whole blood, after the issue of the kinsman of the whole blood, when the common ancestor is a male, after the common ancestor when such ancestor is a female.

(10) In the admission of female paternal ancestors, the mother of the more remote male paternal ancestor and her heirs is preferred to the mother of the less remote male paternal ancestor and her heirs. The rule for the admission of female maternal ancestors is analogous.

(11) Where there is a total failure of the heirs of the purchaser, or where any land is descendible as if an ancestor had been the purchaser, and there shall be a total failure of the heirs of such ancestor, then the land is to descend and the descent is to be traced from the person last entitled, as though he had been the purchaser.[1]

(12) By the Conveyancing Act, 1881,[2] real estate on the death of an intestate may pass to his personal representative, but only for limited purposes, and this devolution ought perhaps not to be considered a descent in the proper sense of the word.

(13) An estate *pur autre vie* passes, in the absence of a special occupant, to the executor or administrator.[3]

In case of the total failure of heirs, even of the person last entitled, the Crown takes the inheritance by escheat as *ultimus heres*, subject to the widow's right of dower, where such right has not been barred, as it

---
[1] 22 and 23 Vict., c. 35, s. 19.
[2] 44 and 45 Vict., c. 41, ss. 4, 30. See p. 145.   [3] P. 43.

generally has been. Escheat applies, since 47 and 48 Vict., c. 71, to incorporeal as well as corporeal hereditaments, that is to franchises, profits *à prendre*, etc.[1]

It should be noticed that in English law the heir cannot renounce, as could the *heres* in Roman law. The estate with all its benefits and burdens descends upon him by act of the law, and he is at once clothed with all its rights and responsibilities. He can, of course, dispose of the inheritance by sale or otherwise as soon as he thinks fit, but until he has made a valid alienation he is regarded by the law as heir.

The full rights of the successor may be limited, as has been already stated,[2] by the occurrence of the temporary interposition of an estate in curtesy or dower. Such estates are, at the present day, of little importance in practice, as they are rarely met with.

A question of some difficulty has arisen as to the application of the Inheritance Act to copyholds. In a case of *Muggleton* v. *Barnett*[3] in 1858 it was held by the Court of Exchequer Chamber that the act did not so apply, but this decision has been disapproved of by such eminent authorities in real property law as Lord St. Leonards and Mr. Joshua Williams, who are of opinion that the act applies as far as the custom of the particular manor allows. Escheat in the case of copyholds is to the lord of the manor, whether they are enfranchised or not.[4] S. 30 of the Conveyancing Act, 1881, does not apply to copyholds.[5] A right analogous to, but less extensive than escheat, is that of seizure

---

[1] The procedure in escheat is now regulated by the Escheat (Procedure) Act, 1887 (50 and 51 Vict., c. 53), and the rules framed in accordance with the act. [2] P. 24.
[3] 2 Hurlstone and Norman's Rep., 653.
[4] 50 and 51 Vict., c. 73, s. 4. [5] *Id.*, s. 45.

quousque, that is, the right of the lord after proclamation at three successive manorial courts to seize the lands, in the absence of an heir or devisee, until some heir or devisee claims admittance. The rights of an heir or devisee under disability are protected by certain sections in the Copyhold Acts.

The main exceptions to the rule of primogeniture in the descent of land occurs in the tenures of gavelkind and borough-English and in the local customs of some manors, as in the case of *Muggleton* v. *Barnett* above. Gavelkind and borough-English are general customs, of the existence of which the court takes judicial notice;[1] manorial customs are particular, and must be proved by evidence. In gavelkind (a variety of socage tenure) all the sons succeed to the inheritance in equal shares; in borough-English (a variety of burgage tenure) the youngest son inherits to the exclusion of his elder brothers. The origin of these tenures has been the subject of much difference of opinion; in borough-English especially some writers have found a survival of the most primitive legal conceptions. It is sufficient in this place to say that gavelkind is now almost confined to Kent, and borough-English to certain manors and to some ancient boroughs, such as Nottingham.[2] The heir in these exceptional tenures is generally known as the customary heir, the term heir-at-law being confined to the heir succeeding to real estate held by the ordinary tenure.

Equitable or trust estates descend on intestacy, in

---

[1] The custom of gavelkind received quasi-statutory sanction in the *Consuetudines Cantiæ*, a compilation of uncertain date found in some editions of the statutes.
[2] See the work on *Real Property* in this series. A list of the manors (chiefly in Surrey) where borough-English prevails will be found in Elton, *Tenures of Kent*, p. 167 (1867).

accordance with the maxim of equity that "equity follows the law," in the same way as legal estates. Therefore an equitable estate in gavelkind or borough-English will descend in the same way as a corresponding legal estate. The only difference is in escheat; where an equitable estate fails for want of heirs there is no escheat, but the trustee obtains the legal estate discharged of the trust, that is, the property becomes his own.

A distinction is drawn by the law between an heir *apparent* and an heir *presumptive*. The former is one whose right of succession is indefeasible, provided that he survive the ancestor, *e.g.* an eldest son; the latter is one who would be entitled to succeed in case of the ancestor's immediate death, but whose expectation may be defeated by the birth of a nearer heir,—*e.g.* a daughter, whose succession would be postponed to that of a son born subsequently.

A curious case illustrating the law of intestate succession arose in 1730. The plaintiff was the son of the eldest brother of a deceased intestate. The defendant was his uncle, a younger brother of the deceased. Both claimed to inherit, and the matter was referred to the village schoolmaster. He, acting on the axiom "land cannot ascend but always descends," made his award in favour of the uncle. It was held that the nephew was entitled in equity to relief from the award, notwithstanding the general rule that *ignorantia juris neminem excusat.*[1]

(2) *Personal Estate.*

Succession to personal estate on intestacy depends on rules very different from those governing the

[1] *Lansdown* v. *Lansdown*, Moseley's Rep., 364.

succession to real estate. They are founded on, though not identical with, those of the Roman law, and what mainly distinguishes them from the rules under the Inheritance Act is the absence of any exclusive right of the eldest son. The application of an intestate's personalty after payment of his debts is now regulated by the Statutes of Distribution, of the dates of 1670 and 1685 (22 and 23 Car. II, c. 10, and 1 Jac. II, c. 17, s. 7); and the Statute of Frauds, (1676,) s. 25. The effect of the acts is as follows. The widow takes one-third if there be a child or descendant of a child, one-half if there be no child. The husband of a married woman dying intestate is entitled to the whole of her personalty, and this right does not appear to be affected by the Married Women's Property Act. The shares of the children are two-thirds if there be a widow, the whole if there be no widow. They take in equal shares without distinction between sons and daughters. The descendants of such children as may have died in the lifetime of the intestate stand in the place of their parent or ancestor. Such children as have been advanced by the parent in his lifetime must bring the amount of their advancement into hotchpot, so as to make the estate of all the children to be equal, as nearly as can be estimated.[1] The heir-at-law takes his share of the personalty without respect to the estate which he may take by descent. In default of children or descendants, the father takes half if there be a widow, the whole if there be none. If the father be dead, the mother, brothers, and sisters take in equal shares, subject to the widow's right to one

---

[1] A clause to this effect is very generally inserted in wills. It should be clearly stated in a will, if possible, what kinds of advancement are to be charged against the children.

half. Brothers and sisters of the half blood rank equally with those of the whole blood. The children of a deceased brother or sister stand in *loco parentis* as long as the mother or any brother or sister be living In default of brother or sister or child of brother or sister the mother takes the whole, subject to the widow's half, but a stepmother takes nothing. If there be no mother, the brothers and sisters take equally, subject to the widow's half, and to the share of the descendants of any brother or sister who may have predeceased the intestate. Beyond brothers' and sisters' children there is no right of representation, and the personalty goes *per capita* and not *per stirpes*, *i.e.* among the next of kin in equal shares regardless of the original stock. The degrees of kindred are reckoned on the principle of Roman law, not on that of canon law. Thus a brother is two degrees from a brother, the reckoning being made up to the parent and down again, and each generation counting as a degree. In the canon law the reckoning is according to the degree in which each stands from the common ancestor, so that brothers according to that law are related in the first degree. Cousins are in the fourth degree by Roman and English law, in the third degree by canon law. This explains why the intermarriage of cousins is forbidden by the Roman Church. Marriages within the fourth degree are prohibited by both systems of law alike, the only difference is what constitutes the fourth degree. If there be no next of kin, the Crown succeeds, as in the case of real estate, subject always to the widow's half. The grant of administration in such cases to a nominee of the Crown, usually the Treasury Solicitor, is regulated by 39 and 40 Vict., c. 18 and 47 and 48 Vict., c. 71. This right of the Crown, though practically the same as escheat, is not called by that name, as escheat proper is confined to real estate.

The rule as to jurisdiction of the courts in suits for a distributive share under an intestacy is the same as that governing the jurisdiction in suits for legacies, except that the question of assent does not arise, the assent of the administrator to a share not making any difference in the rights of parties.[1]

(3) *Titles of Honour.*

The succession to such titles depends as a rule upon the limitations contained in the writ or letters patent creating them.[2] In the case of peerages the writ is no longer in use, except where the eldest son of a peer, generally of at least the rank of earl, is summoned to the House of Lords during his father's lifetime. In such a case the son is as a rule summoned in the name of one of his father's baronies.[3] Succession to ancient peerages by writ—which contained no words of limitation—is presumed to be in the nature of succession to real estate, that is, the eldest male heir succeeds, and, in default of a male heir, the heiress, and, if there be more than one heiress, they all take as joint tenants. But as they cannot all bear the title, none bear it, and the title

[1] P. 62.
[2] Titles of honour as incorporeal hereditaments fall within the definition of "land" in the Settled Land Act, 1882, so that the costs of proceedings taken before the Committee of Privileges of the House of Lords for establishing a claim to a peerage may be ordered to be paid out of settled property. *Re the Earl of Aylesford's Settled Estates*, Law Rep., 32 Chancery Div., 162 (1886).
[3] The latest instance is that of Earl Percy, summoned in 1887 as Baron Lovaine, one of the baronies of his father the Duke of Northumberland.

is said to be in abeyance, as happened recently to the barony of Conyers. This abeyance may be determined by the Crown, in virtue of its prerogative as the fountain of honour, conferring the peerage on one of the joint tenants or one of her descendants, or by the death of all but one of the joint tenants or her descendants, in which case the title devolves by operation of law on the surviving joint tenant or her eldest male descendant. Modern peerages and baronetcies are invariably created by patent; the earliest example of creation by patent was in 1387. They are generally limited to heirs male of the body of the original grantee. There have been a few exceptions, and in such cases the title devolves according to the limitations in the patent. Thus the barony of Nelson, created in 1801, was limited to the father of the grantee and his heirs, and in default of heirs to the sisters of the grantee; the earldom of Nelson (1805) to the sisters of the grantee. The viscountcy of Wolseley (1885) was limited to a daughter, and the barony of Deramore (1885) to a brother. The advantage which a peerage created by patent has over one created by writ is that the former enures to the advantage of descendants, although the original grantee never sit in the House of Lords. To make a peerage by writ transmissible to descendants, it was necessary that the grantee should sit during one, if not two, parliaments. Spiritual peerages and the life peerages conferred under the powers of the Appellate Jurisdiction Act, 1876, are not descendible. A title of honour cannot be disposed of by will, nor can it pass by a shifting clause in the patent, attempting to transfer it to another person on the happening of a certain event.[1]

[1] This was so determined by the Committee of Privileges of the

The law as to Irish peerages is in general accordance with that of English. The Scotch law differs in one important particular. There is no abeyance among co-heiresses, but the eldest bears the title as her *præcipuum*. The presumption in the case of a Scottish peerage is that it descends to heirs male, not heirs general,[1] but the right of heirs general may be established by evidence. Down to the Union, Scotch peerages could be surrendered to the Crown and regranted to a new series of heirs. In 1885 the title of Colonel Erskine to the Earldom of Mar was confirmed by Act of Parliament (48 and 49 Vict., c. 48) on the ground that it was doubtful whether the earldom had ever been surrendered by his ancestor. An Act of Parliament confirming a claim to a peerage appears to be unknown to English law, though there would be nothing unconstitutional in the passing of such an act in a proper case.

House of Lords in the curious case of *The Buckhurst Peerage*, Law Rep., 2 Appeal Cases, 1 (1876).
[1] *The Mar Peerage*, Law Rep., 1 Appeal Cases, 1 (1875).

CHAPTER XI

ADMINISTRATION IN A COURT OF PROBATE

On the death of a person, either testate or intestate, it is necessary for his personal representative or representatives to obtain the authority of the High Court of Justice (Probate, Divorce, and Admiralty Division),[1] of a County Court, or of an officer of Inland Revenue, acting under the authority of the High Court, in order to confer on him or them full rights of dealing with the personal estate of the deceased.[2] The rights of the personal representative do not commence until the death of the deceased has been either proved by producing a copy of the certificate of death or burial, or by presumption of death, which will be made by the court under certain circumstances, such as the fact that a man set sail on a certain vessel, and that such vessel was lost with all on board. There is no period fixed by statute, as in Scotland, after the expiration of which death is pre-

[1] It has been held by Chancery judges that although since the Judicature Acts a judge of the Chancery Division may in theory have jurisdiction to grant or revoke probate, he would not be exercising sound discretion in exercising such jurisdiction, no division but the Probate possessing the requisite machinery for dealing with business of that nature. *Pinney* v. *Hunt*, Law Rep., 6 Chancery Div., 98, (1877); *Bradford* v. *Young*, Law Rep., 26 Chancery Div. 656 (1884).

[2] There are a few exceptions which will be mentioned later.

sumed.[1] With the real estate of the deceased his personal representatives have (with certain exceptions, to be mentioned later) nothing to do. The devisee or heir becomes entitled, by operation of law, to the real estate immediately at the death, or presumed death, of the predecessor. Where there is a will and an executor or executors appointed, it is necessary for him or them to take out probate of the will; where there is no will, or where there is a will with no executor or executors named therein, letters of administration must be taken out. Probate is not granted before the lapse of seven days from the death, administration before the lapse of fourteen days, and both should be applied for within six months, unless in exceptional cases. Probate and letters of administration are granted by the same authority; the main difference in the rights conferred by them is that the executor may do certain acts before obtaining probate, which an administrator cannot do before obtaining letters of administration. The executor has an inchoate right immediately on the death, the administrator has no right at all until the grant of administration. A few exceptions to this rule exist by statute, *e.g.* by 3 and 4 Will. IV, c. 27, s. 6; for the purposes of the act (limitation of actions) the administrator may claim as if there had been no interval between the death and the grant.

(1) *Probate*

The number of executors who may be appointed is unlimited, and every person may be an executor, except those expressly forbidden. In the present state of the law there appears to be no class of persons legally

[1] P. 203.

excluded. If the king or a corporation [1] be appointed, the office is performed by persons named by the executor, such persons in the latter case being called syndics, and taking administration with the will annexed. A married woman, as has been already stated, can be executrix, and in such a case becomes liable to the extent of her separate estate. So can an alien. An infant, if appointed, cannot, by 38 Geo. III, c. 87, s. 6, act until he is of age. Where an infant is sole executor, administration *durante minore ætate* is granted. Where an executor is a bankrupt, a receiver is generally appointed by the Chancery Division; where an idiot or lunatic, administration with the will annexed is granted to a person named by the Probate Division.

The appointment of an executor may be either express or implied. An implied appointment is made by the use in the will of any words from which it can be gathered that the testator wished a certain person to act as executor. Thus a general direction to pay the debts—but not a direction to pay them out of a particular fund—will be sufficient to constitute the person to whom the direction is given an executor, called in such a case executor according to the tenor. Where the appointment of executor applies to more than one person, evidence is admissible to show which person was intended by the testator. But where it is wholly ambiguous, such as "one of my sisters," it is too uncertain for the court to give effect to it, and administration with the will annexed is granted. An alternative executor may be substituted for one who dies or refuses to act. The office of executor may also be limited to

---

[1] Such as, for instance, the Trustees, Executors, and Securities Insurance Corporation.

a certain time, or for certain parts of the estate, in the latter case by what is called a grant save and except. In order to complete the title to deal with the estate, limited administration or a *cæterorum* grant must be obtained for the remaining period or the remainder of the estate.

A person may in one case become executor without either express or implied appointment. If any one intermeddle with the goods of the deceased, or take upon himself any of the duties attaching to the office of executor, he by so doing constitutes himself an executor *de son tort*, or executor of his own wrong. The executor *de son tort* is naturally regarded by the law in no very favourable light. He has all the responsibilities and none of the privileges of an executor properly constituted. Among acts which have been held to make a person executor *de son tort* are receiving the debts of the deceased, realising his property, and carrying on his trade. But offices merely of kindness and charity do not render a stranger liable as executor *de son tort*. Such acts are locking up the goods of the deceased for safety, giving directions for and paying for his funeral, and feeding his cattle.

Up to the time of applying for probate an executor may renounce, provided that he has done no act showing an intention to carry out the will of the testator. The renunciation must be in writing, and may be in either the principal or a district registry of the Probate Division. It may be retracted at any time before it has been actually filed in the registry. Should the executor nominate neither accept nor renounce, a citation is issued to him from the principal registry, and in default of appearance he may be punished for contempt of court, and the administration of the goods of the deceased, under s. 16 of the Court of Probate Act, 1858, devolves as if he had not been appointed executor. The same result follows, by s. 79 of the Court of Probate Act, 1857, where one of several executors renounces. An executor renouncing is not allowed to take representation of the deceased in any other character, such as administrator. Whether an executor renouncing can take a legacy left him is a question of construction. It depends on the words used in the will whether the legacy is made dependent on his acting as executor or not. The office is *primâ facie* a gratuitous one, and if a sum of money be left to the executor, the presumption is that it is to induce him to accept an onerous office. It is also a question of construction depending on the words of the will whether an executor can in any way act in furtherance of the testator's wishes, *e.g.* in the selection of a charity to be benefited by the will. So far is the office considered as gratuitous, that if a solicitor be appointed executor he cannot make the ordinary professional charges without being specially empowered to do so by the testator.

An executorship cannot be transmitted or assigned *inter vivos*, but can pass by will. An executor of an executor (provided that he be sole executor) through any length of series still continues the chain of representation to the testator, but where any administration occurs it breaks the chain. The administrator of an executor (and *a fortiori* the executor of an administrator) is not a representative of the original deceased, and administration *de bonis non* must be taken out to the effects of such deceased. On the death of one of co-executors his interest vests in the survivor or survivors and does not pass to his own executor or executors.

The executor not having renounced, it becomes his duty to prove the will. One or more of the executors nominated in the will may prove it. Where any one nominated does not prove, power is generally reserved —a memorandum of such power being inserted in the grant—for any executor not proving to appear and prove at some future time, such future probate being called a double probate. Probate granted to one executor enables all to act.[1] No security is required from an executor, as it is from an administrator, the testator's confidence in the executor being shown by his appointing him.

Probate is of two kinds—in solemn form and in common form. The former is part of the contentious jurisdiction of the court, and is practically confined to cases where there is any opposition to the grant of probate on the ground of the alleged invalidity of the will. Before probate in solemn form a citation is issued to all persons interested, such as the widow and next of kin, who may appear as interveners. Any one interested who objects to probate in common form may prevent probate in such form by lodging a caveat in the principal or a district registry. Probate in solemn form consists in the witnesses to the will—both where possible—giving evidence in open court, and the formal decision of the court upon their evidence, supporting or otherwise the

---

[1] Only the executor or executors who proved will as a rule be registered as holders of any securities, such as certificates of railway stock possessed by the testator. Where there is any discrepancy in the name or description of the testator in the will and of his name or description in any securities held by him, a statutory declaration of identity is generally required by railway companies, etc.

validity of the will. The party propounding a will, *i.e.* alleging its validity (generally the executor), is bound to call an attesting witness, where the attendance of such witness is obtainable, even though his evidence will be adverse. The court has power to order the production before it of any paper purporting to be testamentary, and a registrar has power to issue subpœnas to produce such papers. Probate in solemn form is one of two cases in which a will devising only real property comes within the jurisdiction of the Probate Division. The other is where an executor is appointed to a will of lands. By the Court of Probate Act, 1857, it is enacted that a will affecting real estate may be proved in solemn form after due citation of the heir and persons interested, that the probate, decree, or order made at the hearing shall ensure to the benefit of all persons interested in the real estate affected, and that the probate copy shall be conclusive evidence of the validity and contents of the will. The contentious jurisdiction of the Probate Division now depends mainly on the Probate Court Acts, 1857 and 1858; the Judicature Acts and Rules of the Supreme Court; and the Probate Rules of 1862, as amended by subsequent rules. The Appendices to the Rules of the Supreme Court, 1883, contain forms of indorsement of writ and statements of claim and defence. As an example of practice, the writ and claim and defence in an action of probate in solemn form may be interesting. The indorsement of the writ is in this form: "The plaintiff claims to be the executor of the last will, dated the   ,
of C. W., late of   , gentleman, deceased, who died on the   day of   ,
and to have the said will established. This writ is

issued against you as one of the next of kin of the said deceased" (*or as the case may be*).¹ The statement of claim runs thus: "The plaintiff is the executor appointed under the will of C. T., late of Bicester, in the county of Oxford, gentleman, who died on the 20th of January 1883, the said will bearing date the 1st of January 1875, and a codicil thereto, the 1st of October 1875. The plaintiff claims: That the Court shall decree probate of the said will and codicil in solemn form of law."²
The statutory form of a statement of defence runs thus—

"1. The said will and codicil of the deceased were not duly executed according to the provisions of the statute 1 Vict., c. 26.

"2. The deceased at the time the said will and codicil respectively purport to have been executed was not of sound mind, memory, and understanding.

"3. The execution of the said will and codicil was obtained by the undue influence of the plaintiff (and others acting with him, whose names are at present unknown to the defendant).

"4. The execution of the said will and codicil was obtained by the fraud of the plaintiff, such fraud, so far as is within the defendant's present knowledge, being [*state the nature of the fraud*].

"5. The deceased, at the time of the execution of the said will and codicil, did not know and approve of the contents thereof [*or*] of the contents of the residuary clause in the said will [*as the case may be*].

"6. The deceased made his true last will, dated the 1st day of January 1873, and thereby appointed the defendant sole executor thereof.

¹ Appendix A, Part III, s. 5.
² Appendix A, section III, No. 2.

"The defendant claims—

"1. That the Court will pronounce against the said will and codicil propounded by the plaintiff.

"2. That the Court will decree probate of the will of the deceased, dated the 1st of January 1873, in solemn form of law."[1]

Trial in the Probate Division is either before the judge alone or before the judge with a common or special jury. A new trial may be granted in a proper case by the Court of Appeal. An issue may also be tried in another court by order of the Probate Division, *e.g.* an issue at assizes of *devisavit vel non*, to try the validity of a devise. An appeal on the facts as well as the law lies from the Probate Division to the Court of Appeal, and thence to the House of Lords. Before the Judicature Acts it lay direct to the House of Lords. How far an appeal lies in non-contentious business is still uncertain: it appears to lie in some cases.[2] The general practice in the Probate Division is in accordance with that of the Queen's Bench Division. Such accordance was the evident intention of the framers of the Court of Probate Act. In one or two cases, however, special rules governing only probate practice occur in the Rules of the Supreme Court, 1883. Thus in probate actions the indorsement of the writ is to show whether the plaintiff sues as creditor, executor, administrator, residuary legatee, legatee, next of kin, heir-at-law, devisee, or in any and what other character.[3] The plaintiff in a probate action must issue his writ of summons out of the central office of the Supreme Court. He cannot

---

[1] Appendix D, section III, No. 2.
[2] *Re Clook*, Law Rep., 15 Probate Div., 132 (1890).
[3] Ord. iii, r. 5.

issue it out of a district registry.¹ The party opposing a will may with his defence give notice that he merely insists on the will being proved in solemn form, and only intends to cross-examine the witnesses produced in support of the will.² This is important in regard to his liability for costs.

The contentious jurisdiction of the Probate Division was to a limited extent conferred on county courts by the acts of 1857 and 1858. The most important section is s. 10 of the act of 1858, which enacts that where it appears by affidavit to the satisfaction of a registrar of the principal registry that the testator in respect of whose estate a grant or revocation of a grant of probate is applied for had at the time of his death his fixed place of abode in one of the districts specified in Schedule (A)³ to the Court of Probate Act, and that the personal estate in respect of which the probate has been granted (exclusive of what the deceased was possessed of or entitled to as a trustee, and not beneficially, but without deducting anything on account of the debts due and owing from the deceased) is under the value of £200, and that the deceased at the time of his death was not seised or entitled beneficially of or to any real estate of the value of £300 or upwards, the judge of the county court having jurisdiction in the place in which the deceased had at the time of his death his fixed place of abode shall have the contentious jurisdiction and authority of the Court of Probate. Trial in the county court is either by the judge alone or by the judge with a jury of five. The County Court Rules of 1889 (rule xlix, forms 347-351) deal with the practice in the county courts. An appeal as of right

---

[1] Ord. v, rr. 1, 2.   [2] Ord. xxi, r. 18.
[3] See Appendix A.

lies from the county court to a divisional court of the Queen's Bench Division of the High Court, from that Court to the Court of Appeal only by leave.

In the vast majority of cases probate in common form is all that is necessary. This is a part of the non-contentious jurisdiction of the Probate Division, and in this part of the practice the Judicature Acts have made no change, s. 18 of the Judicature Act, 1875, specially preserving to the President of the Probate Division the power to make rules in non-contentious and common form business. In order to prove a will in common form the executor in person[1] or by his solicitor applies at (1) the principal registry; (2) a district registry, where the deceased had at the time of his death a fixed place of abode within the district in which the application is made; (3) a proper officer of Inland Revenue, where the personal estate does not exceed £300 without deduction for debts or funeral expenses.[2] In the last case, if the will be at all defective in form, applicants are referred to a registry. The grant is not actually made by the revenue officer, but the will is forwarded by him to a registry and returned by the registry. In order to lead to a grant the executor must produce the original will (or an exemplification or office copy if it have already been proved in another court), must make oath or affirmation in a prescribed form (known as the executor's oath, by which he undertakes to duly administer, exhibit an inventory if necessary, pay debts and legacies, etc.), must produce an official copy of the certifiacte of death or burial of the deceased, and must fill up and swear or

---

[1] Instructions issued by the Probate Division for the guidance of executors proving in person will be found in Appendix C.
[2] A list of the places where Inland Revenue officers are empowered to undertake probate may be obtained at any Inland Revenue office.

affirm the truth of an account of the personal estate of the deceased, a schedule of debts and funeral expenses, and the Inland Revenue affidavit as to the value of the estate. An inventory is not usually required, but may be called for by any person interested. All the necessary documents are supplied at the registry or Inland Revenue office. Should there be any alterations or interlineations in the will or no attestation clause, or should the will be on detached sheets, further affidavits of execution are required from at least one attesting witness, and the will cannot be proved through an Inland Revenue officer. If the attesting witnesses be dead or abroad, or be for any other reason incapable of making an affidavit, affidavits of other persons as to the handwriting of the deceased are accepted. An affidavit as to alterations and interlineations is only required where they are not mentioned in the attestation clause. The executor's oath or affirmation may be taken before a registrar, an Inland Revenue officer, or a commissioner of the High Court of Justice. In due time, after the completion of the preliminaries, and on payment of the probate duty, the account duty (where necessary), and the fees payable in the registry,[1] a probate copy of the will engrossed on parchment and sealed with the seal of the court is issued to the executor. The original will is preserved in the principal registry, where are also deposited all the wills proved in the old Prerogative Court of Canterbury, but not those proved in the bishops' courts, which are still kept in the district registries corresponding to the diocesan registries.

The probate is in general a verbatim copy of the will, with the addition of the dates of death and of grant

[1] For which see Appendix B.

of probate and the sum below which the personal estate of the deceased was sworn. In some cases, however, words or phrases are omitted, such as expressions reflecting on the character of living persons, or the name of a legatee written after the names of the attesting witnesses. Probate may also issue in blank as to a substituted legacy. The probate, unless revoked, becomes evidence for all purposes, and the original will remains deposited in the registry.

It sometimes happens that a will, known to have existed in the testator's lifetime, cannot be found after his death. In such a case the executor may propound the lost will, giving such evidence as he can of its contents. A well-known case in which such evidence was allowed to be given was that of *Sugden* v. *Lord St. Leonards*, decided by the Court of Appeal in 1876.[1] The court, acting upon the evidence of the daughter of the testator as to the terms of the will, which she had seen, and as to declarations made by him, and also upon certain documents and memoranda found among the testator's papers, granted probate of the lost will to the extent to which its terms had been proved.

Probate once granted is conclusive unless revoked. But it may always be revoked for certain reasons, either on citation or on appeal. The principal case of revocation would be where an executor has obtained probate in common form, and being afterwards cited to prove it in solemn form fails to do so. The probate in common form would in such a case be revoked. Other cases might arise where probate had been granted of a forged will, or where a testator, supposed to be dead, afterwards appeared. As a rule *bonâ fide* payments by

[1] Law Rep., 1 Probate Div., 154.

or to an executor acting under a probate afterwards revoked are valid. Such is the express enactment of the Court of Probate Act, 1857. The act further provides that the abatement by revocation of any action brought by an executor is to be entered on the record, and the action is to be continued in the name of the new executor or administrator. The executor has by the same act power to retain and reimburse himself in respect of any payments which might have been lawfully made by the person to whom grants of probate or letters of administration were afterwards made.[1] A county court has jurisdiction to revoke a probate which has been granted by it in a case falling within the pecuniary limit which confers upon it probate jurisdiction.[2]

(2) *Administration.*

Where a person dies wholly or partially intestate, an administrator is appointed by the Probate Division. His rights and duties agree in general with those of the executor, but he is more directly an officer of the court, and his rights date from the grant of letters of administration, not from the death of the testator, as is the case for some purposes with the executor. As a rule, all persons qualified to act as executors are also qualified to act as administrators, but they must have legal capacity to execute the administration bond required by the court. Accordingly, infants, lunatics, or idiots cannot be administrators. If an infant be next of kin, administration *durante minore aetate* is granted to another person. If a bankrupt be appointed, additional security, known as "justifying security," is required. Adminis-

[1] 20 and 21 Vict., c. 77, ss. 76-78.   [2] P. 129.

tratorship is seldom a joint office, as is executorship. A corporation or society is not usually allowed to act as administrator. One of the few examples of the appointment of several persons is the appointment of a board of guardians where a pauper has died intestate and entitled to personal property.[1]

Administration is usually granted in a certain order, preference being given (after husband or wife) to the next of blood who is under no legal disability. The order is—

(a) husband or wife;
(b) child;
(c) grandchild;
(d) other more remote descendant;
(e) father;
(f) mother;
(g) brother or sister;
(h) grandfather or grandmother;
(i) nephew, niece, uncle, aunt, or other collateral;
(j) creditor;[2]
(k) stranger;[2]
(l) the Crown.

Where an intestate dies without any known relations, and without a grant having been made to a creditor or stranger, the grant is made on application to the court by the Treasury Solicitor, or (in the case of the deceased being resident in the counties of Lancaster or Cornwall)

[1] In the United States and in many of the colonies there is an official known as the public administrator. The nearest approach to such an official in England is perhaps the Treasury Solicitor. His jurisdiction is, however, confined to a very limited class of cases.

[2] Such grants are only made "by reason of the insolvency of the estate of the deceased, or other special circumstances," under s. 73 of the Court of Probate Act, 1857.

ORDER OF GRANT

to the nominee of the Queen as Duchess of Lancaster, or of the Prince of Wales as Duke of Cornwall. The practice in grants to the Treasury Solicitor or to the solicitor to the Duchy of Lancaster is regulated by 39 and 40 Vict., c. 18, and 47 and 48 Vict., c. 71. Misconduct or lunacy of husband or wife will be sufficient ground for exclusion. All relations of equal degree have equal right to administer, but the court does not generally make a joint grant, and therefore chooses the person whom the majority of the equal degree select, males being as a rule preferred to females. Any of the next of kin may renounce in proper form, upon which the next in order come in. A citation may be issued, as in the case of executors, calling on those first entitled to accept or renounce. And as in the case of executors no person renouncing may take representation to the deceased in another character. In some cases the person claiming administration may have to bring an interest suit to establish his right.[1]

Letters of administration are not issued till after the lapse of fourteen days from the death of the deceased, unless by special order of the court. If applied for after the lapse of three years, the delay must be explained. Between the time of death and grant the personal estate is vested in the President of the Probate Division. The grant is made by the Probate Division or an officer of Inland Revenue and (in the case mentioned below) by a county court. An oath to administer and exhibit an inventory must be taken. The documents required from the administrator are the copy of the certificate of death or burial of the deceased, a statement of his relationship

[1] A form of statement of claim in such a suit is given in Appendix C, Section III, No. 1 of the Rules of the Supreme Court, 1883.

to the applicant, the affidavit of Inland Revenue (to which is annexed an account of the property of the deceased), and the administration bond. The bond is for double the amount at which the estate to be administered is sworn, and two sureties are required, unless the administrater be the husband (when one is sufficient), or unless the court sees fit to dispense with sureties, as in grants to certain public officials. A married woman or a minor is not accepted as a surety.[1] The stamp on the bond is five shillings, except where the estate does not exceed £100, or where the bond is given by certain relatives of a seaman, marine, or soldier dying on service, when no stamp is required. The papers necessary to lead to the grant, viz., the oath and the Inland Revenue affidavit having been duly executed, the grant will issue, and the administrator then proceeds to distribute to the wife and next of kin, in accordance with the Statutes of Distribution.

The administration of estates of a still smaller maximum value than those falling within the jurisdiction of officers of Inland Revenue is provided for in certain cases by 36 and 37 Vict., c. 52, and 38 and 39 Vict., c. 27.[2] The combined effect of these acts is that the widow and children of an intestate and the children of an intestate widow are enabled, should the whole estate of the deceased not exceed in value £100, and should they reside more than three miles from a registry, to apply to the county court within the district of which the intestate had his or her fixed place of abode at the time of death, and the registrar will fill up the forms,

[1] Certain insurance and other companies make it a part of their business to act as sureties to administration bonds.
[2] This is the only administration (except administration *pendente lite*) which can be granted by a county court.

administer the oath, and do all those acts for the intending administrator or administratrix that would be done for them at the probate registry. The county court registrar may administer oaths and affirmations.

So far only general administration has been treated of. The same law applies, *mutatis mutandis*, to limited and special administrations, the main exception being that in such cases the Inland Revenue and county court officials would have no jurisdiction, their powers being confined to complete administrations of the simplest nature. The principal kinds of limited administration are as follows—

(a) *Cum testamento annexo*, or with the will annexed. Administration of this kind is generally granted where no executor has been named in the will. The administration is general, inasmuch as it deals with the whole of the personalty named in the will, but it differs from the ordinary general administration in that the persons benefited are determined by the will and not by the Statutes of Distribution. Such administration may also be granted to the duly constituted attorney of an executor resident abroad.

(b) *De bonis non administratis*, often contracted into *de bonis non* or *de bonis*. This is a supplementary grant made where the administration of the goods of an intestate has not been completed by the original administrator, *e.g.* where the latter has died before completing title to some of the property of the intestate.

(c) *Durante absentiâ*, granted in certain cases where a near relation entitled to administer is abroad.

(d) *Durante minore ætate*, granted where an infant is sole executor of a will. In this case, as in that of *cum testamento annexo*, the administrator is bound to follow the terms of the will.

(e) *Pendente lite*, granted where there is any suit touching the validity of a will, or for obtaining, recalling, or revoking any probate or grant of administration. The Court of Probate Act, 1857, enables the court to appoint such administrator or any other person to be receiver of the real estate of the deceased, with a right to such reasonable remuneration as the court shall determine.[1]

Limited grants are made in other cases, the Probate Division having a wide discretion in such matters. Examples are grants *durante dementiâ*, during the lunacy of an executor or administrator;[2] *ad colligenda bona defuncti*, where no application is made by the next of kin or a creditor; and grants until a lost will be found, or until the will of a testator left in India could be transmitted to England. On the expiration of a limited grant, what is called a cessate grant (or a *ceterorum* grant, if the first grant has been limited as to amount) issues to the person who ought to have been administrator in the first instance, but for the circumstance of his minority, absence, etc. Special administration is that granted under 38 Geo. III, c. 87, and s. 18 of the Court of Probate Act, 1858, by which the Probate Division is empowered to grant such administration after the expiration of twelve months from the death of the deceased, where the executor or the person who ought to be administrator is out of the jurisdiction.

In a few cases title to the personal estate of the

---

[1] Ss. 70-72. The court may require security by bond from a receiver of real estate (21 and 22 Vict., c. 95, s. 21).

[2] On the death of the committee of a lunatic intestate, the judge in lunacy may order some fit person to transfer to a new committee, or into court, any stock to which the lunatic is entitled (53 Vict., c. 5, s. 133).

EXEMPTIONS FROM PROBATE & ADMINISTRATION

deceased may be made without the necessity of taking out probate or letters of administration. These cases are:
(1) Soldiers and sailors.[1]
(2) Members of loan societies, to an amount not exceeding £50.
(3) Depositors in savings banks, to an amount not exceeding £100.
(4) Members of friendly, industrial, and provident societies, to the same amount.
(5) Persons who are servants in any public department, to the same amount.

These exemptions depend on a large number of Acts of Parliament which it has not been thought necessary to set out at length. Among the more important of these acts are the Provident Nominations and Small Intestacies Act, 1883, the Savings Bank Act, 1887, and the Superannuation Act, 1887. Characteristic features of the acts are the provisions that a nomination by a depositor or member is in most cases to be equivalent to a will, and that such nomination may be made by any person otherwise entitled to make it at the age of sixteen.

Letters of administration may, like probate, be revoked. It was enacted by 21 Hen. VIII, c. 5, that they cannot be revoked unless for just cause. Such a cause would be the subsequent discovery of a duly executed will. The administrator, acting under letters of administration afterwards revoked is protected to the same extent as the executor acting under a probate afterwards revoked.

[1] P. 77.

CHAPTER XII

THE RIGHTS AND DUTIES OF EXECUTORS AND ADMINISTRATORS

(1) *Rights.*

THE rights in general are the same, the exception being that the executor may do certain acts before probate, which the administrator cannot do before the grant of administration. The testator has shown his confidence in the executor's probity by nominating him to the office. There are also a few more rights of the executor only conferred by statute, among the most important of which is the right of the executor (not of the administrator), given by s. 37 of the Conveyancing Act, 1881, to pay or allow any debt or claim on any evidence that he may think sufficient, and to accept any composition or security for any debt or property claimed, and to allow time for payment of or to settle any debt. The rights of personal representatives may be conveniently grouped under the head of rights with regard to the estate and personal privileges. The rights with regard to the estate may be divided into rights over (1) personal estate in possession, (2) personal estate not in possession, (3) real estate.

(1) The personal representative is entitled to all the personal estate in possession, except the joint estate of the deceased, which passes to the surviving joint owner. Partnership estate is an exception. In the absence of any stipulation that the estate shall pass to the surviving partner, the representative is entitled to have the partnership wound up or continued for the benefit of the estate of the deceased according to the terms of the contract of partnership. Personal estate in possession includes (in addition to what is obviously such, *e.g.* money, furniture, stock in trade, etc.) farming stock and implements of husbandry, the goodwill of a business, the next presentation to a benefice (but not the advowson), emblements, or crops on the testator's lands at the time of his death, rents of land of any tenure,[1] leaseholds, policies of insurance, ships and shares in ships, proceeds of the sale of real estate contracted to be sold by the deceased, personal property over which the deceased had a general power of appointment, and the present value of reversionary property. Heirlooms and fixtures, though *primâ facie* personal, go with the inheritance and not to the personal representative. As between heir or devisee and personal representative, the right of the latter to fixtures is more limited than in many other cases where decision or statute (*e.g.* 14 and 15 Vict., c. 25) has trenched upon the old common law rule that fixtures pass with the inheritance.

Personal estate not in possession comprises *choses in action, i.e.* personal estate to which a person has a right of action, such as debts. Other *choses in action* are stocks and shares (except some which, like New River

---

[1] Including apportioned parts of any rents under the Apportionment Act, 1870.

and Aire and Calder Navigation shares, are real estate), bonds, bills, promissory notes, etc. It is to be noticed that not all stocks and shares are to be included in the personal estate on which stamp duty is payable. Foreign stocks and scrip for foreign loans are assets within the jurisdiction of the court only where they pass by delivery; Indian Government securities, by 23 Vict., c. 5, only where registered in London or enfaced in India to be so registered. Money secured on heritable property and by heritable bonds in Scotland was made chargeable with duty in England by 23 Vict., c. 15. The right to sue on a contract made by the deceased passes to his personal representative, unless the action be one that falls within the old maxim of law *actio personalis moritur cum personâ*. Such actions are those which depend on personal trust or confidence shown in the skill of the deceased, and actions for breach of promise of marriage. In the former class of actions the death of the deceased, though operating as a rescission of the contract, does not deprive the representative of a right of action already vested in the deceased.

The representative of a judgment creditor may (with leave of the court) issue a bankruptcy notice against a debtor of the deceased.

The right to sue for a tort committed against the person or property of the deceased does not as a rule pass to his representative. To this rule certain exceptions have been introduced by statute. By 4 Edw. III, c. 7, a remedy for trespass to the goods and chattels of a testator was given to executors. By 3 and 4 Will. IV, c. 42, s. 2, executors or administrators may bring actions for injuries to the real estate of the deceased, provided that the injury have been committed within

RIGHTS OF ACTION

six months before his death, and that the action be brought within a year after his death. At common law no action lay for damages sustained by the death of a human being. This was altered by Lord Campbell's Act (9 and 10 Vict., c. 93), under which an action is maintainable by the executor or administrator against any person who would have been liable if death had not occurred. The action is to be for the benefit of the wife, husband, parent, or child of the deceased, and the jury are by their verdict to apportion the damages among the persons entitled.[1] If there be no executor or administrator, or if no action be brought within six months of the time of death, it may be brought in the names of the persons entitled to the benefit (27 and 28 Vict., c. 95). The Employers' Liability Act, 1880 (43 and 44 Vict., c. 42) enables the representative of a workman, whose injuries have resulted in death, to bring an action in a county court against the employer in the cases provided for in the act.[2] In addition to the rights of action which he has at common law and by statute, the executor or administrator has certain rights exercisable for the benefit of the estate without action. For instance, he may endorse bills and notes, may distrain for rent, has a power of entry on real estate, generally for breach of covenant, and (if a representative of a last surviving or continuing trustee), may appoint a new trustee or trustees.

Co-executors being considered for many purposes as

[1] Where the death has resulted from a collision at sea, and a suit under Lord Campbell's Act is brought in the Admiralty Division, it must be a suit *in personam* and not *in rem*. *The Vera Cruz*, Law Rep., 10 Appeal Cases, 59 (1884). Damages in such a case are recoverable to the whole amount of loss suffered, although, owing to the negligence of those in charge of both vessels, only half damages would be recoverable for other purposes. *The Bernina*, Law Rep., 13 Appeal Cases, 1 (1888).
[2] See the volume on *Master and Servant* in this series.

one person, one executor can bind another by certain acts, such as payment or release of a debt. But one cannot bind the others by contract, and as a rule all must join in bringing an action. One may, however, proceed alone by originating summons.[1] The power of a single executor to bind the others has led to an important difference in the law as it affects executors and trustees. Where trustees or executors join in a receipt, *primâ facie* all are presumed to have received the money, but it is competent for a trustee to exonerate himself by showing that the money acknowledged to have been received by all was in fact received by one, and that the other joined only for conformity. An executor cannot do this, for it is not necessary for him to join in the receipt, and if he do so join, he is to be considered as assuming a power over the fund, and therefore answerable.[2] The rights of executors in this respect have been recently extended by the Conveyancing Act, 1881, by s. 38 of which, where a power or trust is given to or vested in two or more executors or trustees jointly, then, unless the contrary is expressed in the instrument, if any, creating the power or trust, the same may be exercised or performed by the survivor or survivors of them for the time being.

(3) The powers over real estate of an executor are very limited. Where real estate is converted, the executor has of course the same powers as if it had been originally personal estate. An executor may also be constituted a trustee for sale of real estate; and when so constituted he has the necessary powers of dealing with

---

[1] See p. 159.
[2] *Brice* v. *Stokes*, 2 White and Tudor's *Leading Cases in Equity*, 865.

the property, such powers being, as has just been stated, exercisable by the survivor. When a testator directs that his debts shall be paid by his executors, and also devises real estate to them, either beneficially or on trust, it is a question of intention whether the estate so devised is charged with the payment of the debts. An executor may sue for arrears of rent by 32 Hen. VIII, c. 37. As between devisee or heir and executor or administrator, real estate falling within Locke King's Act is not entitled to be exonerated at the expense of the personal estate.[1] By the Court of Probate Act, 1857, an administrator may be appointed receiver of real estate.[2] The Conveyancing Act, 1881, increases the powers of personal representatives as against heirs and devisees. By s. 4 of the act, where at the death of any person there is subsisting a contract enforceable against his heir or devisee for the sale of any freehold interest, descendible to his heirs general, in any land, his personal representatives have power to convey the land for all the estate and interest vested in him at his death. By s. 30, where an estate or interest of inheritance, or limited to the heir as special occupant, in any tenements or hereditaments, corporeal or incorporeal, is vested on any trust or by way of mortgage in any person solely, the same shall on his death, notwithstanding any testamentary disposition, devolve to and become vested in his personal representatives or representative from time to time, in like manner as if the same were a chattel real vesting in him or them.[3]

[1] P. 160.   [2] P. 138.
[3] This section supersedes provisions to a similar effect contained in the Vendor and Purchaser Act, 1874, and the Land Transfer Act, 1875. It does not include copyhold estate vested in a tenant on trust or by way of mortgage (51 and 52 Vict., c. 73, s. 45).

The personal privileges of an executor or administrator may be divided into retainer and certain legal exemptions from liability, chiefly given by one of Lord St. Leonards' Acts. Retainer is the right of an executor (but not of an executor *de son tort*) to pay himself, if a creditor of the testator, in preference to other creditors of an equal degree, by retaining so much of the legal assets as his debt amounts to. He may retain even though his debt be barred by the Statute of Limitations. An executor or administrator is exempt from liability for payment in good faith in pursuance of a power of attorney if the fact of the death of the donor of the power was not known to him at the time of payment.[1] Nor is he liable in respect of rents, covenants, or agreements of the deceased if he have set apart a sufficient fund to answer any future claim.[2] In order to assist him in obtaining a list of creditors, as well as to release him from subsequent liability should any creditor fail to present his claim until after the assets have been divided, he is entitled to insert in the *London Gazette* and two daily newspapers an advertisement in a prescribed form, the insertion of which will entitle him to successfully defend any action brought against him by an unpaid creditor.[3] In the language of the old pleading such a defence was raised by a plea of *plene administravit* or *plene administravit præter*.[4] If he apply by peti-

---

[1] 22 and 23 Vict., c. 35, s. 26; since extended to persons other than trustees, executors, and administrators by s. 47 of the Conveyancing Act, 1881.

[2] 22 and 23 Vict., c. 35, ss. 27, 28.   [3] *Id.*, s. 29.

[4] The former where all the assets had been administered, the latter where a sum had been set aside to meet a particular claim. Where the plaintiff cannot dispute the defence of *plene administravit*, and there are other assets to be received, he may enter judgment of assets *quando aciderint*, enforceable when the assets come under the control of the executor.

tion to a judge of the Chancery Division for advice, and act on such advice, he is deemed, as far as regards his own responsibility, to have discharged his duty.[1] He may also pay money into the Bank of England to the account of the Paymaster-General under the powers of the Trustee Relief Act, 1847; and may, under the Vendor and Purchaser Act, 1874, s. 9, if the representative of a vendor or purchaser of real estate, obtain from a judge of the Chancery Division on summary application an order in respect of any requisitions or objections or claim for compensation or other question arising out of the contract (not being a question affecting the existence or validity of the contract).

There is no duty incumbent on the executor or administrator to advise those entitled under a will or an intestacy as to their rights. For his own protection he is entitled to employ a solicitor in order to prove the will or obtain a grant of administration, and to fulfil the other necessary duties connected therewith, such as paying the proper duties to the Revenue. He may also—certainly if he be a trustee, probably in any case—in accordance with the principle laid down by the House of Lords in 1883, employ a stockbroker, accountant, or other agent acting within the scope of his business, and if he follow the usual and regular course of business adopted by ordinary prudent men, he will not be liable for the default of the agent.[2] The Trustee Act, 1888, enables an executor or administrator to (*inter alia*) appoint a banker or solicitor to be his agent for certain purposes, indemnifies him for breach of trust committed at the request of a beneficiary and for loss by improper

[1] 22 and 23 Vict., c. 35, s. 30.
[2] *Speight* v. *Gaunt*, Law Rep., 9 Appeal Cases, 1.

investments, enables him to plead the Statute of Limitations in certain cases, to lend money, insure, renew renewable leaseholds, and raise money to meet fines on renewal.

(2) *Duties.*

The first duty of the executor is to bury the deceased; for the expenses of the funeral he may deduct a reasonable sum from the personal estate. This of course does not apply to an administrator, as the funeral must always have taken place before the grant of letters of administration. But after the grant has been made, the expenses of the funeral are recoverable as a first debt against the estate. It should be noticed that, although cremation of a dead body appears not to be illegal, unless done with the intention of avoiding a coroner's inquest, a direction in the will authorising a certain person to cremate the testator's body after death and charge the executors with the expenses will not be enforceable against them in a court of equity.[1] The next duty of the executor is to obtain probate, which, if there be any opposition, must be in solemn form. Probate or administration must be obtained within the period limited by law (in general six months) or the executor or administrator is, by 55 Geo. III, c. 184, s. 37, liable to the penalty of £100 attaching by that Act to any person administering an estate without having taken out a grant of probate or letters of administration and paid the proper stamp duty within six months after the date of the death. By 28 and 29 Vict., c. 104,

[1] *Williams* v. *Williams*, Law Rep., 22 Chancery Div., 659 (1882).

s. 57, administration of personal estate without obtaining probate or administration within (in ordinary cases) six months renders the person administering liable to deliver to the Inland Revenue an account of the estate and pay the proper duties and the costs of the proceedings. By 44 Vict., c. 12, s. 40, any person who ought to obtain probate or letters of administration, or deliver a further affidavit or exhibit an inventory or deliver an account, and who neglects to do so, is liable to pay double the amount of duty chargeable. Any person interested can call upon the executor or administrator to exhibit an inventory and account. The testator's debts should next be paid in a certain order. The order, after payment of funeral and testamentary or administration expenses, is as follows—

(a) Debts due to the Crown.
(b) Debts due to the parish from the deceased as overseer of the poor.
(c) Money due to any friendly society in which the deceased held office.
(d) Money due from him as treasurer or collector to the paving commissioners.
(e) Judgments against him, if duly registered.
(f) Recognisances.
(g) Debts due on instruments under seal, unregistered judgments, rents, and simple contract debts. All these now, since 32 and 33 Vict., c. 46, rank equally, as do dilapidations (if the deceased were a clergyman) since the Ecclesiastical Dilapidations Act, 1871.
(h) Legacies.

It should be noticed that in the case of real assets, *i.e.* where the personal assets are insufficient for the personal debts, or where the realty is charged with the payment of debts, loans under the Land Drainage Acts are a first charge. The case of mortgage debts under Locke King's Act will be dealt with later.[1] An executor or administrator may voluntarily pay a creditor in full after the commencement of an administration action and before judgment, and such a payment will be allowed in passing his accounts. If it be supposed that any debts are outstanding, a notice in accordance with 22 and 23 Vict., c. 35 (see above), should be inserted in the *Gazette*, etc. A legacy becomes due on the death of a testator, but is not payable until the executor has assented to it, which he must do within a year after the testator's death.[2] Where there is no reason to suspect insolvency of the estate and consequent abatement of the legacies, they should be paid as soon as possible. General legacies carry interest at four per cent after the expiration of the year, if then unpaid, unless a future time for payment be fixed by the will, or unless charged on the land, when they bear interest from the testator's death. In the case, however, of a deferred legacy to a minor by a parent or person *in loco parentis*, interest is allowed as maintenance in the absence of other provision for maintenance. A legacy to a minor cannot be paid to him directly, but by the combined effect of 36 Geo. III, c. 52, s. 32, and 35 and 36 Vict., c. 44, a legacy to an infant or a person beyond seas may be paid (after deducting duty) into the Bank of England to the account of the Paymaster-General.

---

[1] P. 160.

[2] This rule as to the executor's year was probably fixed on the analogy of the Statute of Distribution of Charles II, which enacted that no distribution to the next of kin need be made until a year after the death of the intestate.

Legacies cannot be sued for in the Probate Division, but may be recovered in the Chancery or Queen's Bench Division of the High Court, or (where not exceeding £50) in a county court. Before the Judicature Acts a legacy could have been sued for in a superior court of common law only where it had been assented to by the executor. The Court of Chancery always exercised a concurrent jurisdiction on the ground that the executor was a trustee for the legatees, and an exclusive one where the legacy was charged on land. The Judicature Acts do not seem to have made a change in these principles as a matter of practice, though all courts are now enabled to give effect to equitable rights. An action for a legacy cannot, by 37 and 38 Vict., c. 57, s. 8 (the Real Property Limitation Act, 1874), be brought after twelve years, unless, indeed, the executor have assented, when he becomes a trustee and the statute does not run in his favour in certain cases. By s. 8 of the Trustee Act, 1888, these cases are where the claim is founded upon any fraud or fraudulent breach of trust to which the executor was party or privy, or is to recover trust property or the proceeds thereof still retained by the executor or previously received by him and converted to his use. Where the legacy is secured on land by express trust, as between the land charged and the legatee, the right to recover is limited to the time within which it might have been recovered had there been no express trust, the legatee being relegated to his personal right against the trustee. This seems to be the effect of the Real Property Limitation Act, 1874, as read with the Trustee Act, 1888. An administrator must administer within a year after the grant. The period of limitation for a claim against an administrator by any one entitled to the share of an intestate's estate is, by 23 and 24 Vict., c. 38, s. 13, twenty years. S. 8 of the Trustee Act, 1888, applies, *mutatis mutandis*, to claims against an administrator. The duty of both executor and administrator is to take reasonable care of the estate, as by sale and insurance and by investment of funds. Any loss by unreasonable delay in realisation of the assets must be made good by the executor or administrator. The investments authorised now depend on the Trust Investment Act, 1889, under which an executor (unless expressly forbidden by the will) or administrator may invest at his discretion in the securities named by the act.[1]

The liabilities of a personal representative are (*a*) those which survive against him in his representative character; (*b*) those which he imposes on himself by his own act. The principle of law applicable to the representative is clearly stated in a judgment by Lord Justice Bowen. "By the English law an executor represents the debts and property, but not the person of the testator. It seems to have been thought that there would be an injustice in making the executor stand in the place of the dead man when the causes of action were purely personal."[2]

(*a*) Contracts entered into by the deceased are enforceable against his representatives to the extent of the assets coming into their hands, unless the contract was one personal to the deceased—as a contract to marry, or to do some work depending on confidence shown in

---

[1] See Appendix A. Where the beneficiaries are all *sui juris*, it is sometimes convenient to let the investments remain, and make a division of securities with cash payments for equalisation. This arrangement may or may not be confirmed by deed.

[2] *Phillips* v. *Homfray*, Law Rep., 24 Chancery Div., 456 (1883).

the particular person, such as to write a book. Where the contract is joint, the burden of it passes to the survivor or survivors, unless, as is the better opinion, in the case of partnership debts. A partnership debt being several as well as joint, the assets of the deceased partner may be resorted to by creditors of the partnership. A covenant relating to land not of inheritance, and a covenant, contract under seal, or bond or obligation under seal, now operate, by the Conveyancing Act, 1881, to bind the executors and administrators.[1] The representative who is sued is, like the representative suing, bound by the provisions of the Apportionment Act, 1870. With regard to torts committed by the deceased, such as libel, as a general rule the liability is not transmissible to the representatives, and the doctrine of *actio personalis moritur cum personâ* applies. The law, as laid down by the Court of Appeal in the case just cited, is to the effect that, apart from cases of breach of contract, a remedy for a wrongful act done by a deceased person cannot be pursued against his estate, unless property or the proceeds or value of property belonging to another person have been appropriated by the deceased person and added to his estate. By 3 and 4 Will. IV, c. 42, s. 2, an action of trespass or trespass on the case may be maintained against the executors or administrators for any wrong committed by the deceased in his lifetime to another, in respect of his property, real or personal, provided that such injury was committed within six months before such person's death, and that the action be brought within six months after the executors or administrators shall have taken upon themselves administration to the estate. It will be noticed that this

[1] Sections 58, 59.

provision differs in two particulars from the part of the section which gives the representatives a remedy for injuries to the estate of the deceased.[1] The remedy is only for injuries to real estate, and the limit of time fixed for bringing the action is a year from the death.

·(b) An executor or administrator may impose a personal liability on himself beyond his representative liability, and such liability may arise either from contract or from tort. The main examples of the latter would be the liability of an executor *de son tort*,[2] and of an executor proper for *devastavit*, that is, for misapplication of the assets under his control, as by investment in unauthorised or wasting securities, but not for mere loss without wilful default. As to express contract, it is provided by the Statute of Frauds (29 Car. II, c. 3, s. 4) that no action shall be brought whereby to charge any executor or administrator upon any special promise to answer damages out of his own estate, unless the agreement upon which such action shall be brought, or some memorandum or note thereof, shall be in writing and signed by the party to be charged therewith, or some other person thereunto by him lawfully authorised. The statute does not apply to contracts other than express contracts of the kind mentioned. Thus, if an executor take possession of land formerly in the occupation of the deceased, he may be personally liable for rent due after the death. He may also become liable, on general principles of equity, by admission of assets, even though the estate be really insufficient to meet the claims on it. Should he carry on the testator's trade in the absence of express directions in the will to that effect, he may be liable for any loss, while his

[1] P. 142. [2] P. 123.

fiduciary position gives him no right to take advantage of any profit. He may, however, complete existing contracts, and may receive dividends on stock or shares standing in the name of the deceased. It is a question of fact, which the courts have frequently had to decide, whether the liability of an executor as shareholder is in his personal or his representative character. A question of some difficulty may arise how far an executor incurs the liability of a trustee. He is a trustee for some purposes and not for others. The most important cases in which he incurs the liability of a trustee are after assent to the legacies, when he becomes a trustee for the legatees, and under 11 Geo. IV and 1 Will. IV, c. 40, by which he becomes a trustee of any undisposed of residue for the benefit of the next of kin, unless it be clear that the will intends him to take it for his own benefit. The intention is to be ascertained from the words of the will itself. A gift of the residue without reference to his office, to a person constituted earlier in the will executor and trustee has been held to be a gift for his own benefit.[1] An executor may always be, and very commonly is, constituted by the will a trustee, especially a trustee for sale. The near approach of an executor or administrator to a trustee is shown by the fact that in many Acts of Parliament, *e.g.* the Trustee Acts, 1850 to 1888, the Succession Duty Act, 1853, the Trust Investment Act, 1889, and the Lunacy Act, 1890, the word "trustee," as used in the acts, includes executor or administrator. The difference in the liability of executors and trustees as to receipts has already been mentioned.[2]

[1] *Williams* v. *Arkle*, Law Rep., 7 House of Lords, 606 (1875).
[2] P. 144.

As to practice, there is a provision in the Rules of the Supreme Court, 1883, enabling executors and administrators to sue and be sued on behalf of or as representing the property or estate, without joining the persons beneficially interested.[1] The representative character of the plaintiff must appear on the indorsement of the writ.[2] If the representative character be denied, it must be denied specifically.[3] Claims by or against an executor or administrator as such, may be joined with claims by or against him personally, provided the last-mentioned claims are alleged to arise with reference to the estate in respect of which the plaintiff or defendant sues or is sued as executor or administrator.[4] A cause or matter is not abated by reason of the death of any of the parties, if the cause of action survive or continue; and whether the cause of action survives or not, there is to be no abatement by reason of the death of either party between the verdict or finding of the issues of fact and the judgment; but judgment may in such case be entered, notwithstanding the death. The court or a judge has power to order that the personal representative shall be made a party or be served with notice, or to make an order for new parties.[5] Where any change has taken place by death in the parties entitled or liable to execution, it can only issue by leave of the court or a judge.[6] Similar rules of practice are contained in the County Court Rules, 1889, and Ord. xxx. of those rules is chiefly occupied with costs of forms and judgments where executors and administrators are parties.

[1] Ord. xvi, r. 8.
[2] Ord. lii, r. 4.
[3] Ord. xxi, r. 5.
[4] Ord. xviii, r. 4.
[5] Ord. xvii, rr. 1, 2, 4.
[6] Ord. xlii, r. 23 (a).

CHAPTER XIII

ADMINISTRATION IN A COURT OF EQUITY

THE question of the validity of a will is, as has been already stated, one for the consideration of the Probate Division or a county court; the question of the persons entitled to take under a will or an intestacy and of the meaning of words used in a will is for a court of equitable jurisdiction, generally by means of an action of administration or an originating summons. The court of equity thus becomes *par excellence* the court for the construction of wills, though to a smaller extent, *e.g.* in questions of pedigree and in bankruptcy, the Queen's Bench Division and other courts deal with construction. The jurisdiction of the court of construction follows and is supplementary to that of the court of probate; it only begins when a grant of probate or administration has been granted by the latter, and it accepts the decision of the latter as to the grant. The usual courts which determine the administration of the estate of a deceased are (1) the Chancery Division of the High Court of Justice, (2) a court having jurisdiction in bankruptcy, (3) the Court of Chancery of the County Palatine of Lancaster, (4) a county court in its equitable jurisdiction.

158 ADMINISTRATION IN A COURT OF EQUITY

(1) In most cases the distribution of the assets of a deceased person, real or personal, when it comes before a court of justice at all, falls within the jurisdiction of the Chancery Division, to which by s. 34 of the Judicature Act, 1873, are assigned all causes or matters for the administration of the estates of deceased persons. An administration action may be brought by any person interested, as a legatee, devisee, next of kin, or creditor. As a rule, all parties interested must be before the court. The defendant, at any rate the principal defendant, is usually the personal representative of the deceased. The judgment or order pronounced at the hearing ordinarily directs accounts to be taken of the personal estate of the deceased, his debts and funeral expenses, and (where there is a will and it is not a creditor's action) of the legacies and annuities bequeathed, and an inquiry to be made as to what parts of his personal estate are outstanding or undisposed of. If the administration extend to real estate, the judgment or order directs inquiries to be made as to what real estate the deceased died seised of or entitled to, and as to the incumbrances affecting the same, and if necessary directs the real estate to be sold with the approbation of the judge. Sometimes an account is directed to be taken of the rents and profits received by the trustees.[1] The Judicature Act, 1875, s. 10, provides that in the administration of the assets of a person who died insolvent the same rules shall prevail as to the respective rights of secured and unsecured creditors, as to debts and liabilities provable, and as to the valuation of annuities and future and contingent liabilities, as may be in force for the time being under the law of bankruptcy. The Rules of the Supreme

[1] 2 Daniell's Chancery Practice, c. xvii, s. 3 (11).

Court, 1883, contain many provisions as to administration, the most important of which are those relating to the procedure by originating summons, introduced as a new remedy by the rules. By Order lv, rule 3, the executors or administrators of a deceased person or any of them, and any person claiming to be interested in the relief sought as creditor, devisee, next of kin, or heir-at-law or customary heir, may (*inter alios*) take out, as of course, an originating summons returnable in the chambers of a judge of the Chancery Division for such relief of the nature or kind following as may by the summons be specified, and as the nature of the circumstances may require; that is to say, the determination, without an administration of the estate, of any of the following questions or matters :—(*a*) any question affecting the rights or interests of the person claiming to be creditor, devisee, legatee, next of kin, or heir-at-law; (*b*) the ascertainment of any class of creditors, legatees, devisees, next of kin, or others; (*c*) the furnishing of any particular accounts by the executors or administrators, and the vouching (when necessary) of such accounts; (*d*) the payment into court of any money in the hands of the executors or administrators; (*e*) directing the executors or administrators to do or abstain from doing any particular act in their character as such executors or administrators; (*f*) the approval of any sale, purchase, compromise, or other transaction; (*g*) the determination of any question arising in the administration of the estate. It has been held that this rule applies only to matters which before the rule would have been determined by an administration action.[1]

---

[1] For other rules of practice see Ord. xvi, rr. 32-47, and *ante*, p. 156. Costs are provided for by Ord. lxv, r. 1, under which the

The determination of any incidental position arising respecting the management or administration of the trust property or the assets of any testator or intestate may by 22 and 23 Vict., c. 35, s. 30, be obtained by the executor or administrator by petition or summons for the opinion, advice, or direction of a judge of the Chancery Division at chambers. In the administration of assets the court follows a certain order in directing the payment of debts. The order is (*a*) the general personal estate, (*b*) real estate devised for the purpose of paying debts, (*c*) real estate descended, (*d*) real or personal property devised or bequeathed charged with the payment of debts, (*e*) general legacies, lands comprised in a residuary devise, specific legacies and devises, (*f*) property over which the deceased had a general power of appointment. The personal estate is not, however, the primary fund where it is exempted by express words or manifest intention, or where the debt forming the charge is in its nature real (as in the case of portions to be raised out of lands by a power of appointment), or where the debt was not contracted or adopted by the deceased, or in cases coming within Locke King's Act (17 and 18 Vict., c. 113) and the amending acts of 1867 (30 and 31 Vict., c. 69) and 1877 (40 and 41 Vict., c. 34). The effect of these acts is to make a mortgage debt or any other equitable charge, including a lien for unpaid purchase money, primarily payable out of the mortgaged lands, whatever be their tenure, and whether the deceased have died testate or intestate, unless the deceased have by will or deed or other document signified any contrary or other intention.

court has discretion to order an executor or administrator to pay costs unnecessarily incurred.

The act of 1867 enacts that the contrary or other intention must be express or by necessary implication, not merely by a general direction for the payment of debts out of the personal estate. These acts only apply where the debt is on real or leasehold estate, and where it was of the deceased's own contracting. As a rule parol evidence is not receivable to show an intention of exonerating the real estate.[1]

It should be noticed that in administration of the assets the court applies the doctrine of conversion, which has been defined as "that change in the nature of property by which, for certain purposes, real estate is considered as personal, and personal estate as real, and transmissible and descendible as such." To effect a conversion there must be an imperative, not merely an optional, direction by the testator. Locke King's and the other acts do not apply to real estate directed to be considered as personal estate by the doctrine of conversion. If therefore land be devised in trust for conversion, it is not the primary fund for payment of a debt charged on it by the testator. Nor will the court presume conversion in favour of a charity. The doctrine of conversion of course cannot apply unless there be a will. If the purpose of the conversion fails, as by lapse of legacies to be raised out of land, a resulting trust of the property intended to have been converted arises in favour of the heir-at-law. This was first held by Lord Thurlow in a famous case,[2] which was the foundation of Lord Eldon's success at the bar. He succeeded in convincing the court of the soundness of the proposition

[1] The whole law of the order of administration of assets is fully considered in the notes to the case of *Duke of Ancaster* v. *Mayer*, 1 White and Tudor's Leading Cases in Equity, 630.

[2] *Ackroyd* v. *Smithson*, 1 Brown's Chancery Cases, 502 (1780).

of law just stated. In many wills a clause postponing conversion at the discretion of the trustees is inserted. Such a clause is of great advantage where the property to be converted is likely to be fluctuating in value. The conversion which has been spoken of is conversion by the act of the testator. There is another kind of conversion, which is done by the act of the court. Where personal estate is given in terms amounting to a general residuary bequest to be enjoyed by persons in succession, the interpretation the court puts upon the bequest is that the persons indicated are to enjoy the same thing in succession, and in order to carry out that intention the court as a general rule converts into permanent investments so much of the personalty as is of a wasting or perishable nature, such as annuities or leaseholds, and also reversionary interests.[1] One of the main objects of an administration is to satisfy the creditors as far as the assets suffice. In accordance with this object it is a rule of practice, known as "marshalling the assets," that where one claimant has more than one fund to resort to and another claimant only one, the first claimant is to resort to that fund to which the second cannot resort. Assets are not marshalled in favour of a charity. The main reason for the rule of marshalling was the desire of the court to put specialty and simple contract debtors on an equal footing. This has, however, now been expressly done by 3 and 4 Will. IV, c. 104, and 32 and 33 Vict., c. 46. The effect of these acts, and of the Judicature and

[1] It should be noticed that property may be reconverted, i.e. revert to its original state. This generally happens where the donee prefers to take it in its original state ; for instance, where land is devised on trust, to sell and pay the purchase-money to A, and A gives notice to the trustees that he prefers the land, as he has a right to do.

Bankruptcy Acts, has been to deprive the doctrines of priority and marshalling of much of their former importance.

(2) Provision is made by the Judicature Act, 1875, s. 10, for the observance in the administration of the estate of a person who dies insolvent of the same rules as to the rights of secured and unsecured creditors, and as to debts and liabilities provable, and as to the valuation of annuities and future and contingent liabilities as may be in force for the time being under the law of bankruptcy. The Bankruptcy Act, 1883, enables the estate of a person dying insolvent to be administered in bankruptcy. The court possessing jurisdiction in such matters is either the High Court on its bankruptcy side or a county court. By s. 125 of the act, any creditor whose debt would have been sufficient to support a bankruptcy petition against a deceased debtor, had such debtor been alive, may present to the court a petition in the prescribed form, praying for an order for the administration of the estate of the deceased debtor according to the law of bankruptcy. The section and the rules framed in accordance with it contain numerous provisions for the carrying out of the administration. There is in bankruptcy proceedings no limit of amount beyond which a county court is deprived of jurisdiction.[1]

(3) An administration action may be brought in the Chancery Court of the County Palatine of Lancaster where a defendant in the action or the property the subject of the action is within the jurisdiction of the court. The jurisdiction is not exclusive, but concurrent with that of the Chancery Division of the High Court.

[1] See the work on *Bankruptcy* in this series.

There is no limit of amount. The practice is in general accordance with that of the High Court.

(4) Equitable jurisdiction was first given to the county courts in 1865 by 28 and 29 Vict., c. 99, the provisions of which have been since superseded by the County Courts Act, 1888. By s. 67 of that Act, a county court is to exercise all the powers of the High Court in actions or matters by creditors, legatees (whether specific, pecuniary, or residuary), devisees (whether in trust or otherwise), heirs-at-law, or next of kin, in which the personal or real or personal and real estate against or for an account or administration of which the demand may be made shall not exceed in amount or value the sum of £500. Sections 68 and 69 provide for the transfer of actions or matters from a county court to the High Court, and from the High Court to a county court. By s. 75 proceedings for the administration of the assets of a deceased person are to be taken in the court within the district of which the deceased person had his last place of abode in England, or in which the executors or administrators, or any one of them, shall have had their or his place of abode. The district courts of the metropolis are, by s. 84, to be treated as one district. Proceedings by originating summons are not competent in the county court; but a practically identical method of obtaining the decision of that court is provided by the County Court Rules, 1889.[1] Under those rules the plaintiff may renounce his right to an order for general administration, and the judge may make an order determining only certain questions submitted. These questions are the same as those named in Ord. lv of the Rules of the

[1] Ord. vi, r. 6.

Supreme Court. The judge has a general discretion as to making or refusing a general administration order.

Appeals lie from the High Court and the Chancery Court of Lancaster to the Court of Appeal, and thence to the House of Lords (in bankruptcy appeals only with leave of the Court of Appeal). From county courts the appeal lies without leave to a divisional court of the High Court of Justice, whose decision is final, unless leave to appeal be given.

CHAPTER XIV

CRIMINAL LAW

At common law there could be no larceny of any instrument concerning land. A will of lands could therefore not be stolen, but a will of personalty could. This difficulty no longer exists, for by 24 and 25 Vict., c. 96, s. 27, any person who shall, either during the life of the testator or after his death, steal, or for any fraudulent purpose destroy, cancel, obliterate, or conceal the whole or any part of any will, codicil, or other testamentary instrument, whether the same shall relate to real or personal estate, shall be guilty of felony, and liable on conviction to a maximum punishment of penal servitude for life.

Forgery of a will with intent to defraud is a felony, making the offender liable to the same punishment, 24 and 25 Vict., c. 98. It has been held that there may be a conviction for the forgery of the will of a living person and even of an imaginary person. By 24 and 25 Vict., c. 98, s. 21, it is felony, punishable with a maximum term of fourteen years penal servitude, with intent to defraud to demand, receive, or obtain, or cause or procure to be delivered or paid to any person, any chattel, money, security for money, or other property whatsoever, under, upon, or by virtue of any forged or altered instrument whatsoever, knowing the same to be forged or altered, or under, upon, or by virtue of any probate or letters of administration, knowing the will, testament, codicil, or testamentary writing on which such probate or letters of administration shall have been obtained to have been forged or altered, or knowing such probate or letters of administration to have been obtained by any false oath, affirmation, or affidavit.

Concealment of wills is provided for by 22 and 23 Vict., c. 35, s. 24, and 23 and 24 Vict., c. 38, s. 8. The combined effect of these sections is that any seller or mortgagor of land, or of any chattels real or personal, or choses in action conveyed or assigned to a purchaser or mortgagee, or the solicitor or agent of such seller or mortgagor, who shall conceal any will material to the title in order to induce him to accept the title offered or produced to him, with intent to defraud, shall be guilty of misdemeanor, and punishable with a maximum term of two years' imprisonment.

Forgery of the seal or signature of a registrar or district registrar, or of a court or person authorised to administer oaths in the Probate Division, is by 20 and 21 Vict., c. 77, s. 28, and 21 and 22 Vict., c. 95, s. 33, a felony punishable with a maximum term of penal servitude for life. Taking a false oath before such a court or person is by s. 34 of the same act made perjury, and punishable as such.

CHAPTER XV

SUCCESSION IN ITS RELATION TO THE REVENUE

THERE are five kinds of duties payable on the death of a testator or intestate, known as probate, account, legacy, succession, and estate duties. Of these the probate and account duties are payable out of the general assets of the deceased, the legacy, succession, and estate duties are payable by the persons who benefit by the legacy or the succession. The duties as a whole are sometimes known by the name of the "death-duties."[1] The law governing the incidence and collection of these duties now depends on a large number of Acts of Parliament, and it is much to be desired in the interests of simplicity that a consolidating act should be passed. Probate duty was first introduced in 1694, legacy duty in 1780, succession duty in 1805, account duty in 1881, and estate duty in 1889. Up to 1880 a higher duty was payable on administration than on probate, but the Customs and Inland Revenue Act of that year (superseded as to the amount of duty by the correspond-

[1] This term, whether introduced by Mr Gladstone or not, has become well-known since his adoption of it. It appears to be a translation of the German *Sterbgefälle*. A book has lately been published with the title of *A Handbook to the Death Duties*, by S. Buxton, M.P., and G. S. Barnes, 1890.

ing act of 1881) equalised the duties in the two cases. The duties in all cases are denoted by stamps. By the Local Government Act, 1888, four-fifths of one half of the probate duties are to be distributed among county councils in relief of local taxation.[1] In addition to these five duties there are also some smaller stamp duties of a miscellaneous character.

(1) *Probate Duty.*

The probate and account duties are now regulated by the Customs and Inland Revenue Act, 1881 (44 Vict., c. 12), as amended by the corresponding act of 1889 (52 Vict., c. 7). The stamp duties on affidavits for probates and letters of administration, in the case of persons dying domiciled in the United Kingdom, are as follows (except in cases of persons dying on and after 1st June 1881, whose whole personal estate and effects, without any deduction for debts or funeral expenses,[2] does not exceed £300, of persons falling within the Small Intestacies Acts of 1873 and 1875, and of any common seaman, marine, or soldier slain or dying in Her Majesty's service [3]) :—

DUTY.

Where the estate and effects are above the value of £100 and not above the value of £500.	At the rate of £1 for every full sum of £50 and for any fractional part of £50 over any multiple of £50.

---

[1] 51 and 52 Vict., c. 41, ss. 21-23.
[2] Testamentary expenses are excluded by the words of s. 28, which does not allow deductions of voluntary debts "payable under any instrument which shall not have been *bonâ fide* delivered to the donee thereof three months before the death of the deceased." Funeral expenses must be reasonable to be allowed, s. 28. By the same section debts do not include voluntary debts, or debts charged on real estate.
[3] P. 77.

Where such estate and effects are above the value of £500 and not above the value of £1000.	At the rate of £1 : 5s. for every full sum of £50 and for any fractional part of £50 over any multiple of £50.
Where such estate and effects are above the value of £1000.	At the rate of £3 for every full sum of £100 and for any fractional part of £100 over any multiple of £100.

Provision is made for the return of duty overcharged, or the payment of further duty where it has been undercharged.

Where the value of the property, after the deductions named, does not exceed £300, grants may be obtained, on application to a collector or supervisor of excise, for a uniform fee of fifteen shillings for fees of court and expenses. If the estate be under £100, no stamp duty is payable. If the estate exceed £100 but not £300, a stamp duty of thirty shillings in addition to the fifteen is payable. If the estate be afterwards found to have been under-estimated, full duty is payable, and no allowance is made for the fixed duty already paid. Under the acts for the relief of widows and children of intestates,[1] where the whole estate and effects of the intestate do not exceed in value £20, five shillings is the sum payable for duty; where they exceed £20, the sum of five shillings and the further sum of one shilling for every £10 or fraction of £10 by which the value shall exceed £20. The management and collection of probate duty depend, in addition to the act of 1881, on 55 Geo. III, c. 184.

(2) *Account Duty.*

The account duty is at the same rate as the probate duty. It satisfies the legacy or succession duty only where the latter duty is at the rate of one per cent.

[1] P. 136.

The property on which the duty is payable includes (*a*) a *donatio mortis causâ* and *bonâ fide* made twelve months before the death of the deceased; (*b*) property voluntarily transferred to the deceased and any other person jointly, so that a beneficial interest accrues to the latter by survivorship; (*c*) property passing by a voluntary settlement, with a reservation of a life interest to the settlor, or with any trust in favour of a volunteer, and whether made for valuable consideration or not; (*d*) money received under a policy of life assurance, whether the policy is wholly or partially kept up by the assured, for the benefit of a donee. The amount of the stamp duty (five shillings per cent) payable on the settlement is, if it have been duly paid, to be returned to the person delivering the account. The account is to be delivered by every person who, as beneficiary, trustee, or otherwise, acquires possession or assumes the management of any personal property of the foregoing description, on retaining, distributing, or disposing of the same, and in any case within six months after the death of the deceased.[1] The account must be verified by oath or affirmation.

(3) *Legacy Duty.*

Legacy duty depends mainly on 36 Geo. III, c. 52, 55 Geo. III, c. 184, and 44 Vict., c. 12. Many other gifts besides legacies proper are chargeable with the duty. Among such gifts are residue,[2] rent-charges, annuities, benefits derived from appointments under powers of money charged on real estate, and even

[1] 44 Vict., c. 12, ss. 38, 39, as amended by 52 Vict., c. 7, s. 11.

[2] The executor is bound to deliver to the Inland Revenue a residuary account as well as legacy receipts.

forgiveness of a debt due to the testator. Leaseholds fall within the Succession Duty Act. The question as to what is and what is not the subject of legacy duty is a very difficult one, and one on which there have been very numerous decisions. Legacy for the purposes of the Legacy Duty Acts is defined by 8 and 9 Vict., c. 76, s. 4, to be "every gift by any will or testamentary instrument of any person, which, by virtue of any such will or testamentary instrument,'is or shall be payable or shall have effect or be satisfied out of the personal or moveable estate or effects of such person, or out of any personal or moveable estate or effects which such person hath had or shall have had power to dispose of, or which gift is or shall be payable, or shall have effect or be satisfied out of, or is or shall be charged or rendered a burden upon, the real or heritable estate of such person, or any real or heritable estate, or the rents or profits thereof, which such person hath had or shall have had any right or power to charge, burden, or affect with the payment of money, or out of or upon any moneys to arise by the sale, burden, mortgage, or other disposition of any such real or heritable estate, or any part thereof, whether such gift shall be by way of annuity or in any other form, and also every gift which shall have effect as a donation *mortis causâ*." A sum of money subjected to a limited power of appointment by a marriage settlement is exempted by the section. Legacy duty attaches not only on gifts by will, but also on the devolution of shares under an intestacy. No legacy duty is payable on legacies charged on real estate, or where the whole personal estate does not amount to £100,[1] or where the duty of thirty shillings has been paid on estates not

[1] 43 Vict., c. 14, s. 13.

exceeding £300, or in respect of any legacy, residue, or share of residue where the one per cent duty has been paid on the affidavit or inventory or account.[1] Legacy duty is now payable on pecuniary legacies or shares under the amount or value of £20.[2] The duty becomes payable upon every retainer or other satisfaction or discharge; so that in a legacy devolving in succession upon several persons, the duty is payable at each devolution. The person primarily liable to pay the duty is the executor or administrator, and the commissioners of Inland Revenue have power to enforce returns from him;[3] but trustees and legatees may be called on to pay if the duty have not already been paid. The duty may be proceeded for by the attorney-general on information, or by summary proceedings under 28 and 29 Vict., c. 104, and the Crown is entitled to four per cent interest on duty in arrear. With respect to property the subject of an administration action, the court makes provision for payment of the duty. The duties (subject to the exceptions introduced by the act of 1881) depend on the schedule to 55 Geo. III, c. 184. They are as follows. If the legacy accrues to a child or descendant of a child, or the father or mother, or any lineal ancestor, £1 per cent. If to a brother or sister, or any descendant of a brother or sister, £3 per cent. If to a brother or sister of the father or mother of the deceased, or any descendant of such brother or sister, £5 per cent. If to a brother or sister of a grandfather or grandmother of the deceased, or any descendant of such brother or sister, £6 per cent.

[1] 44 Vict., c. 12, ss. 33, 41.
[2] *Id.* s. 42. It had previously been common to make gifts of nineteen guineas in order to avoid payment of legacy duty.
[3] 16 and 17 Vict., c. 51, s. 48.

If to any person in any other degree of collateral consanguinity to the deceased, or to any stranger in blood, £10 per cent. The only case in which such duties are not payable (unless where an exemption attaches) appears to be where the commissioners of Inland Revenue have, in pursuance of the power conferred on them by 44 Vict., c. 12, s. 43, accepted composition for the legacy duty payable under a will. This section affects only legacy duty payable under a will; where it is payable under an intestacy, 36 Geo. III, c. 52, s. 33, seems still to apply. That section enables composition to be accepted not merely at the discretion of the commissioners, but only after the lapse of two years from the death and where it appears that it will require time to collect the effects or be difficult to ascertain the residue.

Certain exemptions from the duty (irrespective of amount, with which alone the act of 1881 deals) are allowed by 36 Geo. III, c. 52, 39 Geo. III, c. 73, 55 Geo. III, c. 184, and 26 and 27 Vict., c. 87. These are legacies to or for the benefit of the Royal Family or for the husband or wife of the deceased, or consisting of books, prints, etc., or other specific articles given in trust for any body corporate, any of the Inns of Court, or any endowed school, not for the purposes of sale, or any fund expressly set apart for the payment of duty, or legacies bequeathed out of the estate and effects of a deceased depositor in a savings bank, where the whole of the estate and effects do not exceed £50.

When the duty is paid, a proper receipt must be given, and any one paying the duty without taking a proper receipt is by 36 Geo. III, c. 52, liable to a penalty of £10. The duty must be paid within twenty-one days of the date of the receipt. If not paid within three months after date, the person neglecting to pay incurs a penalty of ten per cent on the amount or value of the legacy.

An executor or administrator who shall have given notice in writing to the commissioners of Inland Revenue for any claim to legacy duty in respect of any fund in his hands which he intends to distribute, and shall have delivered all particulars, may distribute the fund after satisfaction of duty, and shall be entitled to a certificate discharging him from liability.[1]

No person is under a will or administration to be liable for payment of legacy or succession duty after the expiration of six years from settlement of the account, where such account was full and true and contained all material facts; and no executor, administrator, or trustee is to be liable after the expiration of six years, if it be proved to the satisfaction of the commissioners that the account was true to the best of his knowledge, information, and belief.[2] Where the person liable to pay legacy or succession duty resides in London, the duty is payable by personal application at Somerset House, where he resides elsewhere it can be paid, and the necessary forms sent, through the post. The forms can be obtained at any money-order post-office and the postage is free.

(4) *Succession Duty.*

The principal provisions of the law as to succession duty are contained in the Succession Duty Act, 1853 (16 and 17 Vict., c. 51), which imposed on succession to real and settled personal property a duty at the same rate as that attaching by the Legacy Duty Acts. By the Customs and Inland Revenue Act, 1888, legacies

[1] 43 Vict., c. 14, s. 12.   [2] 52 Vict., c. 7, s. 14.

charged on real estate were made liable to succession duty, and by the same act a duty was imposed on all successions in addition to that payable under the act of 1853, viz. ten shillings per cent where the successor is the lineal issue or lineal ancestor of the predecessor, and in all other cases one pound ten shillings per cent.[1]

Succession duty is payable only on property which is not subject to legacy duty; in no case is more than one of the duties payable on the same property. The Succession Duty Act is long and complicated, and has given rise to numerous decisions; its main provisions are as follows. The term "real property" includes leaseholds, the term "personal property" includes money payable under any engagement and money secured on heritable property in Scotland—s. 1. Succession liable to duty under the Act is defined as "every past or future disposition of property by reason whereof any person has or shall become beneficially entitled to any property or the income thereof upon the death of any person dying after the time appointed for the commencement of this act,[2] either immediately or after any interval, either certainly or contingently, and either originally or by way of substitutive limitation, and every devolution by law of any beneficial interest in property or the income thereof upon the death of any person dying after the time appointed for the commencement of this act to any other person, in possession or expectancy." "Successor" denotes the person entitled, "predecessor" the settler, disposer, testator, obligor, ancestor, or other person from whom the interest of the successor is derived—s. 2. Joint tenants taking by survivorship are successors—s. 3. General powers of appointment, extinction of determin-

[1] 51 Vict., c. 8, s. 21.   [2] 19th May 1853.

able charges, dispositions accompanied by the reservation of a benefit to the grantor or any other person, and dispositions to take effect at periods depending or death, or made for the purpose of evading duty, confer successions—ss. 4, 5, 7, 8. Any person chargeable with duty under this act or the Legacy Duty Acts, if married to a wife or husband of nearer consanguinity than himself or herself to the predecessor, is to pay only the rate of duty with which the wife or husband would have been chargeable—s. 11. The duty is payable where the same person is successor and predecessor under a disposition made by himself, if at the date of the disposition he is entitled to the property comprised in the succession expectantly on the death of any person dying after 19th May 1853, and such person shall have died during the continuance of such disposition—s. 12.[1] Only one duty is payable on each succession; but in the case of a transmitted succession (*i.e.* where the interest of a successor passes by death to another successor before the first successor becomes entitled in possession), duty at the highest rate payable by either successor is payable by the ultimate successor—s. 14. Successions subject to trusts for charitable or public purposes are liable to duty at the ten per cent rate—s. 16. No duty is payable where the succession is under £100 in value, or in respect of property chargeable under the Legacy Duty Acts—s. 18.[2] The duty is payable on the successor becoming entitled

---

[1] The object of this section was to prevent any one with a vested estate tail in remainder from diminishing by his own act the rate of succession duty which would have been payable if he were not to deal with the estate tail until it vested in possession; *Lord Braybrooke v. Attorney-General*, 9 House of Lords Cases, 150 (1861).

[2] The provision in this section exempting successions which if they were legacies under £20 would not be liable to duty has been repealed by 52 Vict., c. 7, s. 10.

in possession, and in the case of outstanding interests on their determination—s. 20. The interest of a successor in real property is to be considered as an annuity[1] equal to the annual value of the property, and the duty chargeable is payable in eight equal half-yearly instalments, the first to be paid at the expiration of twelve months after the successor has become entitled— s. 21.[2] Rules are given for valuing land, houses, timber, advowsons, property subject to beneficial leases, manors, mines, property taken by corporations, converted property, etc.—ss. 22-31. Certain allowances are made to the donee of a general power of appointment who has already paid duty on a limited interest, and also for incumbrances other than contingent incumbrances—ss. 33-35. No allowance is to be made for a contingency on the happening of which the property may pass to another person, but in such a case a proportionate return of the duty is to be made—s. 36. Allowances are also made for duty payable on a succession paid by mistake, etc., or on property relinquished—ss. 37, 38 (52 Vict. c. 7, s. 10). The commissioners of Inland Revenue may compound for duties, or receive them in advance, or commute future duties—ss. 39-41. The duty is a first charge on the property—s. 42. Besides the successor, a trustee (which includes an executor or administrator),[3] guardian, committee, tutor, curator, or husband is accountable for the duty, but only to the extent of the property or funds actually received or disposed of by him—s. 44. Notice of succession is to be given to the commissioners

---

[1] These annuities are calculated according to a table in the schedules to the act.
[2] An alternative mode of payment is provided by 51 Vict., c. 8, s. 21, and the commissioners are empowered to allow discount for payment in advance.
[3] S. 1

SUCCESSION DUTY

of Inland Revenue, and a return of the property made —s. 45 (52 Vict., c. 7, s. 10). The penalty for not giving notice is a sum equal to ten per cent on the amount of duty payable, and the same for not paying within twenty-one days after the amount has been ascertained—s. 46. A stamped receipt must be given, and the commissioners may give a certificate of discharge on application—s. 51. Such a certificate is a protection to a *bonâ fide* purchaser for valuable consideration and without notice, notwithstanding any suppression, misstatement, or insufficiency of assessment—s. 52. When any suit is pending for the administration of property chargeable with legacy or succession duty, the court is to provide for the payment of the duty—s. 53. The modes of recovery of duty by the Crown are the same as those used for the recovery of legacy duty. An appeal lies from the decision of the commissioners to the Queen's Bench Division or (where the sum in dispute does not exceed £50) to a county court. The law as to certificates of discharge under 43 Vict., c. 14, s. 12, as to exemption from duty under s. 13 of the same Act and 44 Vict., c. 12, and as to cesser of liability after six years under 52 Vict., c. 7, is the same as in the case of legacy duty. The latter act also provides that a purchaser for valuable consideration or a mortgagee is exempt from liability to succession duty after the expiration of a period varying according to circumstances, but twelve years at most, after notice of succession given to the commissioners of Inland Revenue.

(5) *Estate Duty.*

This duty depends on the Customs and Inland Revenue Act, 1889 (52 Vict., c. 7), and is payable in addition to the ordinary duties. It is only of temporary incidence, and attaches only to large estates. Where the estate on which probate or account duty is payable exceeds in value £10,000, a statement of the value of the estate is to be delivered by the person applying for probate or administration, and a duty of £1 per £100 or fraction of £100 is to be paid on such statement. Where the value of any succession exceeds £10,000, and where the value of the succession alone does not exceed £10,000, but such value, together with the value of any other benefit taken by the successor under a will or intestacy, exceeds £10,000, a statement is to be delivered and duty paid at the same rate as in the last case. The estate duty is not to be chargeable in respect of the estate of any person dying on or after 1st June 1896. A penalty of double the amount of duty is incurred by neglect to deliver a statement by the person who ought to do so, and four per cent is chargeable on arrears.

(6) *Other Duties.*

These are regulated by the Stamp Act, 1870. A copy or extract of or from an original will or codicil, the probate or probate copy of a will or codicil, or any letters of administration or any confirmation of a testament is chargeable, in the case of an instrument chargeable with any duty not amounting to one shilling, with the same duty as such instrument, in any other case, one shilling. A certificate of valuation of the estate by a professional valuer is required by the Inland Revenue, and the valuation must be stamped with a stamp varying in amount.[1] Where the amount of the valuation does not exceed £5 the stamp is threepence. It increases gradually up to £500, beyond which sum it is £1. A grant or licence under the sign-manual to take and use a surname and arms or a surname only in compliance with the injunctions of any will must bear a £50 stamp.

[1] Except in valuations for estate duty under 52 Vict., c. 7.

CHAPTER XVI

CONFLICT OF LAWS

THE opinions of jurists, the decisions of courts, and the legislation of parliaments have in the case of property left by will taken three main directions.

(1) The whole property of the testator may be subject to the law of his domicil (domicil may be defined with sufficient accuracy for the present purpose as the place where the testator had his permanent residence at the time of his death).[1] This is the view of Savigny, and the practice of the German courts is in accordance with his view.

(2) The whole property may be subject to the law of the place where it happens to be at the time of the testator's death. This is in accordance with a rule of law much in favour on the continent, known as the rule of *locus regit actum*, applying primarily to contracts, thence transferred to succession.

(3) Moveable property may be subject to the law of the domicil; immoveable (including leaseholds) to that

---

[1] Domicil for the purpose of succession must be more fully established than for some other purposes, *e.g.* contract or divorce. In *Brodie* v. *Brodie*, 30 Law Journal (Probate), 185 (1861), the court dissolved a marriage on evidence of domicil which would have been insufficient for succession.

of the place where it is—the *lex loci rei sitæ*, as it is expressed by the text-writers. This is the view taken by the United Kingdom and the United States.

Testamentary capacity is governed by the law of the testator's domicil. The form of the testamentary instrument is in most countries valid if it be good by either the law of the domicil or the law of the place where it be made, at the option of the testator. The old rule of the English common law was to allow only the former alternative. It is still the law, and has been confirmed by legislation, in many of the states in the United States. The occasional hardships caused by such a state of the law were illustrated by a well-known case of *Bremer* v. *Freeman*, before the judicial committee of the Privy Council in 1859. It was held in that case that the will of an English lady domiciled at Paris, and made in the English form, was insufficient to pass her personal property in England, though it was admitted that it passed real property in India.[1] In order to obviate such difficulties for the future, an act, commonly known as Lord Kingsdown's Act, was passed in 1861 (24 and 25 Vict., c. 114). The act provides that every will and other testamentary instrument made out of the United Kingdom by a British subject, whatever be the domicil of such subject, shall, as regards personal estate, be held to be well executed for the purpose of probate if it be made (1) according to the forms required either by the law of the place where it was made, or (2) by the law of the place where the testator was domiciled when it was made, or (3) by the laws then in force in that part of Her Majesty's dominions where he had his domicil of origin. With regard to a will

[1] 10 Moore, Privy Council Cases, 361.

made in the United Kingdom by a British subject, it is well executed, as regards personal estate, if executed according to the forms required by the laws for the time being in that part of the United Kingdom where it is made. Subsequent change of domicil does not revoke the will. It will be noticed that the act does not affect wills of real property, which must conform to the law of the place where the property is situate, nor does it affect wills of aliens, so that an alien domiciled abroad cannot make a valid will in England in the English form, unless, indeed, the English and foreign forms coincide. On the same day on which Lord Kingsdown's Act was passed (August 6, 1861) another Act (24 and 25 Vict., c. 121) received the royal assent. By the terms of this act Her Majesty in council is empowered, under convention with any foreign state, to direct by order in council that no British subject resident at the time of his death in the foreign country named in such order shall be deemed under any circumstances to have acquired a domicil in such country unless he shall have been resident in such country for one year immediately preceding his decease, and shall have made and deposited in a public office of such foreign country (such office to be named in the order in council) a declaration in writing of his intention to become domiciled in such foreign country.[1] A similar provision is made as to subjects of the foreign country acquiring a domicil in the United Kingdom. The act does not apply to foreigners naturalised in any part of Her Majesty's dominions. Under certain circumstances foreign con-

[1] In spite of this provision, a *de facto* domicil, for the purposes of succession, may be acquired by a British subject who has not conformed to the law of France so as to obtain full civil rights there. *Hamilton v. Dallas*, Law. Rep., 1 Chancery Div., 257 (1875).

sular officers in British dominions may, on obtaining authority from the proper court, take possession and have the custody of the personal property of a deceased foreigner belonging to the country of the consular officer, may apply the property in payment of his debts and funeral expenses, and may retain the surplus for the benefit of the persons entitled thereto.

The construction of a will is governed by the law of the domicil of the testator, as he must be supposed to have used the language of his domicil, unless, indeed, he express himself in the technical language of another country. But a mere use of some Scotch legal terms, such as "dispone" and "liferent," is not sufficient of itself to induce the court to apply Scotch principles of interpretation to a will made by a domiciled Englishman.[1]

The persons who are to take under a will or an intestacy are decided by different rules, according as the property is moveable or immoveable. Moveables take their legal character from the domicil of the owner, and the distribution of the goods and the class of persons entitled to benefit are regulated by the same law. The rule as to immoveable property is different. The persons entitled to succeed to that must be entitled by the law of the place where the property is situate. Most of the cases on the subject have turned upon the question of illegitimacy. In a well-known case in the House of Lords in 1840 it was held that a child legitimate in Scotland by the marriage of its parents after its birth was not legitimate for the purpose of inheriting real property in England. On the other hand, it was held that a child in a similar position, legitimate by the law of England but not by the law of Holland, was so far

[1] *Doe v. Vardill*, 7 Clark and Finelly's Rep., 911.

legitimate as to be entitled to share in personal property in England as one of the next of kin of the deceased.[1] In order that such a child may be legitimate for the purpose of succession, it is essential that the father should at the time of its birth and of the subsequent marriage be domiciled in a country the law of which allows legitimation *per subsequens matrimonium*.[2] The principle on which these cases were decided was well expressed by Lord Justice James in the latter case. "Heirship is an incident of land, depending on local law. . . . Kinship is an incident of the person, and universal." On the same principle it has been held that leaseholds in England belonging to a domiciled Scotchman devolved on intestacy by English law,[3] and that a Scotchman making a will disposing of personalty locally situate in England could not exclude his children from their *legitim*.[4] Difficult questions have arisen as to how far the English legal restrictions on the disposition of real property apply to property of that nature situated out of England. The question of public policy, already mentioned in the chapter on construction, becomes important here. For instance, the law of mortmain was held not to extend to British India,[5] or to the island of Grenada in the West Indies,[6] or to British Honduras.[7] A devise of real estate in England for the maintenance of a charity in Scotland was held to be void.[8] On the other hand, a bequest by a domiciled Englishman of

[1] *Re Goodman's Trusts*, Law Rep., 17 Chancery Div., 266 (1881).
[2] *Re Grove*, Law Rep., 40 Chancery Div., 216 (1888).
[3] *Duncan v. Lawson*, Law Rep., 41 Chancery Div., 394 (1889).
[4] *Hog v. Lashley*, 6 Brown's Parliamentary Cases, 577 (1792).
[5] *Mayor of Lyons v. East India Company*, 1 Moore's Privy Council Cases, 175 (1836).
[6] *Attorney-General v. Stewart*, 2 Merivale's Rep., 143 (1811).
[7] *Jex v. M'Kinney*, Law Rep., 14 Appeal Cases, 77 (1888).
[8] *Curtis v. Hutton*, 14 Vesey's Rep., 537 (1808).

money to be laid out in the purchase of lands in Scotland, to be settled in a manner which would have been void in England for remoteness, was held to be good.[1] The law of perpetuities was held to apply to a gift in the Straits Settlements.[2] Trusts in the strict sense of the word, not merely constructive, could probably not be affixed by an English testator to lands situate abroad, especially in a country where anything like the English equitable estate is unknown.

The law of the domicil determines whether a deceased person died testate or intestate. The legal representation of the deceased, collection of effects, and administration are governed by *lex sitûs*, that is, the law of the place where the property, moveable or immoveable, is situate at the time of the death of the deceased. "The court of the domicil," said Lord Westbury, "is the *forum concursus* to which the legatees under the will of a testator, or the parties entitled to distribution of the estate of an intestate, are required to resort."[3] This is, especially as to the word "required," since the case of *Ewing* v. *Orr-Ewing*, perhaps too broadly stated, for in that case Lord Selborne said that recourse must be had not always or necessarily to the courts of the domicil but always and necessarily to the law of the domicil. The *forum* of the domicil is, however, in most cases the most convenient one, though the English courts have no doubt asserted their jurisdiction when even a very small part of the property of the deceased has been in England. In *Ewing* v. *Orr-Ewing* such an assertion of jurisdiction led to some conflict between the English and

[1] *Fordyce* v. *Bridges*, 2 Phillips's Rep., 497 (1848).
[2] *Yeap Cheah* v. *Ong Cheng*, Law Rep., 6 Privy Council, 381 (1875).
[3] *Enohin* v. *Wylie*, 10 House of Lords Cases, 1 (1862).

Scotch courts. The testator in that case was a domiciled Scotchman, his personal estate in Scotland was of the value of £460,000, that in England of £25,000, and before the trial all the English assets had been removed into Scotland. The House of Lords held that the English Chancery Division had under these circumstances jurisdiction to administer the whole estate, both Scotch and English.[1] The Court of Session in Scotland refused to accept the English decision on the ground that it was contrary to international comity. On appeal from the Scotch decision, the House of Lords held that the claim of exclusive competency made by the Court of Session was not supported by statute or authority, but that under the circumstances a *primâ facie* case of convenience in favour of administration in Scotland had been made out.[2] The ultimate effect of this and other cases appears to establish that the question of what tribunal is to administer the estate of the deceased is one of convenience rather than of right.[3] As to minor matters falling within this part of the subject, the priorities of creditors are determined by the *lex fori*, that is, the law of the tribunal of administration, without regard to the law of the domicil. The questions of currency and interest are determinable by the same law. Thus interest at four per cent (the English rate) will be all allowed by an English court, though the personalty is in a country where a higher rate is allowed.

A will executed abroad is generally required to be

[1] Law Rep., 9 Appeal Cases, 34 (1884).
[2] *Ewing* v. *Orr-Ewing*, Law Rep., 10 Appeal Cases, 453 (1885).
[3] The mere fact that probate of a will has been granted by an English court is not conclusive evidence that the testator was domiciled in England.

clothed with the authority of a court of the country where any property affected by the will is situate, for a grant of probate or anything corresponding to it is not extra-territorial in effect. A will disposing of property wholly situated abroad is not admitted to probate in England, and where the testator was domiciled abroad the English probate is limited to English assets where there is property in England. A foreign probate is conclusive both as to the grounds on which it was granted and the period for which its authority continues. As to the United Kingdom, there are statutory provisions for the carrying into effect of probate or confirmation granted in one kingdom in one of the other kingdoms. By 20 and 21 Vict., c. 79, s. 94, an English probate or letters of administration may be sealed in Ireland, and being duly stamped shall have the same operation in Ireland as if it had been granted by the Probate Division of the High Court of Justice in Ireland. S. 95 provides for the opposite case of sealing an Irish probate in England. By 21 and 22 Vict., c. 56, s. 12, confirmation of the executor of a person who died domiciled in Scotland, when produced in the Principal Registry in England together with a certified copy of the interlocutor of the commissary finding that such deceased person died domiciled in Scotland, is to be sealed with the seal of the English court, and has the same effect as an English probate or letters of administration. S. 13 makes a similar provision for sealing the confirmation in Dublin. S. 14 provides for the due indorsement by the commissary clerk in Edinburgh of an English or Irish probate or letters of administration, which, when duly stamped, will have the same effect as a confirmation.

Duties.—On the death of a foreigner probate duty is payable on any assets, the disposition of which was governed by an English probate or letters of administration, in the same way as though he were a natural-born British subject. The liability to legacy and succession duty of foreign assets of a British testator or intestate, or of British assets of a foreign testator or intestate, has been the subject of numerous decisions, from which it is perhaps possible to extract the following principles.

(1) Liability to legacy duty seems to attach more directly to the person than does liability to succession duty. Legacy duty is therefore not as a rule payable when the testator is domiciled abroad, unless the fund has been collected and placed in this country by the executor, in which case any subsequent devolution of the property, even in favour of a person domiciled abroad, becomes liable to the duty.

(2) The estate of a foreigner engaged in trade in England is liable to legacy duty. In one case the liability was held to extend even to the estate of an *attaché* of a foreign embassy.[1] But in this case the testator had acquired an English domicil before his appointment as *attaché*.

(3) Succession duty on personal property may be payable where legacy duty is not payable, *e.g.* on settled property in this country the property of a testator domiciled abroad. It is payable by a foreigner who benefits by the succession and is payable under certain circumstances on foreign moveable property, *e.g.* funds of a foreign government or trading corporation comprised in a British settlement, vested in trustees subject

[1] *Attorney-General* v. *Kent*, 1 Hurlstone and Coltman's Rep., 12 (1862).

to British jurisdiction, and recoverable by action in a British court.[1]

(4) Succession duty on real property in this country is payable where the succession is to a person domiciled abroad and in favour of a successor domiciled abroad. For the purposes of succession rent charges and estates *pur autre vie* are real property, even though they descend like personal property.

(5) On the principle of *Doe* v. *Vardill* and *Re Goodman's Trusts* it has been held that children legitimated by the subsequent marriage of their parents are for the purposes of succession duty to real property strangers in blood and chargeable with duty at ten per cent,[2] but for the purposes of legacy duty are so far legitimate that they only pay duty at one per cent.[3]

[1] *Re Cigala's Trusts*, Law Rep., 7 Chancery Div., 351 (1877).
[2] *Atkinson* v. *Anderson*, Law Rep., 21 Chancery Div., 100 (1882).
[3] *Skottowe* v. *Young*, Law Rep., 11 Equity, 474 (1871).

CHAPTER XVII

SCOTLAND

THE Scotch law of succession is entirely independent of the English, and few of the acts which have been cited (except those relating to the Revenue) are operative in Scotland. Legislation on the subject of testamentary disposition began at a very early date, the earliest being a clause in the *Statuta Gilde* (attributed to the reign of Alexander III, 1249-1286), enabling guild-brethren to bequeath legacies to the guild. The law of intestate succession was also regulated by acts of the Scottish Parliament.

Up to 1868 the great difference between the English and Scotch law was that in the latter system wills of immoveables were not allowed. The usual means of obtaining disposition of heritage after death was a trust disposition and settlement[1] by deed *de præsenti*, under which the truster disponed the property to trustees according to the trusts of the settlement, reserving a life interest. Thus something very similar to a testamentary disposition was secured by means resembling those employed in England before the Wills Act of Henry VIII. The main disadvantage of the trust disposition was that

[1] This term is still properly used to denote a testamentary disposition of heritable property, while "testament" strictly applies only to a disposition of moveables.

it was liable to be overthrown by the heir, who could reduce *ex cavite lecti* all voluntary deeds made to his prejudice within sixty days before the death of his ancestor. In 1868 the Titles to Land Consolidation Act (31 and 32 Vict., c. 101, s. 20) made it competent to any owner of lands to settle the succession to them in the event of death by testamentary or *mortis causâ* deeds or writings duly executed in the manner required or permitted in the case of any testamentary writing by the law of Scotland. This is of course subject to the children's *legitim* and to the widow's right of terce if they have not accepted any other provision. In 1871 reduction *ex capite lecti* was abolished by 34 and 35 Vict., c. 81. A will of immoveables, which may be partly written and partly printed, must be executed with the formalities of a deed, and duly registered in the Register of Sasines. A clause of consent to registration is usually contained in the disposition. The executor or trustee must apply the lands for the purposes of the will. *Rei interventus* will not constitute an improbative will a valid conveyance *inter vivos*. As the law stands at present, a will, if not holograph, must be executed in the presence of two witnesses at least, with the solemnities enforced by the Act 1681, c. 5 (in effect very much the same as those of the English Wills Act),[1] or in the presence of a notary or of the minister of the parish where the testator resides. Where the testator cannot write, a justice of the peace, notary, or parish minister may subscribe the will for him in his presence and by his authority before two witnesses. The witnesses to a will

---

[1] In addition to the provision that the testing clause was to contain the name of the writer of the instrument. This, though no longer necessary, is still generally inserted.

must be in all cases at least fourteen years of age and subject to no legal incapacity, such as insanity, blindness, or interest. The disability of a woman as witness was removed by the act of 1868. As to wills of moveables, there are several important points in which they differ from English wills, the influence of Roman law being more marked. Males may make a will at fourteen, females at twelve. A nuncupative legacy is good to the amount of £100 Scots (£8:6:8). A holograph testament is good without witnesses, but it must be signed as well as written by the testator, differing in this from the old English holograph. By the Conveyancing Act, 1874, such a will is presumed to have been executed on the date which it bears. There is not a complete power of disposition of moveables, as in England. The moveable property of the deceased is subject to *jus relictæ*, or the widow's right to half if there be no child or children,[1] and the *legitim*, or bairns' part, half if there be no widow, one-third if there be a widow. Only the remainder is disponible as dead's part.[2] *Legitim* depends on survivance and is not transmissible on predecease of a person prospectively entitled to it. Both *jus relictæ* and *legitim* may be excluded by discharge or satisfaction, as by provision in the contract of marriage. By the Married Woman's Property Act, 1881, s. 7, the children of any woman who may die domiciled in Scotland have the same right to *legitim* out of her moveable estate as they would have had out of their father's estate.

[1] The Married Woman's Property Act, 1881 (44 and 45 Vict., c. 21, s. 6), gives a similar right to the husband.
[2] Up to 1855 the executor had a right under the Act 1617, c. 14, to one-third of the dead's part, but this right was abolished by 18 and 19 Vict., c. 23.

Both heir and executor in Scotch law are more extensive terms than in English law. An heir includes an heir in heritage or by destination, whether by tailzie or otherwise, and also a person who succeeds to moveables as a legatory or next of kin. An executor can only be appointed by writing. He is either nominative (appointed by the testator) or dative or executor-creditor, the latter two appointed by the court, and corresponding in most respects to the English administrator. Caution is required from the latter two, but not from the former. The rights and duties of the heir and executor correspond in most essential respects to those which have been already treated under English law.[1] The executor is bound to pay all debts *pari passu* except privileged debts. Many sections of recent Acts of Parliament simplify completion of title by an executor, *e.g.* he may complete though there is no direct conveyance to him, and he may do so by notarial instrument in a prescribed form. The apparent heir may pursue for and discharge rents and perform certain other acts necessary for the advantage of the estate before his title is complete. By 30 and 31 Vict., c. 97, s. 18, the resignation of a trustee who is also executor infers resignation as executor. "Trustee" in the Trusts (Scotland) Acts does not, as in the English Acts, expressly include an executor by the interpretation clauses of the acts. Where an executor is also trustee his power of investment is now regulated by the Trusts (Scotland) Amendment Act, 1884. By the common law doctrine of passive representation, the heir or executor was liable to be sued for

---

[1] In Scotch cases and text-books, English decisions are constantly cited as authorities on the law of succession, especially in construction of testamentary documents. The converse is not the case.

implement of the obligations of the deceased. The Roman principle of *beneficium inventarii* was first conferred by the Act 1695, c. 24, under which the heir became liable only to the value of the heritage exhibited in inventory. The Conveyancing Act, 1874, provided in more general terms that "an heir shall not be liable for the debts of his ancestor beyond the value of the estate of such ancestor to which he succeeds." As the law stands at present, the heir or executor is liable only to the amount of the succession, except where he has made himself liable by passive title. The principal examples of passive title are vitious intromission in the case of moveables, *gestio pro herede*, or behaviour as heir, and *præceptio hereditatis*, or premature taking of the succession in the case of heritables.

Before the executor has authority to act, he must obtain confirmation, which includes both the probate and the letters of administration of English procedure. In order to obtain confirmation, an inventory must be duly exhibited. Confirmation granted to an executor-creditor may, by 4 Geo. IV, c. 98, s. 4, be limited to the amount of his debt. A judicial factor may be appointed on petition of creditors of the deceased. Without confirmation by the court interference by the executor becomes a vitious intromission. The only exception is made in the case of privileged debts, which are deathbed and funeral expenses, a year's rent, servants' wages for a year or less term, and the expenses of confirmation. Debts due by an officer of a friendly society to the society, and of a clergyman of the Church of Scotland to the Widows' Fund, are also privileged. Confirmation of testaments of moveables originally fell, as in England, under the cognisance of the church courts, and was expressly recognised as part of the ecclesiastical jurisdiction by *Regiam Majestatem*. This ecclesiastical jurisdiction, continued through the Commissary Courts at Edinburgh (constituted by Queen Mary in 1563) and the local commissaries until modern times, when the rights of these courts were first transferred and then abolished by a series of enactments from 4 Geo. IV, c. 97, to the Sheriff Courts Act, 1876. The act of George IV placed the commissary jurisdiction in the sheriff courts; by the Act of 1876, the sheriffs sit as sheriffs in testamentary matters, no longer as commissaries. Commissary clerks (except the commissary clerk of Edinburgh) were abolished by the Act of 1876. Confirmation, where the whole moveable estate does not exceed £300, is regulated by 44 Vict., c. 12, as in England. It is granted, whether on a will or an intestacy, by the sheriff clerk. The fees and stamp-duty are the same as in England.[1] An eik is an addition to a confirmation made on discovery after confirmation of additional effects of the deceased.

The duties payable to the revenue are the same as in England. It has been held that "disposition," as used in the Succession Duty Act, 1853, is a general term for any alienation, and is not confined to a disposition in its technical meaning in Scotch law. In addition to duties to the revenue, casualties may be payable to the superior. By the Conveyancing Act, 1874, the only casualties that can now be stipulated for on the succession of an heir or the acquisition of a singular successor are to take the form of a fixed sum, payable at fixed

---

[1] The act of 1881 superseded previous acts of 1875 and 1876, under which the powers of the sheriff clerk were limited to estates not exceeding £150.

intervals. By the interpretation clause of the act "casualties" includes only relief and composition, and sums payable in lieu of these. Casualties created prior to 1st October 1874, and payable on the death of the vassal, may be redeemed. The Conveyancing Act, 1887, enacts that where heritable estate is conveyed to trustees for the benefit of the heir of the testator, the casualty payable by the heir is to be the same as would have been payable had he taken the estate by direct succession. Provision is made by the Local Government (Scotland) Act, 1889, Part II, for the payment of part of the probate duties for certain purposes therein mentioned, the most important being the relief from payment of school fees in state-aided schools in Scotland.

Vitiation of a will, or wilful destruction or mutilation of testamentary documents, if done to suppress evidence, is a crime.

Lands vested in the Church were held to have been given for superstitious uses, and were by the Act 1587, c. 29, vested in the Crown. But mortifications of land may still be made for the use of a charity, to be held by the trustees of the charity in fen or in blench, subject to the general control of the Court of Session under its *nobile officium*. A conveyance of lands (which includes a *mortis causâ* conveyance) duly recorded, made for religious or educational purposes by s. 29 of the act of 1868 vests not only the disponees but also their successors in the lands. By s. 113 of the same act, a sum in lieu of casualties is leviable on charity lands by the superior every twenty-five years. The Mortmain Acts do not apply to Scotland. Scotch law does not "abhor perpetuities," and an entail containing prohibitory, irritant, and resolutive clauses[1] could not have been defeated until the Rutherford Act (11 and 12 Vict., c. 36). By the same act the Thellusson Act was repealed as far as related to Scotland, the act as it originally stood having extended to the whole of Great Britain.

The Married Woman's Property (Scotland) Acts, 1877 and 1881, have enabled a married woman to dispose of her property by will, but to an extent much more limited than that given by the English Act of 1882. The Act of 1877 applies only to wages and earnings of a married woman, or any money or property acquired by the exercise of any literary, artistic, or scientific skill. The Act of 1881 applies only to moveables and the rents of heritable property. In these cases only is the *jus mariti* excluded (unless, indeed, it be excluded by express provision).

Rules of construction have been of use chiefly in determining the destination of moveables or heritage, especially the latter. They are in general accordance with those recognised in English law, but there are of course some special ones depending on the technicalities of the Scotch system. Thus before the distinction between fees of heritage and fees of conquest was abolished by the Conveyancing Act, 1874, a destination to "A and his heirs of line" carried the property to the heir of heritage to the exclusion of the heir of conquest. "Heirs female" carries the estate to a son's daughter rather than to a daughter. In "heirs and children" heirs is the ruling term, and the estate goes to the eldest son. The rule in *Shelley's Case* does not apply in Scotland. *Jus accrescendi* is always a question of intention. That is, it

---

[1] A clause authorising registration in the Register of Entails is now equivalent to these clauses.

depends on the intention of the testator to be gathered from his disposition whether, when a gift is provided to a class and one of the class dies, his share is to go to the survivors or to his personal representatives. The doctrine of radical right is an important rule of construction. It is to the effect that, where the trust does not exhaust the estate, the truster retains the radical title. It has been a question often difficult of decision what words give the beneficial interest to the grantee and what words on the other hand make him simply a trustee. In some cases rules of construction depend on statute. An example is s. 28 of the act of 1874, enacting that where no term of entry is stated in a conveyance, the entry shall be at the first term of Whitsunday or Martinmas. The doctrine of *cy-près* is recognised in Scotland. The principles of its exercise are in effect the same as those acknowledged in England.

The law of intestate succession differs in many respects from that in use in England; the right, however, of the eldest son to succeed to heritable property is the same in both systems. A distinction is drawn in Scotland between universal and singular succession, the former being the succession of the heir, like that of the Roman *heres*, to the whole inheritance; the latter the succession of a disponee by title of purchase, such as a legatory. The law regulating intestate succession depends partly on common law, partly on statute, and is different with regard to heritables and moveables. In heritables (which include leaseholds) the succession opens first in favour of descendants, the eldest son,[1] if

[1] It should be noticed that by the Scotch doctrine of *legitimatio per subsequens matrimonium* an eldest son might become heir who would not be entitled to succeed in England. See the case of *Doe v. Vardill*, p. 185.

there be one, taking all. Female descendants in the same degree of relationship succeed as heirs-portioners in equal shares, but the eldest has the mansion-house as her *præcipuum* and also any title of honour or dignity descendible from the intestate. Next come collaterals, brothers and sisters, a younger brother (in cases of succession to a brother) taking in preference to an elder. Then come ascendants, the father taking first, after him his brothers and sisters, then the grandfather, and so on. There is no succession through the mother. The full-blood is preferred to the half-blood. The Crown takes as *ultimus heres* in default of relations. Since the act of 1874, s. 37, the distinction previously existing between succession to fees of conquest and succession to fees of heritage has ceased to exist. The right of any person to an estate in land by succession as heir may by s. 13 of the same act be challenged within twenty years of his infeftment as heir and his entering into possession. The heir-at-law of a sole or last surviving trustee, being of full age and not subject to any legal incapacity, may by s. 43 complete a title to the land held in trust.

The heir on the death of the ancestor does not, as in England, attain his full rights by simple survivorship. The Scotch theory of law is the same as the Roman. The inheritance is only offered to the heir, and he must do some act from which acceptance of it may be presumed. He has six months (before the act of 1868 it was a year and a day) to deliberate whether he will accept the inheritance. Should he decide to accept, his title must be completed by service as heir, by adjudication on a trust bond, or (in case of lands held of a subject superior) by writ or precept of *clare constat*, a mode of admission by the superior. Service is either general or special, general where the ancestor was not infeft, special where the ancestor was infeft. Up to 1847 service depended on the verdict of a jury. The procedure has recently been much simplified, and now depends mainly on the acts of 1868 and 1874. Both kinds of service now proceed by decree on petition to the sheriff of chancery or the sheriff of a county, subject to appeal to the Court of Session.[1] No court need be held when the petition for service is unopposed. A decree of general service is by s. 31 of the act of 1874 equivalent to a *mortis causâ* general disposition, and by s. 9 of the same act the heir obtains a personal right to the land descendible by mere survivance without service. The personal right may be completed by petition in accordance with the act. The right of the heir once vested cannot be divested; *semel heres semper heres.*

In moveables the law of succession is in agreement in the main with that of England. The principal difference is the rule of collation, under which the heir cannot take, as in England, both as heir and next of kin, but he must make his choice, and if he choose the heritable estate, he cannot in addition have his whole share of the moveables. If the heritable estate exceed his share of the moveables, he takes none of the latter, if it be smaller, he only takes enough of the moveables to make his share equal to that of the rest. The half-blood succeeds next after the whole blood, not *pari passu* as in England. The father takes one-half in preference to the brothers and sisters, the mother one-third if she survive the father. A right of representation among next of kin and

---

[1] Forms of service, varying as it is general or special, as the heir is heir of provision, of tailzie, etc., are given in schedules (P) and (Q) of the act of 1868.

heirs of moveables was first given by 18 and 19 Vict., c. 23. The right to heirship moveables was abolished by s. 160 of the Act of 1868. The husband or wife of the deceased has a right to a certain share of the moveables, as has already been stated. Provision is made by the Presumption of Life Limitation (Scotland) Act, 1881, for the disposal of both heritable and moveable estate where the person entitled to it has been absent from Scotland or has disappeared for a period of seven years or upwards. Any person entitled to succeed may present a petition to the Court of Session or (where the value of the estate does not exceed £150) a sheriff court, and the court may grant authority to the petitioner to uplift and enjoy the income, or may sequestrate the estate and appoint a judicial factor. After fourteen years' absence in the case of moveables, twenty years in the case of heritables, the court may grant authority to the petitioner to make up a title to the property as though the absent person were dead.

CHAPTER XVIII

IRELAND

THE will was known to the Brehon law; it was probably of purely ecclesiastical origin, and seems to have been used only for naming a place of burial.[1] The rules of inheritance among the native Irish were up to the seventeenth century considerably different from the English rules. Sons succeeded according to the custom of gavelkind, and illegitimate took their shares with legitimate, daughters being entirely excluded. The chieftain of a sept had his successor nominated during his lifetime, the successor-elect being known as the tanist, and being generally the eldest male of the sept, provided that he was otherwise worthy of the office. Gavelkind was declared void by a resolution of the Irish judges in 1605,[2] and tanistry by a case decided in the Irish Court of Queen's Bench in 1608.[3] The intention evidently was to suppress as barbarous the native Irish customs and to assimilate the law of succession to that of England.

[1] *Senchus Mor*, vol. i. 203 (in the series of Ancient Laws of Ireland).
[2] Sir J. Davis' Rep., 49. The tenure of gavelkind was temporarily revived in Ireland by the Irish Act of 2 Anne, c. 6, which enacted that the lands of a Roman Catholic should on his death be divided among the sons as in gavelkind, but one son becoming a Protestant could take all. This was repealed by the Irish Act of 17 and 18 Geo. III, c. 49.
[3] Sir. J. Davis' Rep., 28.

The law at present is in general accordance with that of England, much of the earlier English legislation having been followed by similar legislation of the Irish Parliament, *e.g.* the Statute of Frauds by 7 Will. III, c. 12, and much of the later legislation, such as the Wills, Conveyancing, and Settled Land Acts applying to Ireland with certain modifications, chiefly in matters of practice. For instance, the registrar of an Irish civil bill court corresponds to the registrar of an English county court, and some matters which would be in the jurisdiction of the Chancery Division in England are in that of the Land Judges in Ireland. The earliest Irish act dealing with wills was passed in 1537 (28 Hen. VIII, c. 18), and followed the English act of Edward III as to the fees for probate demandable by the ecclesiastical courts.

The main differences between English and Irish law are found in mortmain, accumulation, superstitious uses, registry, and devolution of tenancies. The earlier English Mortmain Acts passed before Poyning's Law (10 Hen. VII, c. 22) were introduced into Ireland by that law, but later acts, 9 Geo. II, c. 36, and the Mortmain Act of 1888, do not apply to Ireland.[1] The Thellusson Act of 1800 does not apply to Ireland. The list of charitable uses mentioned in the preamble to 43 Eliz., c. 4, was copied, but not exactly, in the Irish act of 10 Car. I, sess. 3, c. 1, with an important limitation to archbishops and bishops of the right of making grants for charitable purposes. Bequests for masses for the souls of the dead are not void as superstitious.

[1] See the judgment of Lord St. Leonards as Lord Chancellor of Ireland in *Incorporated Society* v. *Richards*, 1 Drury and Warren's Rep., 258 (1841).

They may, however, be void if they tend to perpetuity, as they are not charitable gifts. They tend to perpetuity if they are made to a religious community, not only the existing members, but also their successors, during a period which may extend beyond the limits prescribed by the rule against perpetuities. A registry of memorials of wills of real estate was established in Ireland by the Irish act of 6 Anne, c. 2. It is interesting to note from the preamble that one of the main reasons for passing the act was "for securing purchasers, preventing forgeries and fraudulent gifts and conveyances of lands, tenements, and hereditaments which have been frequently practised in this kingdom, especially by papists, to the great prejudice of the Protestant interest thereof." The practice of the register office now depends on 2 and 3 Will. IV, c. 87, as amended by subsequent acts. Registration, as far as it relates to wills, is facultative, not imperative. In addition to registration as a means of facilitating evidence, wills were often made evidence by private acts of the Irish Parliament. By the Land Law (Ireland) Act, 1881 (44 and 45 Vict., c. 49, s. 3), a tenancy within the act may be bequeathed, and the landlord is bound, subject to objection on reasonable grounds, to accept the legatee as tenant or (in case the tenant dies intestate) the nominee of the personal representatives of the tenant. Where the tenant dies intestate and without leaving any person entitled to his personal estate, the tenancy passes to the landlord, subject to the debts and liabilities of the deceased tenant.

A Court of Probate was established in Ireland in 1857 by 20 and 21 Vict., c. 79. There is a principal registry at Dublin and district registries at Londonderry,

Belfast, Armagh, Ballina, Cavan, Tuam, Mullingar, Kilkenny, Waterford, Limerick, and Cork. The Court of Probate was merged in the High Court of Justice by the Irish Judicature Act, 1877 (40 and 41 Vict., c. 57). Contentious jurisdiction was given to the civil bill courts in testamentary matters by 14 and 15 Vict., c. 57, 20 and 21 Vict., c. 79, and 22 and 23 Vict., c. 31. It extends to cases where the personalty of the deceased is under £200 and he is not beneficially entitled to real estate of the value of £300. The same courts have by 40 and 41 Vict., c. 56, and 45 and 46 Vict., c. 29, jurisdiction in administration actions where the amount does not exceed £500 of personal or £30 of real estate. An appeal lies in most cases to the judge of assize.

The law as to intestate succession and the revenue duties are the same as in England. By the Probate Duties (Scotland and Ireland) Act, 1888,[1] one-fifth of the probate duties is assigned for the relief of local taxation in Ireland.

[1] Repealed as to Scotland by the Local Government (Scotland) Act, 1889.

APPENDIX A.

In the following Acts of Parliament only those sections which are still law and which immediately affect the subject of this volume are set out fully.

WILLS ACT, 1837

(7 Will. IV, and 1 Vict., c. 26)

BE it enacted by the Queen's most Excellent Majesty, by and with the Advice and Consent of the Lords Spiritual and Temporal, and Commons, in this present Parliament assembled, and by the Authority of the same, That the Words and Expressions hereinafter mentioned, which in their ordinary Signification have a more confined or a different Meaning, shall in this Act, except where the Nature of the Provision or the Context of the Act shall exclude such Construction, be interpreted as follows; (that is to say), the Word "Will" shall extend to a Testament, and to a Codicil, and to an Appointment by Will or by Writing in the Nature of a Will in exercise of a Power, and also to a Disposition by Will and Testament or Devise of the Custody and Tuition of any Child, by virtue of an Act passed in the Twelfth Year of the Reign of King *Charles* the Second, intituled *An Act for taking away the Court of Wards and Liveries, and Tenures* in capite *and by Knights Service, and Purveyance, and for settling a Revenue upon His Majesty in lieu thereof,* or by virtue of an Act passed in the Parliament of *Ireland* in the Fourteenth and Fifteenth Years of the Reign of King *Charles* the Second, intituled *An Act for taking away the Court of Wards and Liveries, and Tenures* in capite *and*

Meaning of certain Words in this Act: "Will:" 12 Car. 2. c. 24. 14 & 15 Car. 2. (I.)

by *Knights Service*, and to any other Testamentary Disposition; and the Words "Real Estate" shall extend to Manors, Advowsons, Messuages, Lands, Tithes, Rents, and Hereditaments, whether Freehold, Customary Freehold, Tenant Right, Customary, or Copyhold, or of any other Tenure, and whether corporeal, incorporeal, or personal, and to any undivided Share thereof, and to any Estate, Right, or Interest (other than a Chattel Interest) therein; and the Words "Personal Estate" shall extend to Leasehold Estates and other Chattels Real, and also to Monies, Shares of Government and other Funds, Securities for Money (not being Real Estates), Debts, Choses in Action, Rights, Credits, Goods, and all other Property whatsoever which by Law devolves upon the Executor or Administrator, and to any Share or Interest therein; and every Word importing the Singular Number only shall extend and be applied to several Persons or Things as well as One Person or Thing; and every Word importing the Masculine Gender only shall extend and be applied to a Female as well as a Male. . . .

"Real Estate:"

"Personal Estate:"

Number:

Gender.

III. And be it further enacted, That it shall be lawful for every Person to devise, bequeath, or dispose of, by his Will executed in manner hereinafter required, all Real Estate and all Personal Estate which he shall be entitled to, either at Law or in Equity, at the Time of his Death, and which, if not so devised, bequeathed, or disposed of, would devolve upon the Heir-at-Law or Customary Heir of him, or, if he became entitled by Descent, of his Ancestor, or upon his Executor or Administrator; and that the Power hereby given shall extend to all Real Estate of the Nature of Customary Freehold or Tenant Right, or Customary or Copyhold, notwithstanding that the Testator may not have surrendered the same to the Use of his Will, or notwithstanding that, being entitled as Heir, Devisee, or otherwise to be admitted thereto, he shall not have been admitted thereto, or notwithstanding that the same, in consequence of the Want of a Custom to devise or surrender to the Use of a Will or otherwise, could not at Law have been disposed of by Will if this Act had not been made, or notwithstanding that the same, in consequence of their being a Custom that a Will or a Surrender to the Use of a Will should continue in force for a limited Time only, or any other special Custom,

All Property may be disposed of by Will.

comprising Customary Freeholds and Copyholds without Surrender and before Admittance and also such of them as cannot now be devised;

could not have been disposed of by Will according to the Power contained in this Act, if this Act had not been made; and also to Estates *pur autre vie,* whether there shall or shall not be any special Occupant thereof, and whether the same shall be Freehold, Customary Freehold, Tenant Right, Customary, or Copyhold, or of any other other Tenure, and whether the same shall be a corporeal or incorporeal Hereditament; and also to all contingent, executory, or other future Interests in any Real or Personal Estate, whether the Testator may or may not be ascertained as the Person or One of the Persons in whom the same respectively may become vested, and whether he may be entitled thereto under the Instrument by which the same respectively were created or under any Disposition thereof by Deed or Will; and also to all Rights of Entry for Conditions broken, and other Rights of Entry; and also to such of the same Estates, Interests, and Rights respectively, and other Real and Personal Estate, as the Testator may be entitled to at the Time of his Death, notwithstanding that he may become entitled to the same subsequently to the Execution of his Will.

<small>Estates *pur autre vie;* contingent Interests; Rights of Entry; and Property acquired after Execution of the Will.</small>

IV. Provided always, and be it further enacted, That where any Real Estate of the Nature of Customary Freehold or Tenant Right, or Customary or Copyhold, might, by the Custom of the Manor of which the same is holden, have been surrendered to the Use of a Will, and the Testator shall not have surrendered the same to the Use of his Will, no Person entitled or claiming to be entitled thereto by virtue of such Will shall be entitled to be admitted, except upon Payment of all such Stamp Duties, Fees, and Sums of Money as would have been lawfully due and payable in respect of the surrendering of such Real Estate to the Use of the Will, or in respect of presenting, registering, or enrolling such Surrender, if the same Real Estate had been surrendered to the Use of the Will of such Testator; Provided also, that where the Testator was entitled to have been admitted to such Real Estate, and might, if he had been admitted thereto, have surrendered the same to the Use of his Will, and shall not have been admitted thereto, no Person entitled or claiming to be entitled to such Real Estate in consequence of such Will shall be entitled to be admitted to the same Real Estate

<small>As to the Fees and Fines payable by Devisees of Customary and Copyhold Estates</small>

by virtue thereof, except on Payment of all such Stamp Duties, Fees, Fine, and Sums of Money as would have been lawfully due and payable in respect of the Admittance of such Testator to such Real Estate, and also of all such Stamp Duties, Fees, and Sums of Money as would have been lawfully due and payable in respect of surrendering such Real Estate to the Use of the Will, or of presenting, registering, or enrolling such Surrender, had the Testator been duly admitted to such Real Estate, and afterwards surrendered the same to the Use of his Will; all which Stamp Duties, Fees, Fine, or Sums of Money, due as aforesaid, shall be paid in addition to Stamp Duties, Fees, Fine, or Sums of Money due or payable on the Admittance of such Person so entitled or claiming to be entitled to the same Real Estate as aforesaid.

Wills or Extracts of Wills of Customary Freeholds and Copyholds to be entered on the Court Rolls;

V. And be it further enacted, That when any Real Estate of the Nature of Customary Freehold or Tenant Right, or Customary or Copyhold, shall be disposed of by Will, the Lord of the Manor or reputed Manor of which such Real Estate is holden, or his Steward, or the Deputy of such Steward, shall cause the Will by which such Disposition shall be made, or so much thereof as shall contain the Disposition of such Real Estate, to be entered on the Court Rolls of such Manor or reputed Manor; and when any Trusts are declared by the Will of such Real Estate, it shall not be necessary to enter the Declaration of such Trusts, but it shall be sufficient to state in the Entry on the Court Rolls that such Real Estate is subject to the Trusts declared by such Will; and when any such Real Estate could not have been disposed of by Will if this Act had not been made, the same Fine, Heriot, Dues, Duties, and Services shall be paid and rendered by the Devisee as would have been due from the Customary Heir in case of the Descent of the same Real Estate, and the Lord shall, as against the Devisee of such Estate, have the same remedy for recovering and enforcing such Fine, Heriot, Dues, Duties, and Services as he is now entitled to for recovering and enforcing the same from or against the Customary Heir in case of a Descent.

and the Lord to be entitled to the same Fine, &c. when such Estates are not now devisable as he would have been from the Heir in case of Descent.

Estates pur autre vie.

VI. And be it further enacted, That if no Disposition by Will shall be made of any Estate *pur autre vie* of a Freehold Nature, the same shall be chargeable in the Hands of the

Heir, if it shall come to him by reason of special Occupancy, as Assets by Descent, as in the Case of Freehold Land in Fee Simple; and in case there shall be no special Occupant of any Estate *pur autre vie*, whether Freehold or Customary Freehold, Tenant Right, Customary or Copyhold, or of any other Tenure, and whether a corporeal or incorporeal Hereditament, it shall go to the Executor or Administrator of the Party that had the Estate thereof by virtue of the Grant; and if the same shall come to the Executor or Administrator either by reason of a special Occupancy or by virtue of this Act, it shall be Assets in his Hands, and shall go and be applied and distributed in the same Manner as the Personal Estate of the Testator or Intestate.

VII. And be it further enacted, That no Will made by any Person under the Age of Twenty-one Years shall be valid. No Will of a Person under Age valid;

VIII. Provided also, and be it further enacted, That no Will made by any married Woman shall be valid, except such a Will as might have been made by a married Woman before the passing of this Act. nor of a Feme Covert, except such as might now be made.

IX. And be in further enacted, That no Will shall be valid unless it shall be in Writing and executed in manner hereinafter mentioned; (that is to say), it shall be signed at the Foot or End thereof by the Testator, or by some other Person in his Presence and by his Direction; and such Signature shall be made or acknowledged by the Testator in the Presence of Two or more Witnesses present at the same Time, and such Witnesses shall attest and shall subscribe the Will in the Presence of the Testator, but no Form of Attestation shall be necessary. Every Will shall be in Writing, and signed by the Testator in the Presence of two Witnesses at One Time.

X. And be it further enacted, That no Appointment made by Will, in exercise of any Power, shall be valid, unless the same be executed in Manner hereinbefore required; and every Will executed in manner hereinbefore required shall, so far as respects the Execution and Attestation thereof, be a valid execution of a Power of Appointment by Will, notwithstanding it shall have been expressly required that a Will made in exercise of such Power should be executed with some additional or other Form of Execution or Solemnity. Appointments by Will to be executed like other Wills, and to be valid, although other required Solemnities are not observed.

Soldiers and Mariners Wills excepted.	XI. Provided always, and be it further enacted, That any Soldier being in actual Military Service, or any Mariner or Seaman being at Sea, may dispose of his Personal Estate as he might have done before the making of this Act. . . .
Publication not to be requisite.	XIII. And be it further enacted, That every Will executed in manner hereinbefore required shall be valid without any other Publication thereof.
Will not to be void on account of Incompetency of attesting Witness.	XIV. And be it further enacted, That if any Person who shall attest the Execution of a Will shall at the time of the Execution thereof or at any time afterwards be incompetent to be admitted a Witness to prove the Execution thereof, such Will shall not on that Account be invalid.
Gifts to an attesting Witness to be void.	XV. And be it further enacted, That if any Person shall attest the Execution of any Will to whom or to whose Wife or Husband any beneficial Devise, Legacy, Estate, Interest, Gift, or Appointment, of or affecting any Real or Personal Estate, (other than and except Charges and Directions for the Payment of any Debt or Debts), shall be thereby given or made, such Devise, Legacy, Estate, Interest, Gift, or Appointment shall, so far only as concerns such Person attesting the Execution of such Will, or the Wife or Husband of such Person, or any Person claiming under such Person or Wife or Husband, be utterly null and void, and such Person so attesting shall be admitted as a Witness to prove the Execution of such Will, or to prove the Validity or Invalidity thereof, notwithstanding such Devise, Legacy, Estate, Interest, Gift, or Appointment mentioned in such Will.
Creditor attesting to be admitted a Witness.	XVI. And be it further enacted, That in case by any Will any Real or Personal Estate shall be charged with any Debt or Debts, and any Creditor, or the Wife or Husband of any Creditor, whose Debt is so charged, shall attest the Execution of such Will, such Creditor, notwithstanding such Charge, shall be admitted a Witness to prove the Execution of such Will, or to prove the Validity or Invalidity thereof.
Executor to be admitted a Witness.	XVII. And be it further enacted, That no Person shall, on account of his being an Executor of a Will, be incompetent to be admitted a Witness to prove the Execution of such Will, or a Witness to prove the Validity or Invalidity thereof.

XVIII. And be it further enacted, That every Will made by a Man or Woman shall be revoked by his or her Marriage (except a Will made in exercise of a Power of Appointment, when the Real or Personal Estate thereby appointed would not in default of such Appointment pass to his or her Heir, Customary Heir, Executor, or Administrator, or the Person entitled as his or her next of Kin, under the Statute of Distributions). *Will to be revoked by Marriage.*

XIX. And be it further enacted, That no Will shall be revoked by any Presumption of an Intention on the Ground of an Alteration in Circumstances. *No Will to be revoked by Presumption.*

XX. And be it further enacted, That no Will or Codicil, or any Part thereof, shall be revoked otherwise than as aforesaid, or by another Will or Codicil executed in manner hereinbefore required, or by some Writing declaring an Intention to revoke the same, and executed in the Manner in which a Will is hereinbefore required to be executed, or by the burning, tearing, or otherwise destroying the same by the Testator, or by some Person in his Presence and by his Direction, with the Intention of revoking the same. *No Will to be revoked but by another Will or Codicil, or by a Writing executed like a Will, or by Destruction.*

XXI. And be it further enacted, That no Obliteration, Interlineation, or other Alteration made in any Will after the Execution thereof shall be valid or have any Effect, except so far as the Words or Effect of the Will before such Alteration shall not be apparent, unless such Alteration shall be executed in like Manner as hereinbefore is required for the Execution of the Will; but the Will, with such Alteration as Part thereof, shall be deemed to be duly executed if the Signature of the Testator and the Subscription of the Witnesses to be made in the Margin or on some other Part of the Will opposite or near to such Alteration, or at the Foot or End of or opposite to a Memorandum referring to such Alteration, and written at the End or some other Part of the Will. *No alteration in a Will shall have any Effect unless executed as a Will.*

XXII. And be it further enacted, That no Will or Codicil, or any Part thereof, which shall be in any Manner revoked, shall be revived otherwise than by the Re-execution thereof, or by a Codicil executed in manner hereinbefore required, and showing an Intention to revive the same ; and when any Will or Codicil which shall be partly revoked, *No Will revoked to be revived otherwise than by Re-execution or a Codicil to revive it.*

and afterwards wholly revoked, shall be revived, such Revival shall not extend to so much thereof as shall have been revoked before the Revocation of the whole thereof, unless an Intention to the contrary shall be shown.

A Devise not to be rendered inoperative by any subsequent Conveyance or Act.

XXIII. And be it further enacted, That no Conveyance or other Act made or done subsequently to the Execution of a Will of or relating to any Real or Personal Estate therein comprised, except an act by which such Will shall be revoked as aforesaid, shall prevent the Operation of the Will with respect to such Estate or Interest in such Real or Personal Estate as the Testator shall have Power to dispose of by Will at the Time of his Death.

A Will shall be construed to speak from the Death of the Testator.

XXIV. And be it further enacted, That every Will shall be construed, with reference to the Real Estate and Personal Estate comprised in it, to speak and take effect as if it had been executed immediately before the Death of the Testator, unless a contrary Intention shall appear by the Will.

A Residuary Devise shall include Estates comprised in lapsed, and void Devises.

XXV. And be it further enacted, That, unless a contrary Intention shall appear by the Will, such Real Estate or Interest therein as shall be comprised or intended to be comprised in any Devise in such Will contained, which shall fail or be void by reason of the Death of the Devisee in the Lifetime of the Testator, or by reason of such Devise being contrary to Law or otherwise incapable of taking effect, shall be included in the Residuary Devise (if any) contained in such Will.

A general Devise of the Testator's Lands shall include Copyhold and Leasehold as well as Freehold Lands.

XXVI. And be it further enacted, That a Devise of the Land of the Testator, or of the Land of the Testator in any Place or in the Occupation of any Person mentioned in his Will, or otherwise described in a general Manner, and any other general Devise which would describe a Customary, Copyhold, or Leasehold Estate if the Testator had no Freehold Estate which could be described by it, shall be construed to include the Customary, Copyhold, and Leasehold Estates of the Testator, or his Customary Copyhold and Leasehold Estates, or any of them, to which such Description shall extend, as the Case may be, as well as Freehold Estates, unless a contrary Intention shall appear by the Will.

A general Gift shall include

XXVII. And be it further enacted, That a general Devise of the Real Estate of the Testator, or of the

Real Estate of the Testator in any Place or in the Occupation of any Person mentioned in his Will, or otherwise described in a general Manner, shall be construed to include any Real Estate, or any Real Estate to which such Description shall extend (as the Case may be), which he may have Power to appoint in any Manner he may think proper, and shall operate as an Execution of such Power, unless a contrary Intention shall appear by the Will; and in like Manner a Bequest of the Personal Estate of the Testator, or any Bequest of Personal Property described in a general Manner, shall be construed to include any Personal Estate, or any Personal Estate to which such Description shall extend (as the Case may be), which he may have Power to appoint in any Manner he may think proper, and shall operate as an Execution of such Power, unless a contrary Intention shall appear by the Will. *Estates over which the Testator has a general Power of Appointment.*

XXVIII. And be it further enacted, That where any Real Estate shall be devised to any Person without any Words of Limitation, such Devise shall be construed to pass the Fee Simple, or other the whole Estate or Interest which the Testator had Power to dispose of by Will in such Real Estate, unless a contrary Intention shall appear by the Will. *A Devise without any Words of Limitation shall be construed to pass the Fee.*

XXIX. And be it further enacted, That in any Devise or Bequest of Real or Personal Estate the Words "die without Issue," or "die without leaving Issue," or "have no Issue," or any other Words which may import either a Want or Failure of Issue of any Person in his Lifetime or at the Time of his Death, or an indefinite Failure of his Issue, shall be construed to mean a Want or Failure of Issue in the Lifetime or at the Time of the Death of such Person, and not an indefinite Failure of his Issue, unless a contrary Intention shall appear by the Will, by reason of such Person having a prior Estate Tail, or of a preceding Gift, being, without any Implication arising from such Words, a Limitation of an Estate Tail to such Person or Issue, or otherwise: Provided, that this act shall not extend to Cases where such Words as aforesaid import if no Issue described in a preceding Gift shall be born, or if there shall be no Issue who shall live to attain the Age or otherwise answer the Description required for obtaining a vested Estate by a preceding Gift to such Issue. *The Words "die without Issue," or "die without leaving Issue," shall be construed to mean die without Issue living at the Death.*

VOL. I 15

No Devise to Trustees or Executors, except for a Term or a Presentation to a Church, shall pass a Chattel Interest.

XXX. And be it further enacted, That where any Real Estate (other than or not being a Presentation to a Church) shall be devised to any Trustee or Executor, such Devise shall be construed to pass the Fee-Simple or other the whole Estate or Interest which the Testator had Power to dispose of by Will in such Real Estate, unless a definite Term of Years, absolute or determinable, or an Estate of Freehold, shall thereby be given to him expressly or by Implication.

Trustees under an unlimited Devise, where the Trust may endure beyond the Life of a Person beneficially entitled for Life, to take the Fee.

XXXI. And be it further enacted, That where any Real Estate shall be devised to a Trustee, without any express Limitation of the Estate to be taken by such Trustee, and the beneficial Interest in such Real Estate, or in the surplus Rents and Profits thereof, shall not be given to any Person for Life, or such beneficial Interest shall be given to any Person for Life, but the Purposes of the Trust may continue beyond the Life of such Person, such Devise shall be construed to vest in such Trustee the Fee-Simple or other the whole legal Estate which the Testator had Power to dispose of by Will in such Real Estate, and not an Estate determinable when the Purposes of the Trust shall be satisfied.

Devises of Estates Tail shall not lapse.

XXXII. And be it further enacted, That where any Person to whom any Real Estate shall be devised for an Estate Tail or an Estate in quasi Entail shall die in the Lifetime of the Testator, leaving Issue who would be inheritable under such Entail, and any such Issue shall be living at the Time of the Death of the Testator, such Devise shall not lapse, but shall take effect as if the Death of such Person had happened immediately after the Death of the Testator, unless a contrary Intention shall appear by the Will.

Gifts to Children or other Issue who leave Issue living at the Testator's Death shall not lapse.

XXXIII. And be it further enacted, That where any Person, being a child or other Issue of the Testator, to whom any Real or Personal Estate shall be devised or bequeathed for any Estate or Interest not determinable at or before the Death of such Person, shall die in the Lifetime of the Testator leaving Issue, and any such Issue of such Person shall be living at the Time of the Death of the Testator, such Devise or Bequest shall not lapse, but shall take effect as if the Death of such Person had happened immediately after the Death of the Testator, unless a contrary Intention shall appear by the Will.

WILLS ACT AMENDMENT ACT 219

XXXIV. And be it further enacted, That this Act shall not extend to any Will made before the First Day of January One thousand eight hundred and thirty-eight, and that every Will re-executed or republished, or revived by any Codicil, shall for the Purposes of this Act be deemed to have been made at the Time at which the same shall be so re-executed, republished, or revived; and that this Act shall not extend to any Estate *pur autre vie* of any Person who shall die before the First Day of *January* One thousand eight hundred and thirty-eight. {Act not to extend to Wills made before 1838, nor to Estates pur autre vie of Persons who die before 1838.}

XXXV. And be it further enacted, That this Act shall not extend to *Scotland*. {Act not to extend to Scotland.}

WILLS ACT AMENDMENT ACT, 1852

(15 and 16 Vict., c. 24)

I. Where by an Act passed in the First Year of the Reign of Her Majesty Queen *Victoria*, intituled *An Act for the Amendment of the Laws with respect to Wills*, it is enacted, that no Will shall be valid unless it shall be signed at the Foot or End thereof by the Testator, or by some other Person in his Presence, and by his Direction: Every Will shall, so far only as regards the Position of the Signature of the Testator, or of the Person signing for him as aforesaid, be deemed to be valid within the said Enactment, as explained by this Act, if the Signature shall be so placed at or after, or following, or under, or beside, or opposite to the End of the Will, that it shall be apparent on the Face of the Will that the Testator intended to give Effect by such his Signature to the Writing signed as his Will, and that no such Will shall be affected by the Circumstances that the Signature shall not follow or be immediately after the Foot or End of the Will, or by the Circumstance that a blank Space shall intervene between the concluding Word of the Will and the Signature, or by the circumstance that the signature shall be placed among the Words of the Testimonium Clause or of the Clause of Attestation, or shall follow or be after or under the Clause of Attestation, either with or without a blank Space intervening, or shall follow or be after, or under, or beside the Names or One of {1 Vict. c. 26. When Signature to a Will shall be deemed valid.}

the Names of the subscribing Witnesses, or by the Circumstance that the Signature shall be on a Side or Page or other Portion of the Paper or Papers containing the Will whereon no Clause or Paragraph or disposing Part of the Will shall be written above the Signature, or by the Circumstance that there shall appear to be sufficient Space on or at the Bottom of the preceding Side or Page or other Portion of the same Paper on which the Will is written to contain the Signature; and the Enumeration of the above Circumstances shall not restrict the Generality of the above Enactment; but no Signature under the said Act or this Act shall be operative to give Effect to any Disposition or Direction which is underneath or which follows it, nor shall it give Effect to any Disposition or Direction inserted after the Signature shall be made. . . .

COURT OF PROBATE ACT, 1857

(21 and 22 Vict., c. 77)

Interpretation of Terms.
II. In the Construction of this Act, unless the Context be inconsistent with the Meaning hereby assigned—

"Will" shall comprehend "Testament" and all other Testamentary Instruments of which Probate may now be granted:

"Administration" shall comprehend all Letters of Administration of the Effects of deceased Persons, whether with or without the Will annexed, and whether granted for general, special, or limited Purposes:

"Matters and Causes Testamentary" shall comprehend all Matters and Causes relating to the Grant and Revocation of Probate of Wills or of Administration:

"Common Form Business" shall mean the Business of obtaining Probate and Administration where there is no Contention as to the Right thereto, including the passing of Probates and Administrations through the Court of Probate in contentious Cases when the Contest is terminated, and all Business of a non-contentious Nature to be taken in the Court in Matters of Testacy and Intestacy, not being Proceedings in

COURT OF PROBATE ACT, 1857   221

any Suit, and also the Business of lodging Caveats against the Grant of Probate or Administration.

III. The voluntary and contentious Jurisdiction and Authority of all Ecclesiastical, Royal Peculiar, Peculiar, Manorial, and other Courts and Persons in *England* now having Jurisdiction or Authority to grant or revoke Probate of Wills or Letters of Administration of the Effects of deceased Persons, shall in respect of such Matters absolutely cease; and no Jurisdiction or Authority in relation to any Matters or Causes Testamentary, or to any Matter arising out of or connected with the Grant or Revocation of Probate or Administration, shall belong to or be exercised by any such Court or Person. *Testamentary Jurisdiction of Ecclesiastical and other Courts abolished.*

IV. The voluntary and contentious Jurisdiction and Authority in relation to the granting or revoking Probate of Wills and Letters of Administration of the Effects of deceased Persons now vested in or which can be exercised by any Court or Person in *England*, together with full Authority to hear and determine all Questions relating to Matters and Causes Testamentary, shall belong to and be vested in Her Majesty, and shall, except as hereinafter is mentioned, be exercised in the Name of Her Majesty in a Court to be called the Court of Probate, and to hold its ordinary Sittings and to have its Principal Registry at such Place or Places in *London* or *Middlesex* as Her Majesty in Council shall from Time to Time appoint. . . . *Testamentary Jurisdiction to be exercised by a Court of Probate.*

XIII. There shall be established for each of the Districts specified in Schedule (A) to this Act, and at the Places respectively mentioned in such Schedule, a Public Registry attached to and under the Control of the Court of Probate, hereinafter referred to as "The District Registry." . . . *District Registries to be established as in Schedule (A)*

XVIII. The Registrars, District Registrars, and other Officers of the Court of Probate, except as herein provided, shall be appointed by the Judge. . . . *As to Appointment to Offices.*

XIX. The Registrars and District Registrars shall hold their Offices during good Behaviour, subject to be removed by Order of the Lord Chancellor for some reasonable Cause to be in such Order expressed; and the other Officers of the Court may be removed by the Judge, with the Sanction of the Lord Chancellor. . . . *Tenure of Office of Officers.*

XXIII. The Court of Probate shall be a Court of *The Court to*

222 COURT OF PROBATE ACT, 1857

have Record, and such Court shall have the same Powers, and its throughout all Grants and Orders shall have the same Effect, throughout England all England, and in relation to the Personal Estates in all the same Powers Parts of England of deceased Persons, as the Prerogative as the Prerogative Court of the Archbishop of Canterbury and its Grants and tive Orders respectively now have in the Province of Canterbury, Court within or in the Parts of such Province within its Jurisdiction, and in the Province of relation to those Matters and Causes Testamentary and those Canterbury. Effects of deceased Persons which are within the Jurisdiction of the said Prerogative Court; and all Duties which, by Statute or otherwise, are imposed on or should be performed by Ordinaries generally, or on or by the said Prerogative Court, in respect of Probates, Administrations, or Matters or Causes Testamentary within their respective Jurisdictions,

Suits for shall be performed by the Court of Probate: Provided that Legacies no Suits for Legacies, or Suits for the Distribution of or Distribution Residues, shall be entertained by the Court, or by any not to be Court or Person whose Jurisdiction as to Matters and entertained. Causes Testamentary is hereby abolished.

Power to XXIV. The Court of Probate may require the Attendance examine Witnesses. of any Party in Person, or of any Person whom it may think fit to examine or cause to be examined in any Suit or other Proceeding in respect of Matters or Causes Testamentary, and may examine or cause to be examined upon Oath or Affirmation, as the Case may require, Parties and Witnesses by Word of Mouth, and may, either before or after or with or without such Examination, cause them or any of them to be examined on Interrogatories, or receive their or any of their Affidavits or solemn Affirmations, as

As to the Case may be; and the Court may by Writ require such Production of Attendance, and order to be produced before itself or otherwise Deeds, any Deeds, Evidences, or Writings, in the same Form, &c. or nearly as may be, as that in which a Writ of Subpoena ad testificandum, or of Subpoena duces tecum, is now issued by any of Her Majesty's Superior Courts of Law at Westminster; and every Person disobeying any such Writ shall be considered as in Contempt of the Court, and also be liable to forfeit a Sum not exceeding One Hundred Pounds.

Powers XXV. The Court of Probate shall have the like Powers, of the Court to Jurisdiction, and Authority for enforcing the Attendance of enforce Orders. Persons required by it as aforesaid, and for punishing

Persons failing, neglecting, or refusing to produce Deeds, Evidences, or Writings, or refusing to appear or to be sworn, or make Affirmation or Declaration, or to give Evidence, or guilty of Contempt, and generally for enforcing all Orders, Decrees, and Judgments made or given by the Court under this Act, and otherwise in relation to the Matters to be inquired into and done by or under the Orders of the Court under this Act, as are by Law vested in the High Court of Chancery for such Purposes in relation to any Suit or Matter depending in such Court.

XXVI. The Court of Probate may, on Motion or Petition, or otherwise, in a summary Way, whether any Suit or other Proceeding shall or shall not be pending in the Court with respect to any Probate or Administration, order any Person to produce and bring into the Principal or any District Registry, or otherwise as the Court may direct, any Paper or Writing being or purporting to be testamentary, which may be shown to be in the Possession or under the Control of such Person; and if it be not shown that any such Paper or Writing is in the Possession or under the Control of such Person, but it shall appear that there are reasonable Grounds for believing that he has the Knowledge of any such Paper or Writing, the Court may direct such Person to attend for the Purpose of being examined in open Court, or upon Interrogatories respecting the same, and such Person shall be bound to answer such Questions or Interrogatories, and, if so ordered, to produce and bring in such Paper or Writing, and shall be subject to the like Process of Contempt in case of Default in not attending or in not answering such Questions or Interrogatories, or not bringing in such Paper or Writing, as he would have been subject to in case he had been a Party to a Suit in the Court and had made such Default; and the Costs of any such Motion, Petition, or other Proceeding shall be in the Discretion of the Court. *Order to produce any Instrument purporting to be testamentary.*

XXVII. The Registrars and District Registrars shall respectively have full Power to administer Oaths; and all Persons who at the Commencement of this Act shall be acting as Surrogates of any Ecclesiastical Court, and any other Persons whom the Judge shall, under the Seal of the Court, from Time to Time appoint, shall respectively have *Registrars, &c. to have Power to administer Oaths.*

224 COURT OF PROBATE ACT, 1857

Power to appoint, also, Commissioners to administer Oaths, &c. full Power to administer Oaths and perform such other Duties in reference to Matters and Causes Testamentary as may be assigned to them from Time to Time by the Rules and Orders under this Act; and the Persons so appointed shall be styled "Commissioners of Her Majesty's Court of Probate:" Provided, that any Party required to be examined, or any Person called as a Witness or required or desiring to make an Affidavit or Deposition under or for the Purposes of this Act, shall be permitted to make his solemn Affirmation or Declaration instead of being sworn in the Circumstances and Manner in which a Person called as a Witness or desiring to make an Affidavit or Deposition would be permitted so to do under the Common Law Procedure Act, 1854, in Cases within the Provisions of that Act; and any Person who shall wilfully give false Evidence, or who shall wilfully swear, affirm, or declare falsely in any Affidavit or Deposition before the Court of Probate, or before any Registrar, District Registrar, or Commissioner of the Court, shall be liable to the Penalties and Consequences of wilful and corrupt Perjury.

Penalty on forging or counterfeiting Seals or Signatures of Officers. XXVIII. If any Person forge the Signature of any Registrar, District Registrar, or Commissioner for taking Oaths, or forge or counterfeit any Seal of the Court of Probate, or knowingly use or concur in using any such forged or counterfeit Signature or Seal, or tender in Evidence any Document with a false or counterfeit Signature of such Registrar, District Registrar, or Commissioner, or with a false or counterfeit seal, knowing the same signature or seal to be false or counterfeit, every such Person shall be guilty of Felony, and shall upon Conviction be liable to Penal Servitude for the Term of his Life or any Term not less than Seven Years, or to Imprisonment for any Term not exceeding Three Years, with or without Hard Labour.

Practice of the Court. XXIX. The Practice of the Court of Probate shall, except where otherwise provided by this Act, or by the Rules or Orders to be from Time to Time made under this Act, be, so far as the Circumstances of the Case will admit, according to the present Practice in the Prerogative Court.

Rules and Orders to XXX. And to the Intent and End that the Procedure and Practice of the Court may be of the most simple and

COURT OF PROBATE ACT, 1857

expeditious Character, it shall be lawful for the Lord Chancellor, at any Time after the passing of this Act, with the Advice and Assistance of the Lord Chief-Justice of the Court of Queen's Bench, or any One of the Judges of the Superior Courts of Law to be by such Chief-Justice named in that Behalf, and of the Judge of the said Prerogative Court, to make Rules and Orders, to take effect when this Act shall come into operation, for regulating the Procedure and Practice of the Court, and the Duties of the Registrars, District Registrars, and other Officers thereof, and for determining what shall be deemed contentious and what shall be deemed non-contentious Business, and, subject to the express Provisions of this Act, for fixing and regulating the Time and Manner of appealing from the Decisions of the said Court, and generally for carrying the Provisions of this Act into effect; and after the Time when this Act shall come into operation it shall be lawful for the Judge of the Court of Probate from Time to Time, with the Concurrence of the Lord Chancellor and the said Lord Chief-Justice, or any One of the Judges of the Superior Courts of Law to be by such Chief-Justice named in this Behalf, to repeal, amend, add to, or alter any such Rules and Orders as to him, with such Concurrence as aforesaid, may seem fit. *be made for regulating the Procedure of the Court.*

XXXI. Subject to the Regulations to be established by such Rules and Orders as aforesaid, the Witnesses, and where necessary the Parties, in all contentious Matters where their Attendance can be had, shall be examined orally by or before the Judge in open Court: Provided always, that, subject to any such Regulations as aforesaid, the Parties shall be at liberty to verify their respective Cases, in whole or in part, by Affidavit, but so that the Deponent in every such Affidavit shall, on the Application of the opposite Party, be subject to be cross-examined by or on behalf of such opposite Party orally in open Court as aforesaid, and after such Cross-examination may be re-examined orally in open Court as aforesaid by or on behalf of the Party by whom such Affidavit was filed. *Mode of taking Evidence in contentious Matters.*

XXXII. Provided, That where a Witness in any such Matter is out of the Jurisdiction of the Court, or where, by reason of his Illness or otherwise, the Court shall not think fit to enforce the Attendance of the Witness in open Court, *Court may issue Commissions or give*

Orders for Examination of Witnesses abroad, or who are unable to attend.

it shall be lawful for the Court to order a Commission to issue for the Examination of such Witness on Oath, upon Interrogatories or otherwise, or if the Witness be within the Jurisdiction of the Court to order the Examination of such Witness on Oath, upon Interrogatories or otherwise, before any Officer of the said Court, or other Person to be named in such Order for the Purpose; and all the Powers given to the Courts of Law at *Westminster* by the Acts of the Thirteenth Year of King *George* the Third, Chapter Sixty-three, and of the First Year of King *William* the Fourth, Chapter Twenty-two, for enabling the Courts of Law at *Westminster* to issue Commissions and give Orders for the Examination of Witnesses in Actions depending in such Courts, and to enforce such Examination, and all the Provisions of the said Acts, and of any other Acts for enforcing or otherwise applicable to such Examination, and the Witnesses examined, shall extend and be applicable to the said Court of Probate and to the Examination of Witnesses under the Commissions and Orders of the said Court, and to the Witnesses examined, as if such Court were One of the Courts of Law at *Westminster*, and the Matter before it were an Action pending in such Court.

Rules of Evidence in Common Law Courts to be observed.

XXXIII. The Rules of Evidence observed in the Superior Courts of Common Law at *Westminster* shall be applicable to and observed in the Trial of all Questions of Fact in the Court of Probate.

Common Law Judges may sit, on Request of Judge of Court.

XXXIV. It shall be lawful for the Judge of the Court of Probate to sit, with the Assistance of any Judge or Judges of any of the Superior Courts of Law at *Westminster*, who, upon the Request of the Judge of the Court of Probate, may find it convenient to attend for that Purpose.

Court may cause Questions of Fact to be tried by a Jury before itself, or direct an Issue to a Court of Law.

XXXV. It shall be lawful for the Court of Probate to cause any Question of Fact arising in any Suit or Proceeding under this Act to be tried by a Special or Common Jury before the Court itself, or by means of an Issue to be directed to any of the Superior Courts of Common Law, in the same Manner as an Issue may now be directed by the Court of Chancery, and such Question shall be so tried by a Jury in any case where an Heir-at-Law, cited or otherwise made

Party to the Suit or Proceeding, makes Application to the Court of Probate for that Purpose; and in any other Case where all the Parties to the Suit or Proceeding concur in such an Application, and where any Party or Parties other than such Heir-at-Law make a like Application (the other Party or Parties not concurring therein), and the Court shall refuse to cause such Question to be tried by a Jury, such Refusal, of the Court shall be subject to Appeal as herein provided. . . .

XXXVIII. Where the Court of Probate directs an Issue, it shall be lawful for such Court to direct such Issue to be tried either before a Judge of Assize in any County or at the Sittings for the Trial of Causes in *London* or *Middlesex*, and either by a Special or Common Jury, in like Manner as is now done by the Court of Chancery. . . . *{Court may direct where Issues shall be tried.}*

XLVI. Probate of a Will or Letters of Administration may, upon Application for that Purpose to the District Registry, be granted in Common Form by the District Registrar in the Name of the Court of Probate and under the Seal appointed to be used in such District Registry, if it shall appear by Affidavit of the Person or some or One of the Persons applying for the same that the Testator or Intestate, as the Case may be, at the Time of his Death had a fixed Place of Abode within the District in which the Application is made, such Place of Abode being stated in the Affidavit, and such Probate or Letters of Administration shall have effect over the Personal Estate of the Deceased in all Parts of *England* accordingly. *{Probates and Administration may be granted in Common Form by District Registrars, if it shall appear by Affidavit that the Testator, &c. had a fixed Place of Abode.}*

XLVII. Such Affidavit shall be conclusive for the Purpose of authorising the Grant, by the District Registrar, of Probate or Administration; and no such Grant of Probate or Administration shall be liable to be recalled, revoked, or otherwise impeached by reason that the Testator or Intestate had no fixed Place of Abode within the District at the Time of his Death; and every Probate and Administration granted by any such District Registrar shall effectually discharge and protect all Persons paying to or dealing with any Executor or Administrator thereunder, notwithstanding the Want of or Defect in such Affidavit, as is hereby required. *{Affidavit to be conclusive for authorizing Grant of Probate.}*

XLVIII. The District Registrar shall not grant Probate or Administration in any Case in which there is Contention as to the Grant until such Contention is terminated or disposed of by Decree or otherwise, or in which it otherwise appears to him that Probate or Administration ought not to be granted in Common Form.

District Registrars not to make Grants where there is Contention, &c.

XLIX. Notice of every Application to any District Registrar for the Grant of Probate or Administration shall be transmitted by such District Registrar to the Registrars of the Principal Registry by the next Post after such Application shall have been made; and such Notice shall specify the Name and Description, or Addition (if any), of the Testator or Intestate, the Time of his Death, and the Place of his Abode at his Decease, as stated in the Affidavit made in support of such Application, and the Name of the Person by whom the Application has been made, and such other Particulars as may be directed by Rules or Orders under this Act; and no Probate or Administration shall be granted in pursuance of such Application until such District Registrar shall have received a Certificate, under the Hand of one of the Registrars of the Principal Registry, that no other Application appears to have been made in respect of the Goods of the same deceased Person, which Certificate the said Registrar of the Principal Registry shall forward as soon as may be to the District Registrar; all such Notices in respect of Applications in the District Registries shall be filed and kept in the Principal Registry, and the Registrars of the Principal Registry shall, with reference to every such Notice, examine all Notices of such Applications which may have been received from the several other District Registries, and the Applications which may have been made for Grants of Probate or Administration at the Principal Registry, so far as it may appear necessary to ascertain whether or no Application for Probate or Administration, in respect of the Goods of the same deceased Person, may have been made in more than One Registry, and shall communicate with the District Registrars as Occasion may require in relation to such Applications.

As to Transmission of Notice of Application for Grants of Probate, &c. to District Registrar.

L. In every Case where it appears to a District Registrar that it is doubtful whether the Probate or Letters of Administration which may be applied for should or should

District Registrar in case of Doubt as

COURT OF PROBATE ACT, 1857 229

not be granted, or where any Question arises in relation to the Grant, or Application for the Grant, of any Probate or Administration, the District Registrar shall transmit a Statement of the Matter in question to the Registrars of the Court of Probate, who shall obtain the Directions of the Judge in relation thereto, and the Judge may direct the District Registrar to proceed in the Matter of the Application according to such Instructions as to the Judge may seem necessary, or may forbid any further Proceeding by the District Registrar in relation to the Matter of such Application, leaving the Party applying for the Grant in question to make Application to the Court of Probate through its Principal Registry, or, if the Case be within its Jurisdiction, to a County Court. {to Grant to take the Directions of the Judge.}

LI. On the First *Thursday* of every Month, or oftener if required by any Rules or Orders to be made in that Behalf, every District Registrar shall transmit to the Registrars of the Principal Registry a List, in such Form and containing such Particulars as may be from Time to Time required by the Court of Probate, or by any Rules or Orders under this Act, of the Grants of Probate and Administration made by such District Registrar up to the last preceding *Saturday,* and not included in a previous Return, and also a Copy, certified by the District Registrar to be a correct Copy, of every Will to which any such Probate or Administration relates. {District Registrars to transmit Lists of Probates and Administrations, and Copies of Wills.}

LII. Every District Registrar shall file and preserve all original Wills of which Probate or Letters of Administration with the Will annexed may be granted by him, in the Public Registry of the District, subject to such Regulations as the Judge of the Court of Probate may from Time to Time make in relation to the due Preservation thereof, and the convenient Inspection of the same. {District Registrars to preserve original Wills.}

LIII. Caveats against the Grant of Probates or Administrations may be lodged in the Principal Registry or in any District Registry, and (subject to any Rules or Orders under this Act) the Practice and Procedure under such Caveats in the Court of Probate shall, as near as may be, correspond with the Practice and Procedure under Caveats now in use in the Prerogative Court of *Canterbury*; and immediately upon a Caveat being lodged in any District Registry, the {As to Caveats.}

District Registrar shall send a Copy thereof to the Registrars to be entered among the Caveats in the Principal Registry; and immediately upon a Caveat being entered in the Principal Registry, Notice thereof shall be given to the District Registrar of the District, if any, in which it is alleged the Deceased resided at the Time of his Decease, and to any other District Registrar to whom it may appear to the Registrar of the Principal Registry expedient to transmit the same. . . .

<small>Registrar of County Court to transmit Certificate of Decree for Grant or Revocation of Probate.</small>
LV. On a Decree being made by a Judge of a County Court for the Grant or Revocation of a Probate or Administration in any such Cause, the Registrar of the County Court shall transmit to the District Registrar of the District in which it shall have been sworn that the Deceased had at the Time of his Decease his fixed Place of Abode a Certificate under the Seal of the County Court of such Decree having been made, and thereupon, on the Application of the Party or Parties in favour of whom such Decree shall have been made, a Probate or Administration in compliance with such Decree shall be issued from such District Registry; or, as the Case may require, the Probate or Letters of Administration theretofore granted shall be recalled or varied by the District Registrar according to the Effect of such Decree.

<small>The Judge of the County Court to decide Causes and enforce Judgments as if in other Cases.</small>
LVI. The Judge of any County Court before whom any disputed Question shall be raised relating to Matters and Causes Testamentary under this Act shall, subject to the Rules and Orders under this Act, have all the Jurisdiction, Power, and Authority to decide the same and enforce Judgment therein, and to enforce Orders in relation thereto, as if the same had been an ordinary Action in the County Court.

<small>Affidavit of the Facts giving the County Court Jurisdiction to be conclusive unless disー</small>
LVII. The Affidavit as to the Place of Abode and State of the Property of a Testator or Intestate which is to give contentious Jurisdiction to the Judge of a County Court under the previous Provisions shall, except as hereinafter provided, be conclusive for the Purpose of authorising the Exercise of such Jurisdiction, and the Grant or Revocation of Probate or Administration in compliance with the Decree of such Judge; and no such Grant of Probate or Administra-

tion shall be liable to be recalled, revoked, or otherwise impeached by reason that the Testator or Intestate had no fixed Place of Abode within the Jurisdiction of such Judge or within any of the said Districts at the Time of his Death, or by reason that the Personal Estate sworn to be under the Value of Two hundred Pounds did in fact amount to or exceed that Value, or that the Value of the Real Estate of or to which the Deceased was seised or entitled beneficially at the Time of his Death amounted to or exceeded Three hundred Pounds: Provided that, where it shall be shown to the Judge of a County Court before whom any Matter is pending under this Act that the Place of Abode or State of the Property of the Testator or Intestate in respect of whose Will or Estate he may have been applied to for Grant or Revocation of Probate or Administration has not been correctly stated in the Affidavit, and if correctly stated would not have authorised him to exercise such contentious Jurisdiction, he shall stay all further Proceedings in his Court in the Matter, leaving any Party to apply to the Court of Probate for such grant or Revocation, and making such Order as to the Costs of the Proceedings before him as he may think just. *proved while the Matter is pending.*

LVIII. Any Party who shall be dissatisfied with the Determination of the Judge of the County Court in point of Law, or upon the Admission or Rejection of any Evidence in any Matter or Cause under this Act, may appeal from the same to the Court of Probate, in such Manner and subject to such Regulations as may be provided by the Rules and Orders to be made under this Act, and the Decision of the Court of Probate on such Appeal shall be final. *As to Appeals from County Court.*

LIX. It shall not be obligatory on any Person to apply for Probate or Administration to any District Registry, or through any County Court, but in every Case such Application may be made through the Principal Registry of the Court of Probate, wherever the Testator or Intestate may at the Time of his Death have had his fixed place of Abode: Provided, that where in any contentious Matter arising out of any such Application it is shown to the Court of Probate that the State of the Property and Place of Abode of the Deceased were such as to give contentious Jurisdiction to the Judge of a County Court, the Court of Probate may *Not obligatory to apply for Probate, &c. to District Registries or County Court, but may in every Case be made to Court of Probate.*

send the Cause to such County Court, and the Judge thereof shall proceed therein as if such Application and Cause had been made to and arisen in his Court in the first instance.

Rules and Orders for regulating the Procedure of County Courts under the Act to be made by the Judges now having Authority for the like Purpose.

LX. For regulating the Procedure and Practice of the County Courts, and the Judges, Registrars, and Officers thereof, in relation to their Jurisdiction and Proceedings under this Act, Rules and Orders may be from Time to Time framed, amended, and certified by the County Court judges appointed for the Time being to frame Rules and Orders for regulating the Practice of the County Courts under the Act of the Session holden in the Nineteenth and Twentieth Years of Her Majesty, Chapter One hundred and eight, and shall be subject to be allowed or disallowed or altered, and shall be in force from the Day named for that Purpose by the Lord Chancellor, as in the said Act is provided in relation to other Rules and Orders regulating the Practice of the same Courts; and for establishing Rules and Orders to be in force when this Act comes into operation, the Power given by this Enactment shall be exercised as soon as conveniently may be after the passing of this Act.

Where a Will affecting Real Estate is proved in solemn Form, or is the Subject of a contentious Proceeding, the Heir and Persons interested in the Real Estate to be cited.

LXI. Where Proceedings are taken under this Act for proving a Will in solemn Form, or for revoking the Probate of a Will, on the Ground of the Invalidity thereof, or where in any other contentious Cause or Matter under this Act the Validity of a Will is disputed, unless in the several Cases aforesaid the Will affects only Personal Estate, the Heir-at-Law, Devisees and other Persons having or pretending Interest in the Real Estate affected by the Will shall, subject to the Provisions of this Act, and to the Rules and Orders under this Act, be cited to see Proceedings, or otherwise summoned in like Manner as the Next of Kin or others having or pretending Interest in the Personal Estate affected by a Will should be cited or summoned, and may be permitted to become Parties, or intervene for their respective Interests in such Real Estate, subject to such Rules and Orders, and to the Discretion of the Court.

Where the Will is proved in solemn Form, or its Validity otherwise.

LXII. Where Probate of such Will is granted after such Proof in solemn Form, or where the Validity of the Will is otherwise declared by the Decree or Order in such contentious Cause or Matter as aforesaid, the Probate, Decree, or Order respectively shall enure for the Benefit of all

COURT OF PROBATE ACT, 1857

Persons interested in the Real Estate affected by such Will, and the Probate Copy of such Will, or the Letters of Administration with such Will annexed, or a Copy thereof respectively, stamped with the Seal of Her Majesty's Court of Probate, shall in all Courts, and in all Suits and Proceedings affecting Real Estate, of whatever Tenure (save Proceedings by way of Appeal under this Act, or for the Revocation of such Probate or Administration), be received as conclusive Evidence of the Validity and Contents of such Will, in like Manner as a Probate is received in Evidence in Matters relating to the Personal Estate; and where Probate is refused or revoked, on the Ground of the Invalidity of the Will, or the Invalidity of the Will is otherwise declared by Decree or Order under this Act, such Decree or Order shall enure for the Benefit of the Heir-at-Law or other Persons against whose Interest in Real Estate such Will might operate, and such Will shall not be received in Evidence in any Suit or Proceeding in relation to Real Estate, save in any Proceeding by way of Appeal from such Decrees or Orders. *wise decided on, the Decree of the Court to be binding on the Persons interested in the Real Estate.*

LXIII. Nothing herein contained shall make it necessary to cite the Heir-at-Law or other Persons having or pretending Interest in the Real Estate of a deceased Person, unless it is shown to the Court and the Court is satisfied that the Deceased was at the Time of his Decease seised of or entitled to or had Power to appoint by Will some Real Estate beneficially, or in any Case where the Will propounded or of which the Validity is in question would not in the Opinion of the Court, though established as to Personalty, affect Real Estate, but in every such Case, and in any other Case in which the Court may, with reference to the Circumstances of the Property of the Deceased or otherwise, think fit, the Court may proceed without citing the Heir or other Persons interested in Real Estate; provided that the Probate, Decree, or Order of the Court shall not in any Case affect the Heir or any Person in respect of his Interest in Real Estate, unless such Heir or Person has been cited or made Party to the Proceedings, or derives Title under or through a Person so cited or made Party. *Heir in certain Cases not to be cited, and where not cited not to be affected by Probate.*

LXIV. In any Action at Law or Suit in Equity, where, according to the existing Law, it would be necessary to pro- *Probate or Office Copy to*

234 COURT OF PROBATE ACT, 1857

be Evidence of the Will in Suits concerning Real Estate, save where the Validity of the Will is put in issue.

duce and prove an original Will in order to establish a Devise or other Testamentary Disposition of or affecting Real Estate, it shall be lawful for the Party intending to establish in Proof such Devise or other Testamentary Disposition to give to the opposite Party, Ten Days at least before the Trial or other Proceeding in which the said Proof shall be intended to be adduced, Notice that he intends at the said Trial or other Proceeding to give in Evidence as Proof of the Devise or other Testamentary Disposition the Probate of the said Will or the Letters of Administration with the Will annexed, or a Copy thereof stamped with any Seal of the Court of Probate; and in every such Case such Probate or Letters of Administration, or Copy thereof respectively, stamped as aforesaid, shall be sufficient Evidence of such Will and of its Validity and Contents, notwithstanding the same may not have been proved in solemn Form, or have been otherwise declared valid in a contentious Cause or Matter, as herein provided, unless the Party receiving such Notice shall, within Four Days after such Receipt, give Notice that he disputes the Validity of such Devise or other Testamentary Disposition.

As to Costs of Proof of Will.

LXV. In every Case in which, in any such Action or Suit, the original Will shall be produced and proved, it shall be lawful for the Court or Judge before whom such Evidence shall be given to direct by which of the Parties the Costs thereof shall be paid.

Place of Deposit of original Wills.

LXVI. There shall be One Place of Deposit under the Control of the Court of Probate, at such Place in *London* or *Middlesex* as Her Majesty may by Order in Council direct, in which all the original Wills brought into the Court or of which Probate or Administration with the Will annexed is granted under this Act in the Principal Registry thereof, and Copies of all Wills the Originals whereof are to be preserved in the District Registries, and such other Documents as the Court may direct, shall be deposited and preserved, and may be inspected under the Control of the Court and subject to the Rules and Orders under this Act.

Judge to cause Calendars to be made from

LXVII. The Judge shall cause to be made from Time to Time in the Principal Registry of the Court of Probate Calendars of the Grants of Probate and Administration in the Principal Registry, and in the Several District Registries of the Court, for such Periods as the Judge may think fit, each such Calendar to contain a Note of every Probate or Administration with the Will annexed granted within the Period therein specified, and also a Note of every other Administration granted within the same Period, such respective Notes setting forth the Dates of such Grants, the Registry in which the Grants were made, the Names of the Testators and Intestates, the Place and Time of Death, the Names and Descriptions of the Executors and Administrators, and the Value of the Effects; and the Calendars to be so made shall be printed as the same are from Time to Time completed. *Time to Time in the Principal Registry, and to be printed.*

LXVIII. The Registrars shall cause a printed Copy of every Calendar to be transmitted through the Post or otherwise to each of the District Registries, and to the Office of Her Majesty's Prerogative in *Dublin,* the Office of the Commissary of the County of *Midlothian* in *Edinburgh,* and such other Offices, if any, as the Court of Probate shall from Time to Time by Rule or Order direct; and every printed Copy of a Calendar so transmitted as aforesaid shall be kept in the Registry or Office to which it is transmitted, and may be inspected by any Person on Payment of a Fee of One Shilling for each Search, without reference to the Number of Calendars inspected. *Registrar to transmit printed Copies to certain Offices.*

LXIX. An official Copy of the whole or any Part of a Will, or an official Certificate of the Grant of any Letters of Administration, may be obtained from the Registry or District Registry where the Will has been proved or the Administration granted, on the Payment of such Fees as shall be fixed for the same by the Rules and Orders under this Act. *Official Copy of whole or Part of Will may be obtained.*

LXX. Pending any Suit touching the Validity of the Will of any deceased Person, or for obtaining, recalling, or revoking any Probate or any Grant of Administration, the Court of Probate may appoint an Administrator of the Personal Estate of such deceased Person; and the Administrator so appointed shall have all the Rights and Powers of a General Administrator, other than the Right of distributing the Residue of such Personal Estate; and every such Admistrator shall be subject to the immediate Control of the Court, and act under its Direction. *Administration pendente lite.*

Receiver of Real Estate *pendente lite*. LXXI. It shall be lawful for the Court of Probate to appoint any Administrator appointed as aforesaid or any other Person to be Receiver of the Real Estate of any deceased Person pending any Suit in the Court touching the Validity of any Will of such deceased Person by which his Real Estate may be affected, and such Receiver shall have such Power to receive all Rents and Profits of such Real Estate, and such Powers of letting and managing such Real Estate, as the Court may Direct.

Remuneration to Administrators *pendente lite* and Receivers. LXXII. The Court of Probate may direct that Administrators and Receivers appointed pending Suits involving Matters and Causes Testamentary shall receive out of the Personal and Real Estate of the Deceased such reasonable Remuneration as the Court think fit.

Power as to Appointment of Administrator. LXXIII. Where a Person has died or shall die wholly intestate as to his Personal Estate, or leaving a Will affecting Personal Estate, but without having appointed an Executor thereof willing and competent to take Probate, or where the Executor shall at the Time of the Death of such Person be resident out of the United Kingdom of *Great Britain and Ireland*, and it shall appear to the Court to be necessary or convenient in any such Case, by reason of the Insolvency of the Estate of the Deceased, or other special Circumstances, to appoint some Person to be the Administrator of the Personal Estate of the Deceased, or of any Part of such Personal Estate, other than the Person who if this Act had not been passed would by Law have been entitled to a Grant of Administration of such Personal Estate, it shall not be obligatory upon the Court to grant Administration of the Personal Estate of such deceased Person to the Person who if this Act had not been passed would by Law have been entitled to a Grant thereof, but it shall be lawful for the Court, in its Discretion, to appoint such Person as the Court shall think fit to be such Administrator upon his giving such Security (if any) as the Court shall direct, and every such Administration may be limited as the Court shall think fit.

38 G. 3. c. 87, extended to Administrators. LXXIV. The Provisions of an Act passed in the Thirty-eighth Year of His late Majesty King *George* the Third, Chapter Eighty-seven, shall apply (in like Manner) to all Cases where Letters of Administration have been granted,

and the Person to whom such Administration shall have been granted shall be out of the Jurisdiction of Her Majesty's Courts of Law and Equity.

LXXV. After any Grant of Administration, no Person shall have Power to sue or prosecute any Suit, or otherwise act as Executor of the Deceased, as to the Personal Estate comprised in or affected by such Grant of Administration, until such Administration shall have been recalled or revoked. *After Grant of Administration no Person to have Power to sue as an Executor.*

LXXVI. Where before the Revocation of any temporary Administration any Proceedings at Law or in Equity have been commenced by or against any Administrator so appointed, the Court in which such Proceedings are pending may order that a Suggestion be made upon the Record of the Revocation of such Administration, and of the Grant of Probate or Administration which shall have been made consequent thereupon, and that the Proceedings shall be continued in the Name of the new Executor or Administrator, in like Manner as if the Proceeding had been originally commenced by or against such new Executor or Administrator, but subject to such Conditions and Variations, if any, as such Court may direct. *Revocation of temporary Grants not to prejudice Actions or Suits.*

LXXVII. Where any Probate or Administration is revoked under this Act, all Payments *bonâ fide* made to any Executor or Administrator under such Probate or Administration, before the Revocation thereof, shall be a legal Discharge to the person making the same; and the Executor or Administrator who shall have acted under any such revoked Probate or Administration may retain and reimburse himself in respect of any Payments made by him which the Person to whom Probate or Administration shall be afterwards granted might have lawfully made. *Payments under revoked Probates or Administration to be valid.*

LXXVIII. All Persons and Corporations making or permitting to be made any Payment or Transfer *bonâ fide*, upon any Probate or Letters of Administration granted in respect of the Estate of any deceased Person under the Authority of this Act, shall be indemnified and protected in so doing, notwithstanding any Defect or Circumstance whatsoever affecting the Validity of such Probate or Letters of Administration. *Persons, &c. making Payment upon Probates granted for Estate of deceased Person to be indemnified.*

Rights of an Executor renouncing Probate to cease as if he had not been named in the Will.

LXXIX. Where any Person, after the Commencement of this Act, renounces Probate of the Will of which he is appointed Executor or One of the Executors, the Rights of such Person in respect of the Executorship shall wholly cease, and the Representation to the Testator and the Administration of his Effects shall and may, without any further Renunciation, go, devolve, and be committed in like Manner as if such Person had not been appointed Executor.

Sureties to Administration Bonds.

LXXX. So much of an Act passed in the Twenty-first Year of King *Henry* the Eighth, Chapter Five, and of an Act passed in the Twenty-Second and Twenty-third Years of King *Charles* the Second, Chapter Ten, and of an Act passed in the First Year of King *James* the Second, Chapter Seventeen, as requires any Surety, Bond, or other Security to be taken from a Person to whom Administration shall be committed, shall be repealed.

Persons to whom Grant of Administrations shall be committed shall give Bond.

LXXXI. Every Person to whom any grant of Administration shall be committed shall give Bond to the Judge of the Court of Probate to enure for the Benefit of the Judge for the Time being, and, if the Court of Probate or (in the Case of a Grant from the District Registry) the District Register shall require, with One or more Surety or Sureties, conditioned for duly collecting, getting in, and administering the Personal Estate of the Deceased, which Bond shall be in such Form as the Judge shall from Time to Time by any general or special Order direct: Provided that it shall not be necessary for the Solicitor for the Affairs of the Treasury or the Solicitor of the Duchy of *Lancaster* applying for or obtaining Administration to the Use or Benefit of Her Majesty to give any such Bond as aforesaid.

Penalty on Bond.

LXXXII. Such Bond shall be in a Penalty of double the Amount under which the Estate and Effects of the Deceased shall be sworn, unless the Court or District Registrar, as the Case may be, shall in any Case think fit to direct the same to be reduced, in which Case it shall be lawful for the Court or District Registrar so to do, and the Court or District Registrar may also direct that more Bonds than One shall be given, so as to limit the Liability of any Surety to such Amount as the Court or District Registrar shall think reasonable.

LXXXIII. The Court may, on Application made on Motion or Petition in a summary Way, and on being satisfied that the Condition of any such Bond has been broken, order One of the Registrars of the Court to assign the same to some Person, to be named in such Order, and such Person, his Executors or Administrators, shall thereupon be entitled to sue on the said Bond in his own Name, both at Law and in Equity, as if the same had been originally given to him instead of to the Judge of the Court, and shall be entitled to recover thereon as Trustee for all Persons interested the full Amount recoverable in respect of any Breach of the Condition of the said Bond. . . . *[Power of Court to assign Bond.]*

XCI. One or more safe and convenient Depository or Depositories shall be provided, under the Control and Directions of the Court of Probate, for all such Wills of living Persons as shall be deposited therein for safe Custody; and all Persons may deposit their Wills in such Depository upon Payment of such Fees and under such Regulations as the Judge shall from Time to Time by any Order direct. . . . *[As to Depositories for safe Custody of the Wills of living Persons.]*

XCIII. The Registrars of the Court of Probate shall, within such Period as the Judge shall direct after Probate of any Will or Letters of Administration shall have been granted, deliver or cause to be delivered to the Commissioners of Inland Revenue, or their proper Officer, the following Documents respectively; that is to say, in the Case of a Probate or Administration with a Will annexed a Copy of the Will and the original Affidavit, and in the case of Letters of Administration without a Will annexed such original Affidavit, and in every Case of Letters of Administration a Copy or Extract thereof, and in every Case such Certificate or Note of the Grant as the said Commissioners may require. . . . *[The Registrars to deliver Copies of Wills, &c. to the Commissioners of Inland Revenue.]*

XCV. The Lord Chancellor, with such Assistance as is hereinbefore provided as to Rules and Orders to be made in pursuance of this Act, shall, as soon as conveniently may be after the passing of this Act, fix a Table or Tables of Fees to be taken by the Officers of the Court of Probate, and the Proctors, Solicitors, and Attornies practising therein, including the District Registrars, and the Proctors, Solicitors, and Attornies practising in District Registries, and of Fees to be taken by the Officers of the County Courts, in respect *[Fees to be taken by Officers of Court and by Officers of County Courts.]*

of Business under this Act, and of Fees to be payable in respect of Searches, Inspection, and Printed and other Copies of and Extracts from Records, Wills, and other Documents in the Custody or under the Control of the Court of Probate and the Judge of the Court of Probate, with such Concurrence as is hereinbefore provided in respect of the Amendment of Rules and Orders, is hereby empowered, from Time to Time after this Act shall come into operation, to add to, reduce, alter, or amend such Table or Tables of Fees, as he may see fit : Provided that such Tables of Fees and every Alteration of the same, except so far as respects the Fees which are to be taken by District Registrars, Proctors, and others, for their own Remuneration and to their own Use, shall be subject to the Approval of the Commissioners of Her Majesty's Treasury ; and every such Table of Fees, and every Addition, Reduction, Alteration, or Amendment to, in, or of the same, shall be published in the *London Gazette ;* and no other Fees than those specified and allowed in such Tables of Fees shall be demanded or taken by such Officers and Proctors, Solicitors and Attornies. . . .

Fees not to be paid in Money, but by Stamps. XCVII. None of the Fees payable to the Officers of the Court of Probate, or of any County Court, in respect of Business under this Act, except the Fees of the District Registrars (which are to be taken as their Remuneration, and for their own Use), the Fees of Proctors, Solicitors, and Attornies, and such Fees as may be authorised to be taken for their own Use by Surrogates and Commissioners for administering Oaths, shall be received in Money, but every such Fee shall be collected and received by a Stamp denoting the Amount of the Fee which otherwise would be payable. . . .

No Document to be received or used unless stamped. XCIX. No Document which under this Act, and any Table of Fees for the Time being in force under this Act, ought to have a Stamp in respect of such Fee impressed thereon or affixed thereto, shall be received or filed or be used in relation to any Proceeding in the Court of Probate, or be of any Validity for any Purpose whatsoever, unless or until the same shall have the proper Stamp impressed thereon or affixed thereto : Provided that if any Time it shall appear that any such Document has through Mistake or Inadvertence been received, or filed, or used without having such Stamp impressed thereon or affixed thereto, it shall be lawful for the Judge of the Court of Probate, if he think fit, to order that such stamp shall be impressed thereon or affixed thereto, and thereupon, when a Stamp shall have been impressed on such Document or affixed thereto in compliance with any such Order, such Document and every Proceeding in reference thereto shall be as valid and effectual as if such Stamp had been impressed thereon or affixed thereto in the first instance. . . .

COURT OF PROBATE ACT, 1858

(21 and 22 Vict., c. 95)

X. Where it appears by Affidavit to the Satisfaction of a Registrar of the Principal Registry that the Testator or Intestate in respect of whose Estate a Grant or Revocation of a Grant of Probate or Letters of Administration is applied for had at the Time of his Death his fixed Place of Abode in One of the Districts specified in Schedule (A) to the said "Court of Probate Act," and that the Personal Estate in respect of which such Probate or Letters of Administration are to be or have been granted, exclusive of what the Deceased may have been possessed of or entitled to as a Trustee, and not beneficially, but without deducting anything on account of the Debts due and owing from the Deceased, was at the Time of his Death under the Value of Two hundred Pounds, and that the Deceased at the Time of his Death was not seised or entitled beneficially of or to any Real Estate of the Value of Three hundred Pounds or upwards, the Judge of the County Court having Jurisdiction in the Place in which the Deceased had at the Time of his or her Death a fixed Place of Abode shall have the contentious Jurisdiction and Authority of the Court of Probate in respect of Questions as to the Grant and Revocation of Probate of the Will or Letters of Administration of the Effects of such deceased Person, in case there be any Contention in relation thereto. . . . *Where Personal ty is under 200l. County Court to have Jurisdiction.*

XII. The said Court of Probate Act, Section Fifty-nine, shall, so far as the County Courts or a Judge thereof are concerned, apply to an Application for the Revocation of a Grant of Probate or Administration as well as to an Application for any such Grant. *Sect. 59 of 20 & 21 Vict. c. 77 to apply to Applications for Revocation of Grants.*

COURT OF PROBATE ACT, 1858

Power to make Rules and Orders and frame Scales of Fees for the County Courts.

XIII. The Power and Authority to make Rules and Orders for regulating the Proceedings of the County Courts shall extend and be applicable to all Proceedings in the County Courts under this Act, and also to framing a Scale of Costs and Charges to be paid to Counsel, Proctors, Solicitors, and Attornies, in respect of Proceedings in County Courts, under the said Court of Probate Act or this Act. . . .

An Executor not acting or not appearing to a Citation to be treated as if he had renounced.

XVI. Whenever an Executor appointed in a Will survives the Testator, but dies without having taken Probate, and whenever an Executor named in a Will is cited to take Probate, and does not appear to such Citation, the Right of such Person in respect of the Executorship shall wholly cease, and the Representation to the Testator and the Administration of his Effects shall and may, without any further Renunciation, go, devolve, and be committed in like Manner as if such Person had not been appointed Executor. . . .

Between the Death of the Person deceased and the Grant the Property to vest in the Judge Ordinary.

XIX. From and after the Decease of any Person dying intestate, and until Letters of Administration shall be granted in respect of his Estate and Effects, the Personal Estate and Effects of such deceased Person shall be vested in the Judge of the Court of Probate for the Time being, in the same Manner and to the same Extent as heretofore they vested in the Ordinary.

Second and subsequent Grants to be made where the original Will or the original Letters of Administration are deposited.

XX. All Second and subsequent Grants of Probate or Letters of Administration shall be made in the Principal Registry, or in the District Registry where the original Will is registered or the original Grant of Letters of Administration has been made, or in the District Registry to which the original Will or a registered Copy thereof, or the Record of the original Grant of Administration, have been transmitted, by virtue of a Requisition issued in pursuance of Section Eighty-nine of "The Court of Probate Act"; and for and in respect of such Second or subsequent Grants of Probate or Letters of Administration to be made in a District Registry it shall not be requisite that it should appear by Affidavit that the Testator or Intestate had a fixed Place of Abode within the District in which the Application is made.

COURT OF PROBATE ACT 1858   243

XXI. It shall be lawful for the Court of Probate to require Security by Bond, in such Form as by any Rules and Orders shall from Time to Time be directed, with or without Sureties, from any Receiver of the Real Estate of any deceased Person appointed by the said Court, under Section Seventy-one of "The Court of Probate Act"; and the Court may, on Application, made on Motion or in a summary Way, order One of the Registrars of the Court to assign the same to some Person to be named in such Order; and such Person, his Executors or Administrators, shall thereupon be entitled to sue on the said Security, or put the same in force in his or their own Name or Names, both at Law and in Equity, as if the same had been originally given to him instead of to the Judge of the said Court, and shall be entitled to recover thereon, as Trustee for all Persons interested, the full Amount due in virtue thereof. . . . {The Court of Probate may require Security from a Receiver of Real Estate.}

XXIII. It shall be lawful for a Registrar of the Principal Registry of the Court of Probate, and whether any Suit or other Proceeding shall or shall not be pending in the said Court, to issue a Subpœna requiring any Person to produce and bring into the Principal or any District Registry, or otherwise, as in the said Subpœna may be directed, any Paper or Writing being or purporting to be testamentary, which may be shown to be in the Possession, within the Power, or under the Control of such Person; and such Person, upon being duly served with the said Subpœna, shall be bound to produce and bring in such Paper or Writing, and shall be subject to the like Process of Contempt in case of Default as if he had been a Party to a Suit in the said Court, and had been ordered by the Judge of the Court of Probate to produce and bring in such Paper or Writing. {Registrar may issue Subpœnas to produce Papers, &c.}

XXV. Copies of Wills required to be transmitted by a District Registrar, and certified by him to be correct Copies, under Section Fifty-one of the Court of Probate Act, may be so certified and transmitted under a Stamp provided by the District Registrar for that Purpose, and approved of by the Judge of the Court of Probate. {Copies of Wills may be certified by a Stamp.}

XXVI. Certificates issued from the Principal Registry with reference to Notices of Applications transmitted from the District Registrars under Section Forty-nine of the Court of Probate Act need not be under the Hand of a {Certificates from the Principal Registry may be stamped.}

244   COURT OF PROBATE ACT, 1858

Registrar of the Principal Registry, as required by the said Act, but may be issued under a Stamp provided for that Purpose, and approved of by the Judge of the Court of Probate.

Requisitions may be issued for the Transmission of a single Paper.

XXVII. Whereas Doubts have been entertained whether a Requisition can be issued under Section Eighty-nine of the Court of Probate Act for the Transmission of One or more Papers only, not being all the Papers and Documents in the Custody of the Person to whom any such Requisition may be addressed; Be it therefore enacted and declared, That the said Section shall be construed to extend to all Requisitions, whether for the Transmission of One or of more Records, Wills, Grants, Probates, Letters of Administration, Administration Bonds, Notes of Administration, Court Books, Calendars, Deeds, Processes, Acts, Proceedings, or other Instruments relating exclusively or principally to Matters or Causes Testamentary.

Power to enforce Decree as to Costs.

XXVIII. The Judge of the Court of Probate, and the Registrars of the Principal Registry thereof, shall respectively, in any Case where an Ecclesiastical or other Court having Testamentary Jurisdiction had previously to the Eleventh Day of *January* One thousand eight hundred and fifty-eight made any Order or Decree in respect of Costs, have the same Power of taxing such Costs, and enforcing Payment thereof, or of otherwise carrying such Order or Decree into effect, as if the Cause wherein such Degree was made had been originally commenced and prosecuted in the said Court of Probate: Provided that in taxing any such Costs, or any other Costs incurred in Causes depending in any such Courts before the Time aforesaid, all Fees, Charges, and Expenses shall be allowed which might have been legally made, charged, and enforced according to the Practice of the Prerogative Court of *Canterbury.*

Letters of Administration granted in Ireland not to be resealed in England until sufficient Bond is given.

XXIX. Letters of Administration granted by the Court of Probate in *Ireland* shall not be resealed, under Section Ninety-five of the Twentieth and Twenty-first *Victoria*, Chapter Seventy-nine, until a Certificate has been filed under the Hand of a Registrar of the Court of Probate in *Ireland* that Bond has been given to the Judge of the Court of Probate in *Ireland* in a Sum sufficient in Amount to cover the Property in *England* as well as in *Ireland* in respect of which such Administration is required to be resealed. . . .

XXXI. In Cases where it is necessary to obtain Affidavits, Declarations, or Affirmations to be used in the Court of Probate from Persons residing in Foreign Parts out of Her Majesty's Dominions, the same may be sworn, declared, or affirmed before the Persons empowered to administer Oaths under the Act of the Sixth of *George* the Fourth, Chapter Eighty-seven, or under the Act of the Eighteenth and Nineteenth of *Victoria*, Chapter Forty-two; provided that in Places where there are no such Persons as are mentioned in the said Acts such Affidavits, Declarations, or Affirmations may be made, declared, and affirmed before any Foreign local Magistrate or other Persons having Authority to administer an Oath. *Affidavits, before whom to be sworn, when Parties making them reside in Foreign Parts.*

XXXII. Affidavits, Declarations, and Affirmations to be used in the Court of Probate may be sworn and taken in *Scotland, Ireland*, the *Isle of Man*, the *Channel Islands*, or any Colony, Island, Plantation, or Place out of *England* under the Dominion of Her Majesty, before any Court, Judge, Notary Public, or Person lawfully authorised to administer Oaths in such Country, Colony, Island, Plantation, or Place respectively, or, so far as relates to the *Isle of Man* and the *Channel Islands*, before any Commissary, Ecclesiastical Judge, or Surrogate, who, at the Time of the passing of the Court of Probate Act, was authorised to administer Oaths in the *Isle of Man* or in the *Channel Islands* respectively, and all Registrars and other Officers of the Court of Probate shall take judicial Notice of the Seal or Signature, as the Case may be, of any such Court, Judge, Notary Public, or Person, which shall be attached, suspended, or subscribed to any such Affidavit, Declaration, or Affirmation, or to any other Document. *Affidavits, before whom to be sworn.*

SUPREME COURT OF JUDICATURE ACT, 1873

(36 and 37 Vict., c. 66)

III. From and after the time appointed for the commencement of this Act the several Courts hereinaftermentioned—(that is to say), . . . the Court of Probate . . . shall be united and consolidated together, and shall constitute, under and subject to the provisions of this Act, one Supreme Court of Judicature for England. . . . *Union of existing Courts into one Supreme Court.*

Constitution of High Court of Justice. V. Her Majesty's High Court of Justice shall be constituted as follows: The first Judges thereof shall be . . . the Judge of the Court of Probate . . .

Jurisdiction of High Court of Justice. XVI. Subject as in this Act mentioned, there shall be transferred to and vested in the said High Court of Justice the jurisdiction which at the commencement of this Act was vested in, or capable of being exercised by, all or any of the Courts following (that is to say);—
(6.) The Court of Probate. . . .

Divisions of High Court of Justice. XXXI. For the more convenient despatch of business in the said High Court of Justice . . . there shall be in the said High Court five[1] Divisions. . . .

(5.) One . . . Division shall consist of two Judges, who, immediately on the commencement of this Act, shall be the existing Judge of the Court of Probate and of the Court for Divorce and Matrimonial Causes and the existing Judge of the High Court of Admiralty, unless either of them is appointed an ordinary Judge of the Court of Appeal. The existing Judge of the Court of Probate shall (unless so appointed) be the President of the said Division, and subject thereto the senior Judge of the said Division, according to the order of precedence under this Act, shall be President.[2]

The said five Divisions shall be called respectively . . . the Probate, Divorce, and Admiralty Division. . . .

Assignment of certain business to particular Divisions of the High Court, subject to Rules. XXXIV. There shall be assigned . . . to the Probate, Divorce, and Admiralty Division of the said High Court
(2.) All causes and matters which would have been within the exclusive jurisdiction of the Court of Probate . . . if this Act had not passed.

SUPREME COURT OF JUDICATURE ACT, 1875

(38 and 39 Vict., c. 77)

Provision as to Rules of Probate, Divorce, and Admiralty Courts, being Rules of XVIII. All Rules and Orders of Court in force at the time of the commencement of this Act in the Court of Probate . . . shall remain and be in force in the High Court of Justice . . . until they shall . . . be altered or annulled by

[1] Since reduced to three.
[2] By 44 and 45 Vict., c. 68, s. 4, the President is an *ex officio* judge of the Court of Appeal.

CUSTOMS AND INLAND REVENUE ACT, 1881   247

. . . any Rules of Court made after the commencement of this Act. The President for the time being of the Probate and Divorce Division [1] of the High Court of Justice shall have with regard to non-contentious or common form business in the Probate Court the powers now conferred on the Judge of the Probate Court by the thirtieth section of the twentieth and twenty-first years of Victoria, chapter seventy-seven, . . . and the said President shall have the powers as to the making of rules and regulations conferred by the fifty-third section of the twentieth and twenty-first years of Victoria, chapter eighty-five.
the High Court, in Substitution for 36 & 37 Vict., c. 66, s. 70.

CUSTOMS AND INLAND REVENUE ACT, 1881
(44 Vict., c. 12)

XXVII. The duties imposed by the Customs and Inland Revenue Act, 1880, upon probates of wills and letters of administration in England and Ireland shall not be payable upon probates or letters of administration granted on and after the first day of June one thousand eight hundred and eighty-one ; and on and after that day, in substitution for such duties, and in lieu of the duties imposed by the said Act upon inventories in Scotland; there shall, save as is hereinafter expressly provided, be charged and paid on the affidavit to be required and received from the person applying for the probate or letters of administration in England or Ireland, or on the inventory to be exhibited and recorded in Scotland, the stamp duties hereinafter specified ; (that is to say),
Grant of duties in respect of probate and letters of administration and on inventories.

Where the estate and effects for or in respect of which the probate or letters of administration is or are to be granted, or whereof the inventory is to be exhibited and recorded, exclusive of what the deceased shall have been possessed of

[1] *Sic.* Admiralty appears to have been temporarily forgotten by the draughtsman.

248   CUSTOMS AND INLAND REVENUE ACT, 1881

A.D. 1881.

	DUTY.
or entitled to as trustee, and not beneficially, shall be above the value of £100, and not above the value of £500	At the rate of one pound for every full sum of £50, and for any fractional part of £50 over any multiple of £50;
Where such estate and effects shall be above the value of £500, and not above the value of £1000	At the rate of one pound five shillings for every full sum of £50, and for any fractional part of £50 over any multiple of £50;
Where such estate and effects shall be above the value of £1000	At the rate of three pounds for every full sum of £100, and for any fractional part of £100 over any multiple of £100;

Provided that an additional inventory, to be exhibited or recorded in Scotland, of any effects of a deceased person, where a former inventory of the estate and effects of the same person has been exhibited and recorded prior to the first day of June one thousand eight hundred and eighty-one, shall be chargeable with the amount of stamp duty with which it would have been chargeable if this Act had not been passed.

Power to deduct debts and funeral expenses where deceased died domiciled

XXVIII. On and after the first day of June one thousand eight hundred and eighty-one, in the case of a person dying domiciled in any part of the United Kingdom, it shall be lawful for the person applying for the probate or letters of administration in England or Ireland, or exhibiting the inventory in Scotland, to state in his affidavit the fact of such domicil, and to deliver therewith or annex thereto a schedule of the debts due from the deceased to persons resident in the United Kingdom, and the funeral expenses, and in that case, for the purpose of the charge of duty on the affidavit or inventory, the aggregate amount of the debts and funeral expenses appearing in the schedule shall be deducted from the value of the estate and effects as specified in the account delivered with or annexed to the affidavit, or whereof the inventory shall be exhibited. A.D. 1881.
in the
United
King-
dom.

Debts to be deducted under the power hereby given shall be debts due and owing from the deceased and payable by law out of any part of the estate and effects comprised in the affidavit or inventory, and are not to include voluntary debts expressed to be payable on the death of the deceased, or payable under any instrument which shall not have been *bonâ fide* delivered to the donee thereof three months before the death of the deceased, or debts in respect whereof any real estate may be primarily liable or a reimbursement may be capable of being claimed from any real estate of the deceased or from any other estate or person.

Funeral expenses to be deducted under the power hereby given shall include only such expenses as are allowable as reasonable funeral expenses according to law.

XXIX. The affidavit to be required or received from any person applying for probate or letters of administration in England or Ireland shall extend to the verification of the account of the estate and effects, or to the verification of such account and the schedule of debts and funeral expenses, as the case may be, and shall be in accordance with such form as may be prescribed by the Commissioners of Her Majesty's Treasury; and the Commissioners of Inland Revenue shall provide forms of affidavit stamped to denote the duties payable under this Act. As to forms of affidavit.

XXX. No probate or letters of administration shall be granted by the Probate, Divorce, and Admiralty Division of the High Court of Justice in England, or by the Probate and Matrimonial Division of the High Court of Justice in Ireland, unless the same bear a certificate in writing under the hand of the proper officer of the court, showing that the affidavit for the Commissioners of Inland Revenue has been delivered and that such affidavit, if liable to stamp Probate or letters of administration to bear a certificate in lieu of stamp duty.

250 CUSTOMS AND INLAND REVENUE ACT, 1881

A.D. 1881.

Provisions as to obtaining probate, &c. where gross value of estate does not exceed 300*l.*

duty, was duly stamped, and stating the amount of the gross value of the estate and effects as shown by the account.

XXXIII. (1.) Where the whole personal estate and effects of any person dying on or after the first day of June one thousand eight hundred and eighty-one (inclusive of property by law made such personal estate and effects for the purpose of the charge of duty, and any personal estate and effects situate out of the United Kingdom), without any deduction for debts or funeral expenses, shall not exceed the value of three hundred pounds, it shall be lawful for the person intending to apply for probate or letters of administration in England or Ireland, to deliver to the proper officer of the court or to any officer of inland revenue duly appointed for the purpose, a notice in writing in the prescribed form, setting forth the particulars of such estate and effects, and such further particulars as may be required to be stated therein, and to deposit with him the sum of fifteen shillings for fees of court and expenses, and also, in case the estate and effects shall exceed the value of one hundred pounds, the further sum of thirty shillings for stamp duty.

(2.) If the officer has good reason to believe that the whole personal estate and effects of the deceased exceeds the value of three hundred pounds, he shall refuse to accept the notice and deposit until he is satisfied of the true value thereof.

(3.) The principal registrars of the Probate, Divorce, and Admiralty Division of the High Court of Justice in England, and of the Probate and Matrimonial Division of the High Court of Justice in Ireland, in communication with the Commissioners of Inland Revenue, shall prescribe the form of notice, and make such regulations as may be necessary with respect to the transmission of notices by officers of Inland Revenue, the steps to be taken for the preparation and filling up of forms and documents, and generally all matters which may be necessary, so as to authorise the grant of probate or letters of administration.

(4.) Officers of Inland Revenue are hereby empowered to administer all necessary oaths or affirmations, and in the case of letters of administration, to attest the bond

CUSTOMS AND INLAND REVENUE ACT, 1881 251

and accept the same on behalf of the President or Judge of A.D. 1881.
the Division.

(5.) Where the estate and effects shall exceed the value of one hundred pounds, the stamp duty payable on the affidavit for the Commissioners of Inland Revenue shall be the fixed duty of thirty shillings, and no more.

XXXIV. (1.) The Intestates, Widows, and Children (Scotland) Act, 1875, and the Small Testate Estate (Scotland) Act, 1876, as amended by the Sheriffs Court (Scotland) Act, 1876, shall be extended so as to apply to any case where the whole personal estate and effects of a person dying on or after the first day of June one thousand eight hundred and eighty-one, without any deduction for debts or funeral expenses, shall not exceed the value of three hundred pounds, whoever may be the applicant for representation, and wheresoever the deceased may have been domiciled at the time of death, and the fees payable under schedule (C.) of each of the two first-mentioned Acts shall not exceed the sum of fifteen shillings, inclusive of the fee of two shillings and sixpence, to be paid to the commissary clerk, or sheriff clerk. *Provision as to inventories where gross value of estate does not exceed 300l. 39 & 40 Vict. c. 24. 39 & 40 Vict. c. 70.*

(2.) In any such case where the estate and effects shall exceed the value of one hundred pounds, the stamp duty payable on the inventory shall be the fixed duty of thirty shillings, and no more.

XXXV. Where representation has been obtained in conformity with either of the two preceding sections, and it shall be at any time afterwards discovered that the whole personal estate and effects of the deceased were of a value exceeding three hundred pounds, then a sum equal to the stamp duty payable on an affidavit or inventory in respect of the true value of such estate and effects shall be a debt due to Her Majesty from the person acting in the administration of such estate and effects, and no allowance shall be made in respect of the sums deposited or paid by him, nor shall the relief afforded by the next succeeding section be claimed or allowed by reason of the deposit or payment of any sum. *Provision in case of subsequent discovery that the value of estate exceeded 300l.*

XXXVI. The payment of the sum of thirty shillings for the fixed duty on the affidavit or inventory in conformity with this Act shall be deemed to be in full satisfaction *Relief from legacy duty in cases under 300l.*

A.D. 1889. of any claim to legacy duty or succession duty in respect of the estate or effects to which such affidavit or inventory relates.

TRUST INVESTMENT ACT, 1889

(52 and 53 Vict., c. 32)

Authorised Investments.

III. It shall be lawful for a trustee, unless expressly forbidden by the instrument (if any) creating the trust, to invest any trust funds in his hands in manner following, that is to say:—

(*a*) In any of the Parliamentary Stocks or Public Funds or Government Securities of the United Kingdom:

(*b*) On Real or Heritable Securities in Great Britain or Ireland:

(*c*) In the Stock of the Bank of England or the Bank of Ireland:

(*d*) In India Three-and-a-half per Cent Stock and India Three per Cent Stock, or in any other Capital Stock which may at any time hereafter be issued by the Secretary of State in Council of India, under the authority of Act of Parliament, and charged on the revenues of India:

(*e*) In any securities the interest of which is or shall be guaranteed by Parliament:

(*f*) In Consolidated Stock created by the Metropolitan Board of Works, or which may at any time hereafter be created by the London County Council, or in Debenture Stock created by the Receiver for the Metropolitan Police District:

(*g*) In the Debenture or Rentcharge or Guaranteed or Preference Stock of any railway company in Great Britain or Ireland incorporated by special Act of Parliament, and having during each of the ten years last past before the date of investment paid a dividend at the rate of not less than three per centum per annum on its ordinary stock:

(*h*) In the stock of any railway or canal company in Great Britain or Ireland whose undertaking is leased in perpetuity or for a term of not less than two hundred years at a fixed rental to any such railway company as is mentioned in sub-section (g) either alone or jointly with any other railway company:

(i) In the Debenture Stock of any railway company in India the interest on which is paid or guaranteed by the Secretary of State in Council of India:

(j) In the "B" Annuities of the Eastern Bengal, the East Indian and the Scinde Punjaub and Delhi Railways, and any like annuities which may at any time hereafter be created on the purchase of any other railway by the Secretary of State in Council of India, and charged on the revenues of India, and which may be authorised by Act of Parliament to be accepted by trustees in lieu of any stock held by them in the purchased railway:

(k) In the stock of any railway company in India upon which a fixed or minimum dividend in sterling is paid or guaranteed by the Secretary of State in Council of India:

(l) In the Debenture or Guaranteed or Preference Stock of any company in Great Britain or Ireland, established for the supply of water for profit, and incorporated by special Act of Parliament or by Royal Charter, and having during each of the ten years last past before the date of investment paid a dividend of not less than five pounds per centum on its Ordinary Stock:

(m) In nominal or inscribed stock issued, or to be issued, by the corporation of any municipal borough, having according to the returns of the last census prior to the date of investment a population exceeding fifty thousand, or by any county council, under the authority of any Act of Parliament or Provisional Order:

(n) In nominal or inscribed stock issued or to be issued by any Commissioners incorporated by Act of Parliament for the purpose of supplying water, and having a compulsory power of levying rates over an area having, according to the returns of the last census prior to the date of investment, a population exceeding fifty thousand, provided that during each of the ten years last past before the date of investment the rates levied by such Commissioners shall not have exceeded eighty per centum of the amount authorised by law to be levied:

(o) In any of the stocks, funds, or securities, for the time being authorised for the investment of cash under the control or subject to the order of the Court:

and also from time to time to vary any such investment.

Purchase at a premium of redeemable stocks.
IV. (1.) It shall be lawful for a trustee under the powers of this Act to invest in any of the stocks, funds, shares, or securities mentioned or referred to in section three of this Act, notwithstanding that the same may be redeemable, and that the price exceeds the redemption value.

(2.) Provided that it shall not be lawful for a trustee under the powers of this Act to purchase at a price exceeding its redemption value any stock mentioned or referred to in sub-sections (g), (i), (k), (l), and (m), which is liable to be redeemed within fifteen years of the date of purchase at par or at some other fixed rate, or to purchase any such stock as is mentioned or referred to in the sub-sections aforesaid, which is liable to be redeemed at par or at some other fixed rate, at a price exceeding fifteen per centum above par or such other fixed rate.

(3.) It shall be lawful for a trustee to retain until redemption any redeemable stock, fund, or security which may have been purchased in accordance with the powers of this Act.

Discretion of trustees.
V. Every power conferred by this Act shall be exercised according to the discretion of the trustee, but subject to any consent required by the instrument (if any) creating the trust with respect to the investment of the trust funds. . . .

Interpretation.
IX. For the purpose of this Act the following terms have the meanings hereinafter respectively assigned to them, that is to say:—

The expression "trustee" shall include an executor or administrator. . . .

APPENDIX B

FEES IN THE PRINCIPAL AND DISTRICT PROBATE REGISTRIES OF THE HIGH COURT OF JUSTICE IN NON-CONTENTIOUS BUSINESS (depending chiefly on rules framed in 1874):

FOR probates or letters of administration with or without a will annexed, under seal, when the gross value of the personal estate does not exceed £300, and (if stamp duty is payable) a stamp of £1 : 10s. is paid upon the affidavit.

A fee to cover all expenses, whether such grant is obtained on personal application or otherwise, 15s.

For probates or letters of administration with will annexed, including double or cessate probates or letters of administration with will annexed, *de bonis non* or cessate, upon which the stamp duty is payable in respect of the value of the Personal Estate of the Testator.

If the Personal Estate is sworn to be—

Under the value of:—				Under the value of:—			
£5	£0	1	0	6,000	£5	0	0
20	0	1	0	7,000	5	5	0
100	0	1	0	8,000	5	10	0
200	0	3	0	9,000	5	15	0
300	0	7	6	10,000	6	0	0
450	0	12	0	12,000	6	5	0
600	0	16	6	14,000	6	10	0
800	1	2	6	16,000	6	17	6
1,000	1	13	0	18,000	7	5	0
1,500	2	5	0	20,000	7	12	6
2,000	3	0	0	25,000	8	2	6
3,000	3	15	0	30,000	8	15	0
4,000	4	10	0	35,000	9	7	3
5,000	4	15	0	40,000	10	6	0

256 FEES

Under the value of:

		£	s.	d.
45,000	.	£11	5	6
50,000	.	12	3	6
60,000	.	13	2	6
70,000	.	15	0	0
80,000	.	16	17	6
90,000	.	18	15	0
100,000	.	20	12	6
120,000	.	21	11	3
140,000	.	23	8	9
160,000	.	25	6	3
180,000	.	27	3	9
200,000	.	29	1	3

Under the value of:

		£	s.	d.
250,000	.	£30	18	9
300,000	.	35	12	9
350,000	.	40	6	3
400,000	.	41	17	6
500,000	.	43	8	9

For every additional £100,000 or any fractional part of £100,000 a further and additional fee of . . . 3 2 6

LETTERS OF ADMINISTRATION,

including letters of administration *de bonis non* or cessate, upon which Stamp Duty is payable in respect of the personal estate of an intestate.

If the personal estate is sworn to be:—

Under the value of:—

		£	s.	d.
£5	.	£0	1	0
20	.	0	1	0
50	.	0	1	0
100	.	0	1	0
200	.	0	4	6
300	.	0	12	0
450	.	0	16	6
600	.	1	2	6
800	.	1	13	0
1,000	.	2	5	0
1,500	.	3	7	6
2,000	.	4	10	0
3,000	.	4	13	9
4,000	.	4	17	6
5,000	.	5	5	0
6,000	.	5	12	6
7,000	.	6	0	0
8,000	.	6	7	6
9,000	.	6	15	0
10,000	.	7	2	6
12,000	.	7	10	0
14,000	.	7	17	6
16,000	.	8	8	9
18,000	.	9	0	0
20,000	.	9	11	3
25,000	.	10	6	3

Under the value of:—

		£	s.	d.
£30,000	.	£11	5	0
35,000	.	12	3	9
40,000	.	13	11	3
45,000	.	15	0	0
50,000	.	16	7	6
60,000	.	17	6	3
70,000	.	20	12	6
80,000	.	23	8	9
90,000	.	26	5	0
100,000	.	29	1	3
120,000	.	30	9	6
140,000	.	33	5	6
160,000	.	36	2	0
180,000	.	38	18	3
200,000	.	41	14	6
250,000	.	44	10	9
300,000	.	46	17	6
350,000	.	49	4	6
400,000	.	51	11	3
500,000	.	53	18	3

For every additional £100,000 or any fractional part of £100,000 a further and additional fee of . . . 4 13 6

The following additional fees are to be taken in the

principal and district probate registries in non-contentious business on personal applications:—

For preparing oaths of executors or administrators, and affidavits for the Inland Revenue Office, for engrossing and collating the will (if three folios of ninety words or under) for clerks; also for administering oaths or affirmations to executors or administrators and for preparing bonds for administrators and attesting execution of bonds, a uniform fee of . . . . . . £0 : 15 : 0

For probates or letters of administration with or without a will annexed under seal—including double or cessate probates or letters of administration with or without a will annexed *de bonis non* or cessate—upon which stamp duty is payable in respect of the personal estate of the testator or intestate:

If the personal estate for or in respect of which stamp duty is payable is under or not exceeding:—

£100	. . £0 1 0		£40,000	. .	£5 18 3
200	. . 0 3 0		45,000	. .	6 7 6
300	. . 0 5 0		50,000	. .	6 17 0
450	. . 0 8 0		60,000	. .	7 6 3
600	. . 0 11 0		70,000	. .	8 5 0
800	. . 0 15 0		80,000	. .	9 3 9
1,000	. . 1 2 0		90,000	. .	10 2 6
1,500	. . 1 10 0		100,000	. .	11 1 3
2,000	. . 2 0 0		120,000	. .	11 10 9
3,000	. . 2 10 0		140,000	. .	12 9 6
4,000	. . 3 0 0		160,000	. .	13 8 3
5,000	. . 3 2 6		180,000	. .	14 7 0
6,000	. . 3 5 0		200,000	. .	15 5 9
7,000	. . 3 7 6		250,000	. .	16 4 6
8,000	. . 3 10 0		300,000	. .	18 11 3
9,000	.· . 3 12 6		350,000	. .	20 18 3
10,000	. . 3 15 0		400,000	. .	21 13 9
12,000	. . 3 17 6		500,000	. .	22 9 6
14,000	. . 4 0 0		And for every additional £100,000 or any fractional part of £100,000, on which stamp duty is payable, a further fee of . . .		1 11 3
16,000	. . 4 3 9				
18,000	. . 4 7 6				
20,000	. . 4 11 3				
25,000	. . 4 16 3				
30,000	. . 5 2 5				
35,000	. . 5 8 9				

Double or cessate probate or letters of administration with the will annexed, *de bonis non* or cessate, upon which no stamp duty is payable, when the personal estate is under £450, are charged with the same fee as a grant under the same sum, £450 or upwards, 12s. 6d. Duplicate or triplicate probate or letters of administration with the will annexed are charged at the same rate.

Exemplification of a probate or letters of administration with the will annexed or ordinary administration, £1 : 1s.

Codicils to wills already proved at the same rate as duplicate probates.

Fees are also chargeable for registering and collating or engrossing and collating wills, for searches and inspection of wills (the fee for search and inspection, which allows inspection of two wills or letters of administration, being one shilling), sealing, notation of domicile, office copies or extracts, collating, attendances, filing, registrar's orders, caveats, receipts for papers, deposit of wills, taxing costs, bonds, oaths, settling advertisements, alterations in grants, notations of alterations, etc., certificates, fiats, notices, perusing and settling oaths, etc.

The fee on administrations upon which no stamp duty is payable is when the personal estate is under £300 the same fee as on a first grant, where it is £300 or upwards the same as in corresponding cases of probate, viz. 12s. 6d.

APPENDIX C

Personal Applications

Rules, Orders, and Instructions as to Personal Applications for grants of probate or letters of administration.

1. Persons wishing to obtain grants of probate or letters of administration without the intervention of a proctor, solicitor, or attorney, must apply in person at the department for personal applications, and not by letter.

2. No such application will be received through an agent of any kind (whether paid or unpaid).

3. The applications of parties who are attended by a person acting or appearing to act as their adviser in the matter will not be entertained.

4. All fees are to be paid in advance in Probate Court stamps.

5. Applications which have in the first instance been made through a proctor, solicitor, or attorney at the principal registry or at a district registry cannot be transferred to this department.

6. Applications for grants of probate or administration in cases which have already been before the court (on motion or otherwise) will not be entertained at this department, but must be made through a proctor, solicitor, or attorney.

7. Whenever it becomes necessary, in the course of proceeding with an application which has been entertained at this department, to obtain the directions of the court, the application will not be proceeded with, but must be placed in the hands of a proctor, solicitor, or attorney.

8. The papers necessary to lead to the grant applied for will be prepared in this department. An applicant is, how-

ever, at liberty to bring such papers, or any of them, filled up, but not sworn to, and the same, if correct, may be received (the usual fee for perusal being charged). All further papers which may be required will be drawn in this department. Testamentary papers once deposited in this department will not be given out unless under special circumstances and by permission of one of the registrars.

9. When it is necessary to administer an oath or take an affirmation, the party shall be sworn or affirmed before some proper authority of the principal registry or of a district registry unless otherwise permitted by one of the registrars.

10. Every applicant for a first grant of probate or letters of administration must produce a certificate of the death or burial of the deceased, or give a reason to the satisfaction of one of the registrars for the non-production thereof.

11. Every applicant must be prepared with a reference to some person of position or character to establish his or her identity.

12. The engrossment of wills and testamentary papers will be made in the registry.

13. Every applicant for a grant of probate or letters of administration shall give under his or her hand a schedule of the property to be affected by the grant in the form hereunto annexed, marked A. (The necessary forms will be provided in the registry.)

14. Legal advice is not to be given to applicants, either with respect to the property to be included in the above-mentioned schedule, or upon any other matter connected with the application, and the clerks in this department are only to be held responsible for embodying in a proper form the instructions given to them; but they will as far as practicable assist applicants by giving them information and directions as to the course which they must pursue.

15. A receipt or acknowledgment of each application will be handed to the applicant, and the production of such receipt will be required of the person who attends to obtain the grant when completed.

16. No clerk or officer of this department is to become surety to any administration bond.

17. All administration bonds in cases of personal ap-

plications are to be executed in this department or in a district registry. If executed in this department the bond must be attested by the chief clerk or senior clerk in attendance.

(A) An Account of the Personal Estate and Effects of deceased.

(No deductions to be made on account of debts owing by deceased.)

	Price of Stocks.	Actual Value.		
		£	s.	d.
Cash in the House and at the Bankers' . Household Goods, Linen, Wearing Apparel, Books, Plate, Jewels, Carriages, Horses, &c., valued at				
Stocks or Funds of Great Britain transferable at the Bank or elsewhere in England, viz. Dividends thereon . . .				
Foreign Stocks or Funds transferable in England, viz. . . . . Dividends thereon				
Leasehold Property— Value per annum . . . . . Ground Rent on do. per annum . . Length of unexpired term . . .				
Rents of Real or Leasehold Property due at the death of the Deceased . . . Do. of Leasehold Property due since the death of the Deceased				
Proprietary Shares or Debentures of Public Companies, viz. . . . . . Dividends or Interest thereon .				
Money out on Mortgage and other Securities Dividends or Interest thereon .				
Book Debts				
Bonds and Bills . . . . . . Notes . . . . Interest thereon , . .				

	Price of Stocks.	Actual Value.
		£ s. d.
Real Estate contracted to be Sold . .		
Personal Estate and Effects left by the Will under some authority enabling the Deceased to dispose of the same as he or she might think fit		
Stock-in-Trade, Farming Stock, and Implements of Husbandry, valued at . .		
Other Personal Property not comprised under the foregoing heads, viz. . .		

APPENDIX D

Forms of Wills

A SIMPLE form of both an English and a Scotch will is appended, not so much as a precedent to be followed as an illustration of the law. Some forms of bequest of a special nature which are likely to be useful are also added. It cannot, however, be too strongly impressed upon intending testators that in all but in the very simplest cases or in some sudden emergency the comparatively trifling sum necessary to obtain professional assistance is money well spent. In the forms punctuation is used in order that they may be more easily read; in wills prepared by counsel or solicitors, as in deeds, stops are not usually inserted, as they may possibly lead to difficulties in interpretation.

An English Will of Real and Personal Estate

(From Davidson's *Concise Precedents in Conveyancing*, No. civ)

I, A. B., of   hereby revoke all wills and testamentary dispositions heretofore made by me, and declare this to be my last will. I bequeath to my wife C. B. all my furniture, plate, plated articles, linen, china, glass, wines, liquors, consumable stores, and articles of household and domestic use and ornament; I bequeath to my said wife the sum of £   to be paid to her within one calendar month after my death,[1] and the further sum of £   to be paid to her within three

---

[1] This provision is commonly made in order that the legatee may not be left without ready money for current expenses.

years after my death, with interest thereon at the rate of £   per cent per annum from the day of my decease, to be paid by equal half-yearly payments, the first thereof to be made at the end of six calendar months from my death; I bequeath to my said wife my leasehold messuage, No.   in   Street, London, she paying the rent reserved by the lease under which I hold the same, and performing and observing the covenants by the lessee and conditions therein contained, and indemnifying my executors and administrators therefrom, and from all actions and demands in respect thereof; I bequeath to my son E. B. and to each of my daughters F. B., G. B., and H. B. the sum of £   ; I devise unto my son J. B., his heirs and assigns,[1] my freehold farm, lands, and hereditaments, situate in or near the parish of   in the county of   , with the appurtenances subject nevertheless in exoneration of my personal estate[2] to the payment of a principal sum of £   now owing to X. Y. on the security of a mortgage thereof, and the interest for the same; and I hereby devise and bequeath all my real and personal estate, except what I otherwise dispose of by this my will or by any codicil thereto, unto my son A. B., his heirs, executors, administrators, and assigns,[3] charged as to my real estate, in aid of my personal estate, with the payment of my debts, and the pecuniary legacies hereinbefore bequeathed. And I hereby appoint my said son A. B. sole executor of this my will. In witness whereof I, the said A. B.,   have to this my will set my hand this   day of   18 .   (Signature of testator.)

Signed and acknowledged by the above-named A. B. as his will in the presence of us, present at the same time, who in his presence and in the presence of each other, have hereunto subscribed our names as witnesses.

(Signatures and descriptions of witnesses.)

[1] In this precedent the children are supposed to be adult, and there is no trust for maintenance of infants or investment of their shares.
[2] These words are not necessary, as a gift to A simply passes to him the fullest estate, real or personal, of the testator in the subject of the gift.
[3] These words are inserted *ex majori cantelâ* in order to avoid the difficulties which have sometimes arisen under Locke King's Act and the acts amending it. See p. 160.

FORM OF A CODICIL SUBSTITUTING A NEW EXECUTOR

This is a codicil to the will of me A. B. of   which will bears date the   day of   18   Whereas by my said will I appointed C. D. executor. Now I revoke my said will as far as the said C. D. is concerned and I substitute E. F. in his place. And I declare that my said will shall take effect in the same manner as if the name of the said E. F. had been originally inserted therein instead of the name of the said C. D., And I confirm my said will in other respects. In witness whereof, etc.

A BEQUEST TO A CHARITY

(From Hayes and Jarman's *Concise Forms*, No. vi)

I bequeath the charitable legacies following (namely) : To the Society for   the sum of   : To etc. And I direct that the said charitable legacies be paid exclusively out of such part of my personal estate as may lawfully be appropriated to such purposes and in preference to any other payment thereout [1] And that the receipt of the Treasurer for the time being of the said Societies respectively shall be a sufficient discharge to my executors for the said charitable legacies respectively.

A DEVISE AND BEQUEST IN TRUST FOR SALE AND CONVERSION FOR WIDOW AND CHILDREN

(From Davidson's *Concise Precedents in Conveyancing*, No. xcix)

I devise and bequeath all my real and personal estate whatsoever (except what I otherwise dispose of by this my

---

[1] The object of this phrase is to prevent the gift to the charity failing in whole or in part through the operation of the rule (p. 162) that the court does not marshal assets in favour of a charity. By the insertion of a direction such as that in the text the debts and funeral and testamentary expenses will be thrown upon the whole fund of pure and mixed personalty, and the charitable legacies will only fail or abate in the event of the entire property, exclusive of the pure personalty, being insufficient for the payment of the debts and funeral and testamentary expenses.

will or any codicil hereto) unto and to the use of C. D. &
E. F., their heirs, executors, and administrators respectively
upon trust, that they the said C. D. & E. F. or the survivors
or survivor of them, or the heirs, executors, or administrators
(as the case may be) of such survivor, shall in such manner,
and under such stipulations, and upon such terms, in all
respects as he or they shall think fit, sell, collect, or otherwise convert into money (according to the nature of the
premises) all such parts of the same premises as shall not
consist of ready money, and may buy in or rescind any
contract for sale or of any other description, and may, for
the purposes aforesaid, execute and do all such assurances
and things as they, or he, shall think fit; And shall, out of
the monies to arise from such sale, collection, and conversion,
and the money of which I shall be possessed at my death,
pay my funeral and testamentary expenses and debts; And
shall invest [*in named securities with power to vary investments*]; And shall pay the income of the said trust monies
and the investments for the time being, representing the
same to my wife G. H. during her life, such income in the
event of her re-marriage to be for her separate use without
power of anticipation, and her receipt alone to be a discharge
for the same; And after her death shall hold the said trust
premises in trust for such of my children living at my death,
and such of my grandchildren living at my death, and being
children of any child of mine having predeceased me, as
being male, attain the age of twenty-one years, or being
female, attain that age, or marry, and if more that one, in
equal shares *per stirpes*, so that my children taking under
this trust shall take in equal shares, and the children taking
under this trust, of any child of mine having predeceased
me, shall take equally between them the share which the
parent would have taken had he or she survived me.

A Scotch Trust Disposition and Settlement

(From 1 *Juridical Styles*, 286)

I, A, having resolved to provide for the settlement of my
affairs in the event of my death, do hereby leave and
bequeath and assign and dispone to and in favour of B. as

his absolute property the whole means, estate, and effects, heritable and moveable, real and personal, of whatever kind and wherever situated, presently belonging and addebted, or which shall belong and be addebted to me at the time of my death; and I nominate the said B. to be my sole executor and administrator; but declaring always that the said B. shall be bound out of my said means and estate to pay all my lawful debts, deathbed and funeral expenses, and also to pay or deliver the following legacies, viz. (specifying them), and also any other legacies or bequests which I may leave, or direct to be paid by any writing under my hand, whether formally executed or not,[1] and I reserve power to revoke or alter these presents in whole or in part; and I reserve my own life-rent; and I dispense with the delivery hereof, and I consent to registration hereof for preservation. In witness whereof these presents, consisting of this and the   preceding pages, with the marginal additions upon pages   and   , all written by   (declaring that the words on the line of page   hereof are written upon an erasure [or, are delete] before subscription) are subscribed by me, the said A, at   on the   day of ·   18   before these witnesses, W. and Y. (fully describing them).[2]

(Signatures of testator and witnesses.)

A Bequest to a Charity in a Scotch Will

(From 2 *Juridical Styles*, 569)

I ordain my said executor to pay and deliver the following legacies......Item, to the Royal Infirmary of Edinburgh the sum of £1000 sterling to be paid upon the receipt of the Treasurer or Secretary thereof for the time being for the purposes of the said infirmary.

---

[1] This would not be a valid clause in an English will. By English law an existing writing may be incorporated, though not duly executed, but no provision can be made for future disposition by informal writing. See p. 31.

[2] By s. 38 of the Conveyancing Act, 1874, the testing clause in use before that act was enabled to be considerably simplified, but the longer form is still commonly used.

A Clause of Mortification

(From 2 *Juridical Styles*, 633)

And farther, for the purpose of establishing four bursaries in the college of M., I do hereby leave and bequeath to the Principal and Professors of the said college of M. the sum of £4000 for maintaining and educating four students in that college, which sum I will and ordain to be invested and employed in manner following, viz. etc.

A Bequest of a Business

(From Bythewood and Jarman's *Precedents in Conveyancing*, vol. vii, p. 777)

I bequeath unto C. D. absolutely all the stock in trade fixtures, machinery, plant, utensils, and effects employed in my trade or business of a   , and also the goodwill of the said trade or business, and all my leasehold interest in the messuage, manufactory, offices, and buildings situate at   in which the said trade or business is carried on, or used for the purposes of the same; but not any money or debts which shall be owing to me in respect of the said trade or business. [*Or*, And also the benefit of all contracts subsisting in respect of the same trade or business, and all book and other debts and monies owing to me in respect of the same; Provided always that the said C. D. shall, to the satisfaction of the executors of this my will, sufficiently indemnify my general estate from all debts and liabilities owing or incurred by me in respect of my said trade or business, and if they shall so require, shall enter into a bond or covenant in that behalf at the cost of my general personal estate.]

A Bequest of an Annuity

(From Bythewood and Jarman's *Precedents in Conveyancing*, vol. vii, p. 824)

I bequeath to C. D. an annuity of £   during his life clear of legacy duty and all other incidental expenses and deductions. And I direct my executors, as soon as convenient after my death, to purchase in their names such an annuity, either from government or from one of the public offices or companies concerned in granting annuities, or upon freehold, copyhold, or leasehold, or other real or chattel real security, from some private person or persons, as my executors shall deem expedient; such annuity to commence from my death and to be paid to the said C. D. by equal quarterly payments, the first of such payments to be made at the expiration of three calendar months from the time of my death. And I direct that until such purchase shall be made, the said annuity shall be paid out of my general personal estate at the times and in manner aforesaid.

An Appointment of Guardians

(From Bythewood and Jarman's *Precedents in Conveyancing*, vol. vii, p. 752)

I appoint jointly with my wife, C. D., the said [*naming the executors*], and the survivors and survivor of them, to be guardians and guardian of my children during their respective minorities; but such guardianship shall cease as to each of the said guardians who shall go to reside abroad, refuse or become incapable to act in the said guardianship, or become bankrupt or insolvent.

I appoint C. D. of   during his life, and after his death such person or persons as he shall by will appoint or nominate, to be guardian or guardians of my children, during their respective minorities.

APPENDIX E

Differences between the Roman and English Will

(1) The primary object of the Roman will was the appointment of a *heres*. Such an appointment was essential to the validity of the will. The primary object of the English will is the disposition of property. The will is valid even though there be no one appointed executor.

(2) A Roman testator could not, unless a soldier, die partly testate and partly intestate. The will must stand or fall as a whole. This is not the case in England.

(3) There is no one in England to whom the *universitas juris* of the testator descends as it did to the Roman *heres*, the English heir-at-law taking only on an intestacy.

(4) The disabilities of testators differed in the two systems. The disability of a slave or a heretic was peculiar to Roman law, of a youth between fourteen and twenty-one to English law.

(5) The whole property may be disposed of in England; at Rome, except by the wills of soldiers, children could not be disinherited unless for specified acts of misconduct. During the greater part of the period of Roman law the heir must also have had a fourth part of the inheritance (the *Quarta Falcidia*) in order to induce him to accept the office. It follows from this that there is in England nothing corresponding to the *querela inofficiosi testamenti*, the Roman remedy for a child entitled to succeed and passed over by the testator.

(6) In English law all wills must be written and must conform to certain statutory requirements; the Romans recognised a nuncupative will and from the time of Augustus

downwards an informal will called *codicilli*. The English codicil is not an informal will, but an addition to a will, read as a part of it, and needing the same formalities of execution.

(7) There is a striking difference, unknown to Roman law, between wills of real and personal estate. Probate is necessary for the latter but not for the former. The Roman *legatum* applied to gifts of both moveables and immoveables; in England "legacy" has long been confined to the former.

(8) The Roman will spoke from the time of making, the English speaks from the time of death. The difference becomes very important in the case of alteration in the position of the testator between the making of the will and his death. As a rule the Roman will could not, the English can, pass after acquired property.

(9) In Roman law in the time of Justinian seven witnesses were required, two are sufficient in England. The Roman witnesses must have been *idonei*, or free from legal disability, and slaves, women, heretics, and others were not good witnesses. In England there appears to be no legal disability.

(10) The English distinction between the court of probate and the court of construction was unknown to Roman law. The same court decided whether a will was duly executed and what was the meaning of the words used in the will.

(11) The Roman will was a public instrument, the English is a private one. This difference rests on historical grounds.

(12) A Roman *paterfamilias* could make a will on behalf of his infant son; this was never the case in England.

(13) A contract to make a will in favour of a certain person, good in England, was void in Roman law.

Several examples of disputed Roman wills and the decisions thereon are given in Valerius Maximus, bk. vi, c. 7 (*De Testamentis Rescissis*), and c. 8 (*De Ratis Testamentis et Insperatis*).

ADDENDUM

THE English law of intestate succession has been modified by the following Act, which received the royal assent too late for any reference to it to be incorporated in the body of the work.

INTESTATES' ESTATES ACT, 1890

(53 and 54 Vict., c. 29)

Intestate's estate not exceeding 500l. to belong to widow where no issue.

1. The real and personal estates of every man who shall die intestate after the first day of September one thousand eight hundred and ninety leaving a widow but no issue shall, in all cases where the net value of such real and personal estates shall not exceed five hundred pounds, belong to his widow absolutely and exclusively.

Intestate's estate exceeding 500l., widow to have a charge for 500l.

2. Where the net value of the real and personal estates in the preceding section mentioned shall exceed the sum of five hundred pounds the widow of such intestate shall be entitled to five hundred pounds part thereof absolutely and exclusively, and shall have a charge upon the whole of such real and personal estates for such five hundred pounds, with interest thereon from the date of the death of the intestate at four per cent per annum until payment.

How charge to be borne as between realty and personalty.

3. As between the real and personal representatives of such intestate, such charge shall be borne and paid in proportion to the values of the real and personal estates respectively.

Above provision to be in addition

4. The provision for the widow intended to be made by this Act shall be in addition and without prejudice to her interest and share in the residue of the real and personal

estates of such intestate remaining after payment of the sum of five hundred pounds, in the same way as if such residue had been the whole of such intestate's real and personal estates and this Act had not been passed. *To share of residue due.*

5. The net value of such real estates as aforesaid shall for the purposes of this Act be estimated in the case of a fee simple upon the basis of twenty years purchase of the annual value by the year at the date of the death of the intestate as determined by law for the purposes of property tax, less the gross amount of any mortgage or other principal sum charged thereon, and less the value of any annuity or other periodical payment chargeable thereon, to be valued according to the tables and rules in the schedule annexed to the statute sixteenth and seventeenth Victoria, chapter fifty-one, and in the case of an estate for a life or lives according to the said tables and rules. *How realty to be valued. [Succession Duties Act, 1853.]*

6. The net value of such personal estate as aforesaid shall be ascertained by deducting from the gross value thereof all debts, funeral and testamentary expenses, of the intestate, and all other lawful liabilities and charges to which the said personal estate shall be subject. *How personalty to be valued.*

7. This Act may be cited as the Intestates' Estates Act, 1890. *Short title.*

8. This Act shall not extend to Scotland. *Extent of Act.*

INDEX

ACCOUNT DUTY, 131, 168-171
  residuary, 171
Accumulation of income, 51, 199, 205
Action of account, 21
  to perpetuate testimony, 40
  form of pleadings, 126-128
  passing to representatives, 142
  against representatives, 152
  for death, 143
  administration, 158
Administration by ordinary, 26
  order of, 134
  of assets, 160
  issue of letters of, 135
  of small estates, 136
  limited, with will annexed, 122, 137
  de bonis non, 124, 137
  durante absentia, 137
  durante minore ætate, 122, 137
  pendente lite, 136, 138
  durante dementia, 138
  ad colligenda bona, 138
  cessate grant, 138
  ceterorum grant, 122, 138
  special, 138
  exemption from, 139
  revocation of, 139
  bond, 26, 74, 133, 136
  when to be obtained, 148
  in court of equity, 157
  action, 158
  of insolvent estate in bankruptcy, 163

Administration, tribunal of, 188
  sealing letters of, 189
Administrator, origin of name, 5
  officer of court, 26
  who cannot be, 133
  oath of, 135
  must give security, 125
  rights of, 140-148
  duties of, 148-156
  liability to costs, 159, 160
Advancement of children, 115
Agnatic relationship, 2-4, 23
Alien, 29, 76, 122, 184
Alienation, restriction on, 55-57
Ambiguity, latent and patent, 93, 94
Ancestor worship, 2, 52
Animism, 2
Annuity, form of bequest of, App. D
Appeal, 128-130, 165
Appointment, power of, 50, 61, 72, 75, 172
  benefit under, subject to legacy duty, 171
  confers succession, 176
Apportionment, 60, 141, 153
Arches, Dean of, 19
Assets by descent, 14, 43
  equitable, 14
  real, 149
  within jurisdiction of court, 142, 190
  division of, 146
  administration of, 158-161
  delay in realising, 152

INDEX

Assets, marshalling, 162
Assurance of land by will, 45, 46
Athenian law, 3, 7

BANKRUPTCY, 122, 133, 142, 157, 158, 163
Beneficium inventarii, 196
Bequest, *see* Legacy
Blind, deaf and dumb, and illiterate person, will of, 83
Bocland, 9
Bona notabilia, 19
Borough, English, 24, 113, 114
Brehon law, 7, 204

CANON LAW, 8, 116
Casualties, 198
Caution from executor, 195
Caveat, 125
Cessate grant, 138
Ceterorum grant, 123, 138
Chancery Division is Court of Construction, 84
  appeal from, 165
  does not grant probate, 120
Charity, gift to, 45, 48, 51, 124, 206
  to be construed cy-près, 103, 104
  form of, App. D
  exempt from Mortmain Act, 47
  assets not marshalled in favour of, 162
  Commissioners, 48
  Roman Catholic, 54
  in Scotland, 198
Chivalry, tenure in, 12
Chose in action, 141
Citation, 123. 125, 135
Codicil defined, 5, 63
  revival of revoked will by, 67
  form of, App. D
Co-executors, 121, 125, 143, 144
Cognatic relationship, 3, 4, 23
Coke's Rules, 11, 37
Collation, 202
Commissary Court, 197
  clerk, 189, 197
Condition repugnant to estate, 55, 56

Condition, precedent and subsequent, 98-100
  impossible, impolitic, or illegal, 98
  in restraint of marriage, 99-101
  not to dispute will, *ib.*
Conditional devise or bequest, 97
  limitation, 97, 98, 100, 101
Confirmation, 189, 196, 197
Conflict of laws, 182-192
Conquest, influence of, on wills, 9
Consistory Court, 19
Construction of wills, 84-108
  principles of law, 85
  authority of cases, *ib.*
  statutory rules, 86
  non-statutory rules, 89
  minor rules, 94, 101
  different from that of deeds, 90
  court of, 85, 157
  cannot rectify mistake, 106
  governed by law of domicil, 185
  in Scotland, 199, 200
Contingent remainder, 41, 49
Contract to make will, 36
  disposing of succession, 36, 37
  not to revoke will, 68
  by acceptance of trust, 74
  one executor cannot bind another by, 144
  right to sue on contract made by deceased, 152
  with deceased, 142
  express by executor, 154
Conversion, 144, 161
Copyholds, will of, 15, 43
  descent of, 24, 112
  seizure *quousque* of, 112, 113
Corporation, gift to, 15, 45, 48
  as executor, 122
  as administrator, 134
Costs, when payable by executor or administrator, 159, 160
County Court, jurisdiction in probate, 21, 62, 120, 129, 130, 133
  in administration, 136, 137
  under Employers' Liability Act, 143
  in suit for legacy, 151
  equitable, 164, 165

INDEX

County Court, appeal from, 129, 130, 165
Cremation, 148
Crown is *ultimus heres*, 111, 116, 134, 201
   may terminate abeyance, 118
   debts, 149
Curtesy, 24, 25, 112
Cy-près, 103, 104, 200

DEATH, action for, under Lord Campbell's Act, 143
   Employers' Liability Act, *ib.*
   certificate of, 120, 135
   presumption of, 120
   duties, 168
Debts, liability of devisee, 13
   heir, 13
   copyholder, 15
   executor, 21, 148, 149, 195, 196
   administrator, 148, 149
   legatee, 21
   ordinary, 26
   in what order payable, 149
   privileged, 196
Delegates, Court of, 20
Depositors in savings banks, etc., 29, 81
Descent, rules of, 109-112
Devastavit, 154
Devise, meaning of, 58
   immediate or executory, 40, 41
   conditional, 97
Devisee, liability for debts, 13, 14
   title accrues at death of testator, 121
Dilapidations, 149
Disposition and settlement, 11, 192, 193, 197, 202
Distribution, Statutes of, 26, 95, 115, 136, 137, 150
Domicil defined, 182
   governs testamentary capacity, 183
   construction of will, 185
   Acts of 1861, 183, 184
Donatio mortis causâ, 61, 171
Dower, 24, 25, 59, 111, 112
Drunkenness, effect on validity of will, 83

Duties, probate, 131, 169, 190, 198, 207
   account, 131, 169
   legacy, 171-175
   succession, 175-179
   estate, 179, 180
   minor, 180, 181
   in Scotland, 197, 198
   in Ireland, 207

ECCLESIASTICAL COURTS, 18
Eik, 197
Emblements, 94, 141
Escheat, 15, 111, 112, 114, 117
Estate, "personal" and real, 10, 141
   tail, 12
   how barred, 49
   quasi entail, 89
   succession duty on, 177
   duty, 179, 180
Evidence to explain intention, 92, 161
Execution, requisites of, 33
Executor, origin of term, 5
   liability for debts, 21, 149, 153
   for costs, 159, 160
   as shareholder, 155
   originally essential to will of personalty, 58
   assent to legacy, 62, 117
   his rights over real estate, 121
   must prove will or renounce, 121, 123, 124
   has inchoate right on testator's death, 121
   number unlimited, 121
   no one legally excluded from the office, 121, 122
   appointment of, express or implied, 123, 124
   alternative, 122
   limited, 122, 123
   de son tort, 123, 146, 154
   of executor, 124
   need not give security, 125
   oath of, 130, 131
   retainer by, 133, 146
   rights of, 140-148
   duties of, 148-156

Executor, rights exercisable without
  action, 143
 receipt by, 144
 when trustee, 144, 155
 investment by, 152
 has year for distributing assets,
  150
 in Scotland, 195
Executory devise, 41, 98
 bequest, 61, 98
Exoneration, 145, 160, 161

FAMILY, primitive, 2
Fees in non-contentious business,
  App. B
Fixtures, 22, 141
Folcland, 9
Forgery of will, 166
 of signature, 167
Forms of wills, App. D
 of pleadings, 126
France, law of, 6, 29, 36
Frauds, Statute of, 13, 14, 18, 36,
  43, 77, 155
Freedom of disposition not universal, 6
Friendly Society, nomination by
  depositor, 29, 139

GAVELKIND, English, 10, 24, 25,
  113, 114
 Irish, 204
Glanvill cited, 13, 18, 23, 24
Guardianship, devise of, 30, 75
 form of, App. D

HALF-BLOOD, 24, 111, 116, 202
Heir, liability for debts, 13, 14
 cannot renounce, 112
 cannot be disinherited but by
  express words, 102
 customary, 113
 apparent and presumptive, 114,
  195
 estate vests on death of testator,
  121
 resulting trust in favour of, 161
 in Scotch law, 195, 199, 200
 portioner, 201
 service as, 201, 202
Heirloom, 37, 42 141

Hereditas, 1
Heres, 6
Heriot, 9, 15, 24
Hindu law, 3, 7
Holograph will, 18, 194
House-Spirit, worship of, 2
Hustings Court, 19

ILLEGITIMATE CHILD, gift to, 100
 cannot succeed as heir, 185
 can succeed as next of kin, 185,
  186
 revenue duty payable by, 191
Immoveables and moveables, 10,
  182, 185, 200
Indefiniteness of gift, 57
Inland Revenue, probate through,
  74, 120, 130, 131, 136, 137,
  170
 affidavit, 135, 136, 149
 duties, 147, 149, 168-181
Insanity, 29, 81
Intention, as a guide to construction, 90-92, 94
 explanation of, 92
 to take effect as far as possible,
  102
 inconsistent, 104
 to benefit executor, 155
 to exonerate real estate, 161
International Law, *see* Conflict of
  Laws
Intestacy, presumption against,
  102
 total or partial, 109
 share on, liable to legacy duty,
  172
 where sued for, 117
Inventory, 130, 131, 135, 149, 196
Investment by executor, 152, 195
Ireland, law of, 204-207

JUDICATURE ACTS, *see* Statutes
Jus accrescendi, 199
 mariti, ib.
 relictæ, 194

KING, will of, 70
 as executor, 122

LANCASTER, Chancery of, 163

Lapse, 60
Larceny of will, 166
Leaseholds liable to succession duty, 171
  are personal property, 10
  are within Locke King's Act, 161
Legacy, meaning of, 58, 172
  kinds of, 59
  executory, 61, 98
  lapse of, 60
  prima facie payable out of personalty, 96
  whether executor renouncing can take, 124
  paid after debts, 149
  interest on, 150, 188
  to infant, 150
  where sued for, 62, 117, 151
  limitation in action for, 151
  duty, 171-175
Legitim, 186, 193, 194
Legitimatio per subsequens matrimonium, 185, 186, 200
Limitations, Statute of, 121, 146, 148
  in claim against executor, 157
  administrator, 152
  for legacy, 151
  for legacy or succession duty, 175, 179, 190, 191
Loan Society, 139
Locke King's Act, 145, 150, 160, 161
Lunatic, will of, 81
  as executor, 122
  as administrator, 135
  intestate, 138

MAINE, Sir H., cited, 2, 4, 7
Malum prohibitum and *malum in se*, 97, 98
Marriage, restraint of, 57, 60, 98-101
  revokes will, 67, 69
  articles, 97
Married woman, will of, 22, 25, 29, 71-73
  as executrix or administratrix, 73
  cannot be surety to administration bond, 136

Marshalling assets, 162
Masses, bequest for, 18, 53, 205
Misdescription, 102
Mohammedan law, 7, 23
Mortgaged estate, exoneration of, 145, 150, 160, 161
Mortification, 198
  form of clause of, App. D
Mortmain meaning of term, 15
  licence in, 16
  provisions of Act of 1888, 45, 46
  exemptions from, 47
  how far extends to land abroad, 186
  does not apply to Scotland, 198
  to Ireland, 205
Mosaic law, 3, 7, 23
Moveables and immoveables, 10, 182, 185, 200

NATURALISATION, 76, 184
Nomination equivalent to will, 29, 139

OCCUPANCY, general, 43
  special, *ib.*, 111
Ordinary, Court of, 19
  power to grant probate, *ib.*
  administration, 26
Originating summons, 144, 159, 164

Pars rationabilis, 17
Partnership estate, 141
  debt, 135
Peerage, succession to, 117-119
Perpetuity, 48-52, 61
  in colonies, 52, 187
  in Scotland, 198
  in Ireland, 206
Personal and real estate, 10, 141
Personalty, will of, history, 16
  intestacy as to, history, 25
  will of, 58-63
  intestate succession to, 114-117
  impure, 45
Power, *see* Appointment
Præcipuum, 201
Precatory trust, 103
Prerogative Court, 19, 20, 131

Presumption of alteration in circumstances, 67
  to explain intention, 92
  against intestacy, 102
  in Court of Probate, 107
  of death, 120
  of Life Limitation Act, 203
Primogeniture, 2, 3, 23, 24, 113, 200
Priority, 149, 163, 188
Privy Council, appeal to, 20
Probate Acts, *see* Statutes
  in Ecclesiastical Courts, 21
  in old county courts, *ib.*
  in Court of Probate, *ib.*
  in Probate Division, *ib.*, 120-133
  not granted by Chancery Division, 120
  is evidence of will, 39, 131, 132
  in common form, 125, 130
  in solemn form, 38, 125, 148
  of will of lands, 38
  double, 125
  conclusive till revoked, 132
  exemption from, 139
  when to be obtained, 148
  duty, 131, 168-170, 189, 198, 207
  sealing, 189
Probate Division cannot entertain action for legacy, 62, 151
  for distributive share under intestacy, 117
  cannot grant probate of King's will, 71
  limited jurisdiction to construe, 84, 107
  authority of, necessary for executor or administrator, 120
  trial in, 128
  appeal from, *ib.*
  discretion in grant of administration, 138
  in Ireland, 206
Property of all kinds may be left by will, 35, 58
Public policy, 44, 99, 100, 105

Quia Emptores, Statute of, 10
Queen, will of, 71

RABBINICAL LAW, 7
Radical right, 200
Rationabilis pars, 17
Real estate, history of will of, 10
  history of descent on intestacy, 23
  will of, 39-58
  descent of, on intestacy, 109-114
  and personal estate distinguished, 10, 141
  power of executor over, 144, 145
  when charged with debts and legacies, 96, 145, 169
  administration of, in equity, 158
Receiver, appointment of, 138, 145
Reconversion, 162
Reduction *ex capite lecti*, 193
Register of Sasines, *ib.*
  of Entails, 199
Registry of will in England, 40
  in Ireland, 206
  probate, 123, 125, 130-132, 136
Relief, feudal, 24, 25
  none against defective execution of will, 106
Remainder, contingent, 48, 49
Remoteness, 50
Renunciation by executor, 121, 123, 124
  not by heir, 112
Residue liable to legacy duty, 171
Restraint of marriage, 57, 60, 98-101
Retainer, 133, 146
Revival of revoked will, 67, 69
Revocation before Wills Act, 11, 38, 69
  since Wills Act, 35, 65-69
  dependent relative, 66
  of probate, 132, 133, 138
  of administration, 138, 139
Roman Catholic religion, gift to, 53
  charity, 54, 104
Roman and English will compared, App. E
  law, 1, 3-8, 10, 12, 16, 23, 31, 36, 43, 59, 61, 63, 73, 94, 98, 101, 112, 115, 116, 194, 196, 201

INDEX

Rules, Lord Coke's, 11, 37
  of descent, 109-112
  of Supreme Court, 126-129, 135, 136
  Probate, 22, 83, 126
  County Court, 129, 156, 164
  for personal applications, App. C

SACRA, 2, 3
Sailor, will of, 29, 77-81, 139, 169
Savings bank, nomination by depositor in, 29, 81, 139
Scotland, law of, 6, 11, 192-203
Secret trust, 64
Security by administrator, 125
  by receiver, 138
  justifying, 133.
  none by executor, 125
Settlement includes will in some statutes, 44, 56
Sheriff court, 197, 202, 203
  clerk, 197
Signature of testator, 33
  of witness, 34
Singular succession, 1, 197, 200
Socage tenure, 12, 24, 113
Soldier, will of, 29, 77, 78, 80, 139, 169
Specialty binding heir, 14
Stamp not needed for will, 28
  on probate, 28, 189
  on letters of administration, *ib.*
  on copies, valuations, and grants of arms, 180, 181
  duties denoted by, 169, 180
Statutes—
  Constitution of Clarendon, 16
  Magna Carta of John, 17, 25
  20 Hen. III, c. 2, 17
  13 Edw. I, c. 1 (*De Donis*), 101
  c. 19, 26
  c. 23, 21
  st. 3, 14
  18 Edw. I, c. 1 (*Quia Emptores*), 10
  4 Edw. III, c. 7, 21, 142
  31 Edw. III, c. 11, 20, 26
  21 Hen. VIII, c. 5, 20, 26, 139
  27 Hen. VIII, c. 10 (Statute of Uses), 12, 14

Statutes—
  28 Hen. VIII, c. 7, 70
  c. 11, 17
  32 Hen. VIII, c. 1 (Wills), 12
  c. 37, 145
  34 and 35 Hen. VIII, c. 5 (Wills), 12
  35 Hen. VIII, c. 1, 70
  1 Edw. VI, c. 14, 53
  43 Eliz., c. 4, 205
  12 Car. II, c. 24, 12, 30, 75
  22 and 23 Car. II, c. 10 (Distribution), 26, 95, 115, 136, 137, 150
  29 Car. II, c. 3 (Frauds), 13, 14, 18, 36, 43, 77, 155
  1 Jac. II, c. 7 (Distribution), 26, 95, 115, 136, 137
  4 and 5 Anne, c. 16, 21
  9 Geo. II, c. 36, 16, 205
  25 Geo. II, c. 6, 13
  36 Geo. III, c. 52, 150, 171, 174
  38 Geo. III, c. 87, 122, 138
  39 Geo. III, c. 73, 174
  39 and 40 Geo. III, c. 88, 71, 199
  c. 98 (Thellusson Act), 51
  43 Geo. III, c. 108, 47, 72
  53 Geo. III, c. 49, 44
  55 Geo. III, c. 184, 148, 170, 171, 173, 174
  c. 192, 15
  10 Geo. IV, c. 7, 54
  11 Geo. IV and 1 Will. IV, c. 20, 78
  c. 40, 18, 155
  c. 41, 77
  3 and 4 Will. IV, c. 27, 121
  c. 42, 142, 153
  c. 74, 12
  c. 104, 162
  c. 105, 25, 59
  c. 106 (Inheritance), 24, 110, 115
  7 Will. IV and 1 Vict., c. 26, (Wills), 13, 15, 17, 18, 28, 30, 33, 34, 35, 38, 41, 42, 43, 44, 58, 60, 63, 65, 67, 68, 69, 72, 75, 77, 78, 79, 80, 86, 87, 88, 89, 90, 205, App. A

Statutes—
3 and 4 Vict., c. 60, 46
4 and 5 Vict., c. 35, 15
7 and 8 Vict., c. 37, 47
8 and 9 Vict., c. 76, 172
9 and 10 Vict., c. 93, 143
10 and 11 Vict., c. 93, 143
14 and 15 Vict., c. 25, 14
15 and 16 Vict., c. 24 (Wills), 33, App. A
16 and 17 Vict., c. 51 (Succession Duty), 155, 171, 173, 175-179, 190, 191, 197
  c. 70, 82
17 and 18 Vict., c. 104, 79
  c. 112, 47
  c. 113, 145, 160, 161
18 and 19 Vict., c. 124, 48
19 and 20 Vict., c. 94, 27
20 and 21 Vict., c. 77 (Probate), 13, 21, 39, 124, 126, 129, 133, 139, 145, 167, App. A
  c. 79, 189
  c. 85, 74
21 and 22 Vict., c. 56 (Probate), 124, 126, 129, 138, 167, 189, App. A
22 and 23 Vict., c. 35, 59, 110, 146, 147, 150, 160, 166
23 Vict., c. 5, 142
  c. 15, 142
23 and 24 Vict., c. 28, 152, 166
  c. 134, 54
24 and 25 Vict., c. 96, 166
  c. 98, 166
  c. 114, 183
  c. 121, 184
25 and 26 Vict., c. 89, 47
26 and 27 Vict., c. 57, 77
  c. 87, 174
28 and 29 Vict., c. 72, 78
  c. 99, 164
  c. 104, 148, 173
  c. 111, 80
30 and 31 Vict., c. 69, 160
32 and 33 Vict., c. 46, 149, 162
33 Vict. c. 14 (Naturalisation), 28, 76
33 and 34 Vict., c. 35 (Apportionment), 60, 141, 153
  c. 97 (Stamps), 28, 181

Statutes—
34 and 35 Vict., c. 43, 149
35 and 36 Vict., c. 44, 150
36 and 37 Vict., c. 52, 136, 169, 170
  c. 66, and subsequent acts, (Judicature Acts, 1873 to 1890), 21, 128, 130, 151, 158, 163, App. A
37 and 38 Vict., c. 57, 151
  c. 78, 40, 145, 147
38 and 39 Vict., c. 27, 136-139, 170
  c. 87, 145
39 and 40 Vict., c. 18, 116, 135
  c. 59, 118
  c. 87, 145
40 and 41 Vict., c. 18, 44, 56
  c. 33, 41, 50
  c. 34, 160
43 Vict., c. 14, 172, 175, 179
43 and 44 Vict., c. 42, 143
44 Vict., c. 12, 149, 169, 171, 173, 174, 179, App. A
44 and 45 Vict., c. 41 (Conveyancing), 56, 97, 110, 111, 112, 140, 144-146, 153, 205
  c. 57, 78
  c. 58, 77
45 and 46 Vict., c. 38 (Settled Land), 44, 55, 56, 205
  c. 39, 50
  c. 75 (Married Women's Property), 22, 25, 56, 71-74, 115
46 and 47 Vict., c. 52 (Bankruptcy), 163
49 and 50 Vict., c. 27, 76
  c. 38, 2
51 Vict., c. 8, 175, 176, 178
51 and 52 Vict., c. 41, 169
  c. 42 (Mortmain), 16, 45-48, 205
  c. 43 (County Courts), 62, 164
  c. 59, 147, 151, 152, 155
  c. 73, 145
52 Vict., c. 7, 169, 175 177-179, 181
52 and 53 Vict., c. 32 (Trust Investment), 152, 155 App. A

Statutes—
  52 and 53 Vict., c. 42, 80
  53 Vict., c. 5, 138, 155
  53 and 54 Vict., c. 29, Addendum, 272
Statutes relating to Scotland—
  Statuta Gilde, 192
  1587, c. 29, 198
  1617, c. 14, 194
  1681, c. 5, 193
  1695, c. 24, 196
  4 Geo. IV, c. 97, 197
  c. 98, 196
  11 and 12 Vict., c. 36, 199
  18 and 19 Vict., c. 23, 194, 203
  30 and 31 Vict., c. 97, 195
  31 and 32 Vict., c. 101 (Titles to Land), 193, 194, 198-203
  34 and 35 Vict., c. 81, 193
  37 and 38 Vict., c. 94 (Conveyancing), 194, 196, 197, 199, 200, 201, 202
  40 and 41 Vict., c. 29, 199
  44 and 45 Vict., c. 21, 194
  c. 47, 203
  47 and 48 Vict., c. 63, 195
  50 and 51 Vict., c. 69, 198
  52 and 53 Vict., c. 50, 198, 207
Statutes relating to Ireland—
  Passed by the Parliament of Ireland—
    10 Hen. VII, c. 22 (Poyning's Law), 205
    28 Hen. VIII, c. 18, 205
    7 Will. III, c. 12, 205
    2 Anne, c. 6, 205
    6 Anne, c. 2, 206
  Passed by the Parliament of the United Kingdom—
    2 and 3 Will. IV, c. 87, 206
    14 and 15 Vict., c. 57, 207
    20 and 21 Vict., c. 79 (Probate), 207
    22 and 23 Vict., c. 31, 207
    40 and 41 Vict., c. 56, 207
    c. 57 (Judicature), 207
    45 and 46 Vict., c. 29, 207
    51 and 52 Vict., c. 60, 207
Succession, its place in a legal system, 1

Succession in Roman law, 1, 3
  in Athenian and other systems, 3
  universal and singular, 1, 197, 200
  origin of, 2
  agnatic, 3
  intestate earlier than testate, 4
  intestate, history of, 23
  modern law of, 109
  to real estate, 24, 109
  to personal estate, 114
  to titles of honour, 117
  duty, 175-179, 190, 191
  Scotch law of, 192-203
  Irish law of, 204-207
Superstitious uses, 53, 60, 64, 205

TANISTRY, 3, 204
Terce, 193
Testament defined, 5, 192
Testamentary character of instrument, 29
Thellusson Act, 51, 61, 199, 205
Titles of Honour, 117-119 201
Tombs, trust for repairing, 51
Torts to person or property of deceased, 21, 142
  by deceased, 153
Trial, 128, 129
Trust, secret, 64
  acceptance of, is contract, 74
  for repair of tombs, 51
  precatory, 103
  resulting, 161
  cannot be attached to land abroad, 187
  disposition and settlement, 192, 197, 202
  form of, App. D
Trustee, married woman as, 7
  estate taken by, 89
  receipt by, 144
  executor when, 144, 178
  in Scotland, 195
  investment by, 152, 195, App. D

UNATTESTED WRITING, incorporation of, 31, 267
Undue influence, 31

United States law, 6, 23, 25, 104, 106, 134, 183
Universal succession, 1, 197, 200
Uses, conveyance to, 11
  Statute of, 12, 14
  superstitious, 53, 60, 64

VALUATION, production of, 180
  stamp on, 181

WAGER OF LAW, 21
Widow, right to dower, *see* Dower
  to one-third of personalty, 115, 116
  under Act of 1890, Addendum, 272
  to terce, 193
  intestate, 136
  as administratrix, 134
Will, Roman, 4
  basis of English, 7
  and English compared, App. E
  defined, 5, 30
  not universal, 6
  in canon law, 8
  could not at one time dispose of whole real estate, 12
  of whole personalty, 17
  nuncupative, 17, 194
  holograph, 18, 194
  of living testator may be deposited, 28
  requisites for validity, 29-35
  in more than one document, 30, 31
  duplicate, mutual, and joint, *ib.*
  execution of, 33
  attestation of, *ib.*
  form of, App. D
  contract to make, 36
  defective in form, 37
  needs no seal, 11, 38
  · or stamp, 28
  of lands itself evidence, 39
  need not be proved, 38

Will of lands must be good by *lex loci rei sitæ*, 184
  registry of, in England, 40
  in Scotland, 193
  in Ireland, 206
  revocation of, 65-69
  revival of, 67, 69
  of special nature—
    king, 70
    married woman, 22, 71
    power of appointment, 75
    guardianship, *ib.*
    alien, 76
    soldier and sailor, 77
    depositor in savings bank, etc., 81
    lunatic, *ib.*
    other cases, 82
  construction of, *see* Construction
  cannot pass title of honour, 118
  evidence of lost, 132
  criminal law relating to, 166, 167, 198
  international law relating to, 182-191
  in Scotland, 192-203
  in Ireland, 204-207
Wills Act, *see* Statutes
  its history, 28
  interpretation clause, 30, 58, 63
  sections affecting real estate, 41, 44
  construction, 44, 86-90
  general law, 35
Witness, no number fixed before Conquest, 9
  credibility of, 13
  signature of, 33-35
  competence of, 34
  gift to, *ib.*
  affidavit by, 108, 131
  evidence at trial, 125, 126
Words construed in ordinary sense, 91
  technical in technical sense, 106

www.ingramcontent.com/pod-product-compliance
Lightning Source LLC
Chambersburg PA
CBHW032053220426
43664CB00008B/988